Advance Praise for *Fear Less*

Trying to be fearless often becomes yet another thing to fail at, but if you can just *fear less*, peace is well within reach. This book is your best guide for achieving that. Dean Sluyter's kind, accessible tone talks *with* you, so you always feel he is by your side as you make the journey.

— Mark Goulston, MD, author of
Get Out of Your Own Way and *Just Listen*

Om meets *Wheeeeeee!* Sluyter careens merrily from the Buddha to Willie Nelson, from prison stories to *The Wizard of Oz*, but it all leads us—step by practical, loving step—toward a life of peace. Who knew that learning how not to be freaked out could be so much fun?

—Michael Kane, author of *Heal Your Broken Heart*

As a recovering alcoholic and not-so-recovered depressed person, I've long been aware that mindfulness would be helpful to my life, but it's just so *intimidating*. Not so with Sluyter, who pairs concrete suggestions with a no-pressure attitude that makes this book feel like it's written by a really smart friend. He also shows how to incorporate the techniques into other programs of recovery—a rare but crucially important component. You'll want to revisit Sluyter's wisdom again and again.

—Katie MacBride, journalist; author of the
"Ask Katie" recovery advice column

In his friendly, easygoing style, Dean Sluyter shows how to surf even the biggest waves of powerful emotions. A delightful and necessary guide to staying sane in these "interesting times."

—Lyn Genelli, marriage and family therapist; author of
Death at the Movies

D0192320

Dean Sluyter has written a beautiful book that shows us how to navigate the free-floating anxiety of everyday fears. He shows us, with insight and humor, how to access the deep silence that is available to everyone. *Fear Less* is rich with inspiration and practices that lead to a more unobstructed view of reality. It is a book to be enjoyed over and over again.

—Edward Viljoen, author of *Ordinary Goodness* and
The Power of Meditation

I especially like the lessons Dean draws from his experiences teaching in prison. I've had the privilege of going behind bars with him and have witnessed his transformative work there. If those men can come out of fear and rage, anyone can.

—Lama Willa Miller, PhD, founder of Natural Dharma
Fellowship; author of *Everyday Dharma*

Dean Sluyter wields his pithy wit and profound wisdom like a laser light, pointing directly to the truth we need to embrace: fear doesn't have to own us any longer. Using various forms of exquisitely simple meditation techniques, the author doesn't just point the way—he takes our hand and gently leads us. Dean equips us with the tools necessary to slay the tyrant that holds us captive in the dungeon of our own making. The dungeon is our mind and the tyrant is fear. Read *Fear Less*—it will help you set yourself free!

—Dennis Merritt Jones, award-winning author of
The Art of Uncertainty, Your (Re)Defining Moments, and
The Art of Abundance

Fear Less

FEAR LESS

LIVING BEYOND FEAR,
ANXIETY, ANGER,
AND ADDICTION

Dean Sluyter

A TarcherPerigee Book

tarcherperigee

An imprint of Penguin Random House LLC
375 Hudson Street
New York, New York 10014

Photograph credits
Pages 102, 103, 126, 127, 128, 129, 130, 131, 132, 133, 156, 197: By the author
Pages 148, 149, 190, 191, 224, 256, 257, 261, 285, 310: Wikimedia Commons
Page 206: © 2016 by Tara Wings Sluyter

TarcherPerigee with tp colophon is a registered trademark of Penguin Random House LLC.

Most TarcherPerigee books are available at special quantity discounts for bulk
purchase for sales promotions, premiums, fund-raising, and educational needs.
Special books or book excerpts also can be created to fit specific needs.
For details, write: SpecialMarkets@penguinrandomhouse.com.

Portions of this book originally appeared, in different form, in
The Huffington Post and *The Mindful Word*.

Library of Congress Cataloging-in-Publication Data
Names: Sluyter, Dean, author.
Title: Fear less : living beyond fear, anxiety, anger, and addiction / Dean Sluyter.
Description: New York : TarcherPerigee, [2018]
Identifiers: LCCN 2017042107 | ISBN 9780143130277 (pbk.)
Subjects: LCSH: Meditation. | Stress management.
Classification: LCC BL627 .S589 2018 | DDC 158–dc23
LC record available at https://lccn.loc.gov/2017042107

Printed in the United States of America
1 3 5 7 9 10 8 6 4 2

Book design by Elke Sigal

For Jim
and
For Rosie

CONTENTS

PART I

COME AND SEE

CHAPTER 1	The Monster Under the Bed	3
CHAPTER 2	Breathe Through Your Feet	14
CHAPTER 3	Relax at the Moment of Contact	17
CHAPTER 4	The Sweetest Dog in the World	22
CHAPTER 5	Would It Help?	25
CHAPTER 6	Resting Bliss Face	33
CHAPTER 7	Snakes on a Plane	37

PART II

REST AS AWARENESS

CHAPTER 8	Settling Happens	43
CHAPTER 9	On-Ramps	51
CHAPTER 10	Testimony	62
CHAPTER 11	Being the Ocean	68
CHAPTER 12	Every Little Thing	78

PART III

OVERDRIVE / HYPERSPACE

CHAPTER 13	Take a Little Walk with Me	99
CHAPTER 14	Drop Your Thoughts	106
CHAPTER 15	The Fire Hose	119
CHAPTER 16	Working In	124
CHAPTER 17	Fear vs. Love	134
CHAPTER 18	Cold, Cold Water	143
CHAPTER 19	In Your Eyes	147
CHAPTER 20	Sit Down. Stand Up.	151
CHAPTER 21	Finding Your Fearless Voice	158
CHAPTER 22	Twelve Steps, Two Thorns	167
CHAPTER 23	Meditating with the iPhone 0	178
CHAPTER 24	You Should Be Dancing	184
CHAPTER 25	Who Needs Sleep?	192
CHAPTER 26	Notice the Sensations	201
CHAPTER 27	Same Boat	211
CHAPTER 28	Decide, Begin, Persist	216
CHAPTER 29	The Buddy System	228

PART IV

VIEW

CHAPTER 30	That Guy	*239*
CHAPTER 31	The Exploded Moment	*249*
CHAPTER 32	Bruegel to the Rescue	*255*
CHAPTER 33	Nothing Sticks	*261*
CHAPTER 34	November 9, 2016	*266*
CHAPTER 35	The Magic Piano	*272*
CHAPTER 36	Lord Shiva Kicks Ass	*279*
CHAPTER 37	Fear of the Lord	*286*
CHAPTER 38	Valley of the Shadow	*292*
CHAPTER 39	Love Is All Around	*303*

Acknowledgments *315*

The capacity for experience is what burns out fear.

—JAMES BALDWIN

THE COWARDLY LION: Somebody pulled my tail!
THE SCARECROW: Oh, you did it yourself.

—*The Wizard of Oz*

PART I

Come and See

CHAPTER 1

The Monster Under the Bed

I was scared of the ball.

They called it a softball, but it seemed plenty hard to me: I had felt it sting my fingers, smack my chest. As it shot toward me, my whole body flinched—that is, when it came toward me at all, as I stood exiled in far right field, where the team hoped I would do the least damage.

I was the skinny, uncoordinated kid: the *spaz*, in the fifth-grade playground lingo of the day. The only game I was good at was dodgeball—not hurling the ball at others, but jumping out of its way. That made perfect sense to me.

Every recess started with the mortifying ritual of choosing teams. The two captains—big Chuck and quick, wiry Ricky—picked boys from best to worst till they finally came to the slow, heavy kid and me, the dreaded dregs. After much disgusted stalling, one captain would sigh dramatically and say, "OK . . . we'll take Fats if you take Spaz."

In the classroom, I had no fear. I cheerfully took over discussions, settling back in my seat and enjoying a chummy tête-à-tête with the teacher, only dimly aware of the restless fidgeting going on all around me. Eventually I noticed Chuck, in the back corner near the door, self-exiled to his own right field, head down, trying for once to be small. Hmmmmm . . . a history question shooting toward him threatened as much danger and humiliation as a softball did for me. Different people, different situations, same feeling. Interesting.

The Cold War was on. In social studies we watched black-and-white propaganda films about communism, with grim narrators and the crablike hammer and sickle squatting over the map of Europe, sprouting evil tentacles of world domination. From time to time, in the middle of a math or geography lesson, the teacher would suddenly shout, "Drop!" We'd fall to our knees and duck and cover under our desks, waiting for a commie A-bomb to come hurtling toward Woodlake Avenue Elementary School, wondering just how effectively our wooden desktops would shield us from the thermonuclear fireball. Hmmmmm . . .

Now we're grownups. Terrorists have replaced Communists, and we've graduated from the playground to other grounds for fear: the office, the boardroom, the bedroom, the barroom. And the newsroom. The last presidential election was fueled by fear, and it's been a white-knuckle ride ever since, with spiking anxiety levels reported by psychologists nationwide. The political is personal.

But no matter who's elected today or impeached tomorrow, our deepest fears persist:

Fear of pain.

Fear of confusion.

Fear of change.

Fear that things will never change, that this is all there is.

Fear of responsibility.

Fear of aging and illness.

Fear of loss, bereavement, abandonment.

Fear that the good times are over, that joy has fled.

Fear of boredom, loneliness, intimacy, violation.

Fear of failure, rejection, humiliation.

Fear of others' opinions, of our own feelings, of being fooled, of blowing it onstage, of being exposed as a bewildered child among the confident adults.

Fear for the planet. We look to the world our children will inherit and wonder if it will be *The Jetsons* or *Mad Max*.

Fear of missing out. For years I was haunted by my high school English teacher's story of his father, who traveled the world, saw the sights, had more adventures than the next ten men, but died screaming—*screaming*—because he felt that, whatever life was all about, he had missed it.

Our fears may be rooted in big traumas haunting the past or big challenges looming in the future, but they cast their shadow over the smallest moments of everyday life right now. We're afraid of wearing the wrong outfit to the party, of sounding stupid if we speak up in the meeting, of getting lost if we take the scenic route. Choices must be made, and we long for the time when we chose out of joy (*Should I play on the slide or the jungle gym?*) rather than fear (*Will it be worse if I tell my partner how I feel or keep it to myself?*).

When we're not sure what to be afraid of, which threat to dodge next and what direction it will come from, our fear mutates into free-floating anxiety. To soothe our anxiety we might fall into addiction, taking refuge in a drug or drink, or in compulsive eating or gambling or gaming or hoarding or sex, or in cutting or starving ourselves, or in magical belief systems or bogus political messiahs—anything that offers to gimme shelter when I feel like I'm gonna fade away. But that sets off new fears: that we'll run out of the drugs or Oreos, or the girl-friend or boyfriend will run out on us, or the belief system will break down when we need it most. Then we lash out in anger at whoever or whatever allegedly threatens our alleged security.

These and the other afflictive emotions—grief, loneliness, guilt, jealousy, confusion, shame, disappointment, resentment, greed, self-righteousness, exasperation, despair—are all deeply connected. Whether they're boiling over into crisis or simmering toxically on a back burner, they're all brewed from fear. They all make us feel unfree and alone. Whether I'm playing my eleventh game of *Candy Crush* and trying to forget I have a term paper to write, or I'm off in a corner with my spoon and my quart of chocolate chip cookie dough ice cream, I feel like I'm all alone and no one must know, even when everyone knows.

Of course, this isn't the whole picture. If you're lucky and you're paying attention, life offers any number of joys and wonders. Many of us manage to sidestep the most destructive habits and scenarios, and to lead reasonably sane, progressive lives. But even in your happiest moments (playing with your healthy, laughing kids), even in your most sublime moments (lost, lost in the music), even in your most thrilling moments (merging in ecstasy with the lover you were born for)—even then, hovering in some dim corner that we try our best to ignore, is the final, definitive fear: your eventual annihilation and that of everything and everyone you love. All this must end. Nevermore, game over, buh-bye, here's your hat, no refunds, no apologies, no exceptions. Death is in the house and demands to be fed. He'll eat you and your little dog too.

And Yet . . .

And yet perhaps you've known people for whom this is all somehow different—who seem to have some deep wisdom, some internal gyroscope that keeps them balanced, some inner silence that inoculates them against the standard craziness and panic. Maybe it was an uncle or aunt, a wise teacher or professor, the nice lady at the corner store, the plumber. Maybe your most inspiring exemplars were movie characters:

Yoda or Obi-Wan Kenobi, Aslan, Gandalf, Mary Poppins, Glinda the Good Witch. But you're at least vaguely aware that there are supposed to have been real people who have embodied that silent wisdom fully—enlightened people, awakened ones, sages.

There are.

Even if we don't know exactly what sages might look like, we're pretty sure they're not racked with anxiety. They're not caught up in anger. And they're not overwhelmed with fear, even fear of death, whether it's Jesus on the cross, Al-Hallaj on the gallows, Socrates drinking the hemlock, or the Buddha calmly calling for his students' final questions while dying of excruciating septic shock. No matter what they undergo, their every breath is breathed from a place of bottomless silence. Just close your eyes for a moment, think of any one of them, and you can practically taste it.

That might seem to put them on some lofty spiritual peak, inaccessible to us ordinary schmoes. But they've all declared that as they are, we can and will be, and that the unshakable silence, whether they call it *nirvana* or *moksha* or *fanaa* or the kingdom of heaven, is within us. Not *might* be within us someday, but *is* within us now. If we reflect back on our lives—the joys, the challenges, the lonely moments out in our own personal right field—we might even sense that, somewhere in the background, that silence has been with us, within us, all along. Our project together will simply be to bring it from the background to the foreground.

Fortunately, that's the most natural thing in the world. All our lives we've been looking for the right thing but in the wrong places, looking outside for what's inside. It's just a matter of settling back into yourself, into the infinite OK-ness that is your own deepest nature. All those words like *fear, loneliness, craving, anger, anxiety, anguish, grief* are finally just different names for deprivation of that OK-ness.

Certainly our fears can seem devastating. We can't just sprinkle a little spiritual pixie dust and shrug them off. But in the light of the deeper truth to which we'll now be opening, our fear is just . . . fear. Unbelievable as it may sound, things are ultimately fine; the awakened ones agree. The sages are here, the grownups, come to shine their brilliant light under the bed and show us there's no monster.

Waking Up

This experience of silence and OK-ness is not something distant or exotic. It's completely intimate to you. In fact, you've probably had glimpses of it.

Some people call it *the zone* and encounter it at moments of peak athletic performance, but it can just as well sneak up on you while you're weeding the garden or washing the dishes, running your sales meeting or playing your ukulele. It comes unbidden. Suddenly you no longer feel stuck in your body. You're watching everything—witnessing it—from some unspecified, unconfined space, while your actions roll on with a wonderful, effortless grace, as if no one is doing them, yet they're done impeccably. Somehow time falls away. Colors might seem brighter, sounds sharper, the air sweeter, as if a veil has fallen from your senses. Everything is deliciously weightless, frictionless, silent, even amid commotion and noise. And although we're not apathetic or numb but vividly awake, there's a deep sense, which has no explanation and needs none, that everything is just fine. At these moments you probably don't stop to ponder your problems (why would you do that?), but if you did, none of them, up to and including death, would appear problematic. It's as if they, like you, are made of pure, open space.

And then, as quietly as it came, the glimpse ends, usually to be forgotten, or dismissed as some passing oddity. But it's not an oddity— that's the promise of the sages. They say it's natural and real to live and breathe from that silence full-time. Then, among other fortunate side effects, our fear, anger, anxiety, and addictions start to thin out and eventually evaporate. We realize that this friction-free, problem-free lightness isn't just some pleasant dream or fleeting high. Against all odds, the heaviness turns out to be the dream, the monster turns out to be the dream. As the great twentieth-century Indian sage Sri Nisargadatta Maharaj said:

> Learn to look without imagination, to listen without distortion: that is all. You will experience peace and freedom from fear.

Accessing that space of freedom is easier than people think. You don't have to change your job or your wardrobe, your philosophy or your diet: those matters are all far more superficial than what we're addressing. No one owns the zone, so it's not inherently Eastern or Western, Buddhist or Christian, or even "spiritual," whatever that means. There's nothing to believe, including anything you read here. My favorite saying of the Buddha is *Ehi-passiko*—"Come and see." Not come and believe, or come and hope, or speculate, or argue. It's pure scientific method. Try something, see what you experience, and if it seems beneficial you'll probably want to do more of it, till you don't have to do it anymore.

The sages who have come and seen didn't live only in ancient times. I've had the good fortune to hang out with more than one. Some have been lamas or rishis in robes, some have been ordinary-looking folks in casual wear. I've spent most of my life following their guidance, confirming it in my own experience, and, with their encouragement, sharing it with others.

What they've taught me, and what I'll be sharing here, consists of *practice* and *view*. Practice is method, technique, stuff you do, and our core practice, the one that has revolutionized my life, is *natural meditation*. Just like on the product labels in the supermarket, *natural* means without artificial ingredients. If we tried to do the things that most people associate with meditation—sit in a strained, uncomfortable posture, or try to push out thoughts, or force our attention to stay concentrated on some object, or concoct some kind of happy-face mood when we really feel like slugging someone—that would be artificial.

If you *try* to meditate, it's, well, trying. But as we've already seen, the zone of great freedom sneaks up on us, "like a thief in the night," as Saint Paul says. So the most natural and effective kind of meditation is not so much *doing* as *being*. It's not going afield in pursuit of some far-out experience but staying right where we are, with the doors and windows of our consciousness wide open, so the thief can make himself at home. As you'll see, it's just a matter of sitting quietly, not pushing stuff out but allowing the silence to pull you in. It's good to sit every day, but because this way of non-effort is so effective, you don't have to devote long hours to it.

Our Syllabus

Before we dive into this core practice, here in Part I we'll warm things up with a few preliminary practices and strategies. Some don't require any sitting at all. You can put them to use right away, applying them in situations where anger, fear, worry, or addictive cravings may arise. They'll help to gently reorient the way you experience life, so that you're less caught up, more grounded and relaxed, in a more friendly relationship with yourself and your world.

In Part II you'll learn to sit in natural meditation. Because it's so simple there's not a lot to learn, but to preserve that simplicity we'll explore the method thoroughly and eliminate the possible ways of making it complicated. We'll walk through a few sessions together and then cover the details of integrating meditation into ordinary life, establishing a regular practice that will keep you, over the weeks and months, opening into the silence with growing clarity and depth.

In Part III we'll introduce several supporting practices—side dishes to go with the main course—and you'll get a sense of which ones you connect with most strongly. Some are eyes-closed meditative techniques with specialized functions, such as breaking out of the sense of isolation that fear can produce, or flushing out the old emotional debris of shame or guilt. Some practices use ordinary activities such as breathing or walking, repurposed to undercut our afflictive emotions. Some can be inconspicuously applied right at the moment when you're trying to muster the courage to board the plane or ask that nice girl or guy for a date, or when you're angry at the rush hour traffic, or when the buzz of anxiety is keeping you from falling asleep. None are difficult, and some are actually a lot of fun. The idea is to make life easier, not harder.

In addition to practice, the other component of awakening, which we'll explore in Part IV, is *view*. View is not mere opinion or idea. As the word implies, it's seeing—seeing clearly, so that we perceive the reality that's right in front of us but was previously obscured by our confused ideas. Suppose one day you notice your neighbor peering at your house with a pair of high-powered binoculars. Is he a spy? A Peeping Tom? Soon all his actions—walking his dog, watering his lawn—become suspect, and your sunny street becomes a dark alley of conspiratorial doom. But then he drops by with binoculars in hand and tells you there's a rare golden-cheeked warbler nesting in your tree: Would you like to take a look? In one moment, your old confusion drops away, and with it your fear and anxiety. Without changing any-thing, everything is fine. It's a beautiful day in this neighborhood.

I've shared practice and view with scientists and musicians, film-makers and lawyers, software engineers and martial artists, addicts and therapists, grad students, prisoners, doctors, and a couple of comedians. I've taught CEOs in the Guatemalan rain forest and car salesmen in New Jersey. Again and again, I've seen that it works. Different people, different situations, same report: the clouds part, the sky clears, the fear and anger and the rest of it start to drain away. Anyone can do it. You may feel sure that you're the one exception, and that's fine. You don't have to believe in it, just try it. Come and see.

There's a track on the Rolling Stones' *Exile on Main St.* that I love: a throbbing, pulsing gospel blues jam in which Mick Jagger sings, preacher-style, about yearning for an experience of Jesus that goes beyond mere belief. It's titled "I Just Want to See His Face."

Does this mean that you'll become a fully awakened, utterly fearless sage overnight? Probably not, but that's OK too. A certain amount of fear, after all, is part of a perfectly healthy alarm system. Nature gives us just enough fear of snakes to make sure we avoid the venomous ones—but if, like one friend of mine, you can't walk into a pet shop because you're afraid the snakes will smash their glass tanks, jump through the air, and attack you, then your alarm system has been cranked up to eleven and needs to be recalibrated. We can do that; we have the technology. And then any remaining traces of fear just become part of the bigger OK-ness. I'm still not wild about dealing with soft-balls or, for that matter, any other kind of sporting equipment. Fine. I once heard the Dalai Lama confess that he's afraid of worms. He gets a good laugh out of it.

The *Bhagavad Gita*, India's classic text of meditation and action, says, "Even a little of this practice delivers from great fear." If, after a little practice, you *fear less*—even one percent less than before—then you're already coming out of the darkness and into the light. You've made it through the worst.

And more light awaits you. You just have to turn toward it. As the poet Hafez wrote:

> *Ever since happiness heard your name*
> *It has been running through the streets*
> *Trying to find you.*

CHAPTER 2

Breathe Through Your Feet

Let's get to it, then.

You're in a conference with your soon-to-be ex and a couple of divorce lawyers . . . or you're waiting for the doctor to call with the results of your biopsy . . . or you're sweating through your third week of sobriety and trying hard to hang on . . . or you're on your umpty-umpth morning commute and feeling your road rage approach the boiling point . . . or you're in the dentist's chair, bracing yourself for the root canal . . .

Those are some serious situations. We're going to start our path of awakening by addressing them with what may seem like a completely unserious technique. In fact, it may seem almost insultingly unresponsive to the gravity of the situation. But appearances can be deceiving. In the immortal words of Spinal Tap, "It's such a fine line between stupid and, uh, clever." Come and see.

Breathe through your feet.

That's it, essentially. Simple, but let's break it down:

You can be sitting, standing, or lying down, with your eyes closed or open, although it's probably best to practice this first with eyes closed.

Bring your attention to the soles of your feet. You might notice that this completely ordinary act of attention takes no effort—as soon as you think of it, it's already happening. You might also notice that it involves a sort of combination of feeling and subtle visual imagining, which you've done all your life. If I say *left ear*, you immediately imagine-feel your left ear, with no effort or learning curve required.

Now, breathe normally, as you already are, but each time you breathe in, imagine-feel that you're breathing in through the soles of your feet. Each time you breathe out, imagine-feel that you're breathing out through the soles of your feet. That's all. Don't worry about how fast or slow or deep or shallow your breathing is, or whether your breathing pattern stays the same or changes. Don't strain to concentrate or focus. Don't try to push away thoughts or sounds or anything else. Don't try to feel any special way. Just breathe through your feet, and let everything else be however it is.

Please take a few moments to do this right now.

. . .

. . .

. . .

OK. Welcome back.

You may notice now that you feel a little less stuck in your head, in the buzzing of thoughts and feelings. Perhaps there's some sense of being more grounded, centered, or refreshed. If you're not sure, that's fine too. Meditative experience (which is what this is) is constantly changing, and we don't worry about whether it seems subjectively "good" or "bad" in any given session.

Now, as you go through your day, you can come back from time to time to this practice of breathing through your feet. Be creative about invoking it in different places and situations. This is your new toy. Anytime you like, you can pull it out of your pocket and play with it: when you're stopped at a red light, standing in line, waiting for your movie to start, working at your computer. Tune in to the technique and get familiar with it when things are fairly relaxed and uneventful.

Then, when the stress hits the fan, you're ready. Even as your plane hits the turbulence, or you're driving through the scary part of town late at night, or you're nervously waiting for the audition or job interview, or you're getting the phone call from the Bad News Boyfriend, you can breathe through your feet and you fear less. You've practiced the drill and you're ready for the fire. Feelings of anger or worry or craving for your drug of choice will still arise. Don't try to suppress those feelings, but don't act them out either. Don't fixate on them or try to distract yourself from them. The feelings are just there, like everything else: the temperature of the air, the color of the walls or the sky. You have to breathe anyway, so just breathe through your feet and you may notice that you're not quite as tightly gripped by the stressful feelings as you were before.

When you go to bed tonight, you may particularly enjoy falling asleep while breathing through your feet. If you normally toss and turn, you may find that this makes sleep a smoother cruise, and if you wake up in the night you can just cruise some more.

See what happens.

CHAPTER 3

Relax at the Moment of Contact

The experience is all too familiar: You know you can no longer put off that onerous phone call to that difficult person. Right outside your window it's a perfect spring day, but all you can feel is dread, like a vise tightening around your temples. In the previous chapter, we referred to this as being "gripped by the stressful feelings." But if we look more carefully, is that really what happens? Do the feelings grip us, or in some way are we gripping them?

No matter what we feel gripped by—whether it's tension, apprehension, obsession, anything—the question is the same, and the answer is important. If it turns out that it's us that's been gripping all along, that's excellent news. That means we can stop. But how would we do that?

It seems obvious that the opposite of gripping is letting go, and "Let go" is advice you'll often hear; in fact, it's become a bit of a cliché in the worlds of therapy and meditation. But it's often construed in a way that backfires. People hear the word *go* and think that the thing they're letting go of is supposed to go away, and then they feel frustrated when it doesn't. They'll often say, "I'm *trying* to let go, but I can't." But that's not letting go. That's insisting that the thought or feeling disappear, which is a backdoor way of holding on to it.

So forget about letting go. Instead, just relax your grip. Then it doesn't matter whether the thought or feeling continues to hang around or not. We can't control that, and we don't have to.

To be clear about this, let's do an experiment. If you happen to have a ball handy, such as a tennis ball or beach ball, please place it on your open palm and grip it tightly from beneath. Walk around the room like this, from the chair to the table to the window, or whatever landmarks are there. This is your mind gripping some thought or feeling. It encounters all the aspects of day-to-day living (all the room's landmarks), but its experiences of them are filtered through the tension of that gripping. Now relax your grip on the ball and walk around some more. The ball may fall away immediately or eventually, or it may remain in your hand, but it doesn't matter. The hand is open and at ease. The landmarks are experienced with clarity, just as they are, without the distorting filter of tension.

Our new practice is simply to take this habit on the road, to apply it in real-life situations. It does require some attention at first to recognize when you're tightening up. Although it may be subtle, there's generally a physical component to that tightening, a sort of bracing of the body. You may feel it in a particular region; for many people it's the neck, lower back, or gut, but it can be anywhere. Notice it, relax your grip, and just sink back into yourself.

Initially, there may be moments when the newness of this approach makes it a little disconcerting. Over the years of using your old approach, you may have come to equate being tense with being conscientious. You may wonder, *Can I really take care of business effectively without my old tightness? Or am I just being flaky and irresponsible?* But once you try the new way a few times, experience will show you that when you're loose you're actually *more* effective. Tightness restricts your range of motion and narrows your vision, keeping you from seeing possible solutions to problems. If you're all wrapped up in fuming at the slow-moving traffic, you may not notice the clear side streets that can get you around it. If you're caught up in anxiety about the impression you're making in your job interview, you may not see the warm smile or hear the gracious comments that the interviewer is making to signal that you're doing fine.

Loose doesn't mean sloppy or undisciplined. It means open enough to be sensitive and responsive, to act in the moment when you have to move faster than you can think. You can see this in great athletes, martial artists, dancers, actors, as well as teachers, parents, and entrepreneurs—there's no way to do what they do if you're tightly coiled. Cary Grant, who exuded supremely cool sophistication on the screen, recognized the importance of coolness in his costars:

> I've worked with Bergman. I've worked with Hepburn. I've worked with some of the biggest stars, but Grace Kelly was the best actress I've ever worked with in my life. That woman was total relaxation, absolute ease—she was totally there.

Years ago, when I was studying the martial art of aikido with my teacher Rick Stickles, I had an experience that brought this point home to me in a very dramatic, physical way. I was practicing for a test where I would have to repel three opponents as they repeatedly rushed me. Aikido, when it's done right, is beautiful to watch, almost dancelike. Rather than clash with your attackers, you use their own energy and, in big, circular, pivoting movements, send them rolling or sailing across the mat. But as the first attacker rushed in to grab me and I tried to execute the throw, I couldn't budge him. We wound up grappling instead, locked in place, as the other two rushed in to take me down. This happened again and again, till suddenly I heard the teacher's voice. Halfway up the stairs to the dressing room, he had paused to watch, and he called out, "Relax at the moment of contact!"

Was I tensing up? That was news to me—I had been too busy tensing up to realize I was tensing up. But now, as the next attacker grabbed me, I relaxed. No longer frozen in my own rigidity, no longer working against my own tension, I felt my shoulders go soft and my energy drop from my upper body to my hips. In the same moment, I pivoted grace-fully and threw the attacker with fluid ease. Wow—*that* was fun! But then, as the next attacker came in, I tensed up again. Once more, Stickles Sensei called out, "Relax at the moment of contact!" and once again I softened, pivoted, and easily made the throw. And again. And again. Every time I popped out of that zone of relaxation, the throw became difficult or impossible. Every time I sank back into it, it was easy. It was like turning a switch on and off. The difference was so stark it was funny.

Anything you can do, you can do better from that place of fluidity and ease. Anything. There's never a reason not to relax. Until it becomes habitual, you do have to think about it and make a deliberate choice. First the challenge comes at you, like one of my three attackers. Maybe it's, *Uh-oh, here comes my crazy neighbor again to complain about my trash cans*, or, *Uh-oh, here I go again, walking to the front of the conference room, to give my presentation and embarrass myself*, or, *Uh-oh, here I am on a first date again, and I really like this person. Do I seem too eager? Or too apathetic? Am I laughing too loud?* The circumstances are different, but the *Uh-oh* is the same, and that's what you have to notice—that's where the physical clenching takes place. Notice how that clenching feels in the body, and then unclench. No one has to teach you how to unclench. You just did it with the ball. You just have to remember *to* unclench.

This is a subtle skill, and it does take time to integrate it into our way of being in the world. It's a matter of replacing an old, turbulent habit with a new, chill one. The change is not merely attitudinal but neurological. We're retraining our nervous system to process experi-ences in a more cooled-out way, so that it doesn't interpret every moment of contact as an occasion for fight-or-flight.

These moments of contact are not always so obvious or dramatic. I once spent a winter in southeast Iowa, on a college campus where the freezing subarctic winds whipped right through my skinny bones. One day, as I walked across the quad with a friend, wretchedly hunching my shoulders and tensing my muscles as usual, he pointed out that it didn't help. "Try dropping your shoulders and relaxing instead," he suggested. I tried it, and damned if I didn't feel a little bit warmer—and a lot more relaxed. That's how you do it. For that winter wind, just substitute the homework you've been putting off, the new job you've been afraid to start, the breakup speech you've been avoiding, the irate driver in the next car—whatever's attacking you—and relax at the moment of contact.

I would like a time machine, please, and just half a minute to visit my nine-year-old self, the wretched spaz standing desolate out in right field, terrified of the ball hurtling toward him—and fated, over the next dozen years, to have puberty, high school, drugs, college, sex, first loves, and first heartbreaks all hurtle toward him as well. (Also some pretty scary encounters with street thugs, cops, and the draft board.) I would tell him: "Pssssst! Dean! Listen up! Relax at the moment of contact! Don't forget!"

There's a further implication here, which would be too much to explain to young Dean in thirty seconds, but which we're now beginning to explore. To relax rather than tighten is to drop our ineffective, imaginary armor and let things be as they are. That's the beginning of a more intimate, accepting relationship with the world, a kind of embrace. There's a beautiful prayer that says, "May all my actions be motivated by love rather than fear." Eventually this embrace becomes love, and love—as you may have heard, and you'll soon see for yourself—casts out fear.

CHAPTER 4

The Sweetest Dog in the World

When your fear kicks in—or your grief, or craving, or anxiety, or rage, or whatever you've got—there are two basic ways to mishandle it. You've probably tried both.

One way is to suppress it. As the word implies, that's a matter of pressing it down. Unfortunately, when you pretend it doesn't exist, it doesn't go away. You've just temporarily pressed it somewhere out of sight, like sweeping dust under a rug. Often it gets pressed down into the body, where it may manifest as back pain, stomach problems, hypertension, or other stress-related ailments.

The other way, essentially the opposite of the first, is to indulge the feeling. Having perhaps tried to suppress the fear or anger or anxiety and failed, we swing in the other direction and let it take over. We sit smack in the middle of it as it becomes our whole reality, both the feeling and the story around it: this thing happened, and then that thing happened, and what if this other thing happens, and oh no oh no oh no oh no . . .

Clearly we need a more skillful way to navigate, one that steers between these two big rocks into the clear waters beyond. Who can help us out here?

Cue the dog!

Please imagine that the sweetest, most loving, most faithful, most empathetic dog in the world is sitting with you right now. You may be so fortunate as to *have* the sweetest dog in the world, in which case you don't have to imagine. (If you're a cat person . . . well, despite the stereotype of aloof disdain, I've met some deeply empathetic cats . . . but not many. Your call.) So here you sit, with the sweetest (let's say) dog in the world. Wow, look at those beautiful eyes—the softest, clearest, most loving eyes imaginable. You can see that he (let's say) is all heart. Go ahead, then, and tell him your story. Hard things happen in this life, and this is your chance to declare them. Pour out your feelings. Go all the way with it, totally spill your guts: all-out indulgence, the indulgier the better. The dog never cuts you off, never questions, never judges, and never loses interest. He pays rapt, loving attention.

Keep pouring out your story and all the feelings connected with it till there's nothing left to pour. Then take a little breather, maybe walk around the block.

And now sit down and go through the story again, but with one big difference. This time, first close your eyes and imagine that *you're* the dog. Feel what it feels like to be under all that doggie fur, inside that doggie metabolism, picking up the subtle aromas of your environment with your sharp doggie nose, looking around the room with your sweet doggie eyes.

And then—oh, here's your dear human friend, the one you love so much. And now your friend is making those funny sounds with the mouth again. They're not *Sit!* or *Stay!*, so they're completely incomprehensible, but that doesn't keep you from listening with unfailing attention and total, unquestioning love. In fact, that makes you the perfect listener. You don't judge or disagree or agree, you don't interpret or try to interject your own stories. You're just wide open to all that *wocka wocka wocka* and to the feelings that it conveys. You can understand feelings, bighearted pooch that you are. So much upsetness!

But it doesn't stick anywhere inside you. It all goes straight to your heart, where it instantly dissolves into perfect, loving, open space.

In this way, just keep listening to the whole story, happily absorbing all those meaningless words, each of them gone and forgotten the moment you hear them, and keep lovingly receiving the feelings as they instantly dissolve in your doggie heart, till it's all been once again told and poured out. And looking out through your eyes of doggie love, really *see* your human friend—so vulnerable, so sincere, just trying to get through life, just wanting to relax and be OK. Fortunately, you're an expert. You can show your friend how it's done, by doing nothing in particular but being as you are.

Good dog!

CHAPTER 5

Would It Help?

In Steven Spielberg's 2015 Cold War thriller *Bridge of Spies*, Mark Rylance plays the captured Soviet mole Rudolf Abel. He has a soft-spoken, deadpan quality, with just a hint of a sardonic smile occasionally crossing his face. In their first jailhouse meeting, Tom Hanks, as James Donovan, the American lawyer assigned to defend Abel, warns him not to speak to anyone else.

> DONOVAN: I have a mandate to serve you. Nobody else does. Quite frankly, everybody else has an interest in sending you to the electric chair.
> ABEL: All right.
> DONOVAN: You don't seem alarmed.
> ABEL (considers for a moment, then shrugs almost imperceptibly): Would it help?

This is the film's most memorable line—people who spot Rylance on the street now call it out to him. For me, it carries an echo of a Yiddish expression I heard a lot growing up: *Gornisht helfn*, meaning "Nothing will help," always uttered in a tone of head-shaking, wouldn't-you-know-it exasperation: just as we thought, life *is* stacked fatally against us. But Abel's question, "Would it help?," is not fatalistic. It's a simple, clear-eyed nod to reality. You may win, you may lose, and worrying won't make any difference, so why subject yourself to it? Why indulge in it? Rylance won an Oscar for his understated performance; audiences recognized the almost palpable stillness that is the root of sanity and dignity in the face of danger. This is how real grownups, who know that worry is an extravagance, carry themselves.

The line also recalls the wisdom of the eighth-century Buddhist sage Shantideva:

> *If there's a solution, what's the point of worrying?*
> *If there's no solution, what's the point of worrying?*

Can you feel the liberative power of this insight? Right now you can acknowledge that absolutely, definitely, positively, in this moment and for the rest of your life, no amount of lost sleep will ever keep your stocks from crashing, or keep your kids safe from the influence of knucklehead friends, or give you a better Gleason score on your prostate biopsy, or make the politicians in Washington obey the instructions you shout at them through the TV screen, or, for that matter, make your old girlfriend or boyfriend come back and beg your forgiveness. Some people call this *resignation*. Fine. The root of that word is *resign*. Worrying is a lot of work and no one's paid me yet, so I resign. Take this job and shove it.

And you really can resign. Many people have, and not just Russian spies. One, apparently, was Alfred Hitchcock. On the set of *Notorious* one day, he was in conference with his cinematographer when a small fire broke out. Hitchcock, never missing a beat, finished his sentence, turned to some stagehands, and said drily, "Will someone please put that fire out?" Then he went on with his conversation. Another non-worrier is Willie Nelson, who, in a recent interview, sounds like a country version of Shantideva:

> I've never seen worrying about anything change it. So I decided not to do it. . . . You know, we're all gonna die. So we all have to say, "OK, I may be next, you may be next, who knows?"

"So I decided not to do it." That simple. This is not a matter of *trying* not to worry. It's not *repressing* worry, pushing it down into your innards where it will fester into an ulcer. It's feeling around, finding where the worry switch is, and pushing it to OFF. Or, rather, it's realizing that you've been repeatedly pushing it to ON, and that you can leave off doing that—resign. It's just a habit. True, Willie is helped by the background mellow of all that weed he smokes, but you're going to have the background mellow of meditation, which is more real and long-lasting and, incidentally, makes your brains clearer instead of fuzzier. As you continue to renew and deepen the clarity and relaxation of meditation, it will become more obvious that worry is not something inflicted on you but something you've chosen to do, and that you therefore can choose to stop. Hitchcock and Willie and Rudolf Abel are not a special breed of people. They're ordinary people who found the switch.

This doesn't mean that you become passive or indifferent, or even that feelings of worry never arise. It means that when those feelings do arise you can apply your new habits. You can breathe through your feet or relax at the moment of contact, or use any of several more methods you'll be learning. That creates space around the worried feelings, so they don't take over the whole screen of your consciousness and you can be more effective in problem-solving, not less.

Where I live, in the Los Angeles area, there are lots of actors scrambling for work. One friend of mine had some meaty featured roles on a couple of popular TV series, and on the strength of that success bought an expensive home in a posh part of town. But then the work started to dry up. He kept getting calls from his agent and going on auditions but not getting the parts. He started having trouble sleeping, worrying about making his mortgage payments. Finally he called me one morning, sounding more relaxed than he'd been in months. "I realized what was going on," he said. "I was convinced that, if I gave myself permission to stop worrying about the jobs, they would stop coming. That doesn't make sense, does it?"

As it happened, a few days later he started getting work again. It was as if once he released his death grip on the thought *I must get a job*, the door swung open and the parts could find him. Do things really work that way? It sounds a bit woo-woo, but I've seen it happen too many times to dismiss it. In particular, I've heard again and again about people who kept searching for the right life partner till they finally gave up and relaxed, deciding that what the hell, maybe they'd just stay single—and then the right person appeared.

Give up. That's a phrase we've been trained to hear as a sad, defeated loser's ending. But giving is a good thing, and up is a good direction. What if to give up really means to offer the outcome up to God, or the universe, or life, and stop trying to own it all ourselves? In fact, outcomes are never really ours to own or give. All we're doing now is acknowledging, as clear-eyed grownups, that in any situation we do what we do and then what happens happens. As the *Bhagavad Gita* says:

> You have control over your actions only. Over the fruits of your actions you have no control.

People often think Eastern scriptures like the *Gita* are full of abstract philosophy or mysticism, but this is the most rational, concrete, liberating pragmatism. Mysticism is what we practice when we try to will our team to win the big game or the rain to stop on our day off. Would it help? Nope. I suspect that all that Law of Attraction stuff is New Age bullshit, and that's good news. It means that yes, we do what we can, as impeccably as we can, and then we're off duty—free.

Once Oprah Winfrey was a guest on Stephen Colbert's show, and they talked about their favorite Bible verses. Colbert, who sometimes teaches Sunday school when he's not making television, said his favorite verse was from the Gospels, Jesus's instruction to the disciples:

I say to you, do not worry, for who among you by worrying can add a hair to his head or an hour to the span of his life?

That's a poetic way of asking, "Would it help?"

I recently found myself echoing Jesus's rhetorical question in talking with a woman who frequently attends the Tuesday evening meditation sessions I lead in Santa Monica. She stopped coming for a while, and when she returned she explained she had been dealing with her father's illness and death. "The hardest part," she said, "was the conflicted feeling. He was suffering a lot and I found myself wanting him to let go, but then how can you wish for your father to die?" When I pointed out that her wish didn't matter, that it had no effect, she exhaled and visibly relaxed. "And that," I said, "is *your* letting go."

This letting go of worry, of futile struggle against what is, works from the smallest annoyance all the way to full-blown crises, when we feel our whole life is melting down. Once my wife and I were on a week-long retreat on beautiful Mount Madonna, in Central California, led by Adyashanti. Adya, whose birth name is Steve, is a perfectly ordinary-looking American fellow with a buzz cut, a boyish voice, and a gentle, prankish sense of humor. A student of his once described him as "Charlie Brown on acid"; I'd say he's the grilled cheese sandwich of awakened sages. At one session, a woman came up to the mike and, choking back her tears, told Adya that she had lost her job and, along with it, her whole sense of her identity. "I just had no more roles . . . I don't have the same interests and ambitions that I used to have in the world. I don't even know who I am in the world anymore." "Isn't it delightful?" Adya responded. "It *should* be!" she said. Then Adya said:

> Well, just try something on for size, OK? You're falling through the sky. You do what everybody does when they fall through the sky—at least for the first time. [Mimes clawing desperately at the air. The woman and the audience laugh.] It's your body looking for orientation, and it can't find any in space, which makes it panic more, which makes it grasp more. It's like a loop, isn't it? So when we fall, it's like a very visceral, deep sense of instantaneous losing of our whole point of reference.
>
> So, imagine that you're falling through the sky, and someone comes falling next to you, and they're just sort of like— [Puts his hands behind his head and leans back, like someone relaxing in a hammock. More laughter.] Of course you would think the person's a little crazy. "Why aren't you panicking?"
>
> Your fear isn't because you're falling. It isn't because you've lost something. Your fear is because you're looking for an orientation that you can't find. You're looking for an identity you can't find. You're looking for things that aren't really there anymore. And it's the looking for them that causes the anxiety and the fear. It's not the falling away. It's the trying to put back together what's fallen away.

Again, there's never a reason not to relax. Clawing the air doesn't help. Trying to reassemble the Humpty Dumpty of our lives doesn't help.

But it's not needed. Yes, of course, when things change dramatically it takes adjustment, and that can be hard, but still your life is never broken; only your old concept of it is broken. Life is what is always emerging from the shell, what you're always living right now.

What about when it's not just our own life, but the whole world that seems to be melting down in crisis? Many people feel that way these days, as they see the environment, human rights, civil liberties, and the notion of truth itself under attack by reckless, sickeningly ignorant chieftains. There are so many fronts to fight on, so many lies to challenge, so many insults to basic decency and kindness that nothing we do seems enough. Some people swing back and forth: they obsessively read every horrific news item till they're choking on stress, then they withdraw completely, then they feel guilty and swing back again. Sometimes the only measure of sanity seems to come from the late-night comedians, but even the laughter they provoke can seem like a stolen consolation, blunting our proper outrage.

But we're not the first to go through such times. In 1946, as the unspeakable slaughter and suffering of the Second World War was giving way to the Cold War and the threat of nuclear holocaust, the great Christian writer C. S. Lewis put this in a letter to a friend:

> One mustn't assume burdens that God does not lay upon us.
>
> It is one of the evils of rapid diffusion of news that the sorrows of all the world come to us every morning. I think each village was meant to feel pity for its own sick and poor whom it can help and I doubt if it is the duty of any private person to fix his mind on ills which he cannot help. (This may even become an escape from the works of charity we really can do to those we know.)
>
> A great many people . . . do now seem to think that the mere state of being worried is in itself meritorious. I don't think

it is. We must, if it so happens, give our lives for others: but
even while we're doing it, I think we're meant to enjoy Our
Lord and, in Him, our friends, our food, our sleep, our jokes,
and the birds' song and the frosty sunrise.

. . . It is very dark: but there's usually light enough for the
next step or so.

This all seems even more valid today than it did when Lewis wrote it.
Now news is diffused even more rapidly, giving us even more opportunities to fix our minds on ills we cannot help and to mistake noble
soliloquies on Facebook for the works of charity we really can do.

And there *are* things you can do. Just take that "next step or so." In
any given situation, in any given moment, there's a most skillful, compassionate way to act. Releasing worry gives us more space to see what
it is. Do what you can do. Don't worry about what you can't do, and
certainly don't go into a tailspin of dejection over it. It won't help. Then,
in whatever light is available, look around. Then take the next step.

CHAPTER 6

Resting Bliss Face

Now we're going to talk about smiling. That may sound peachy to you or it may make you bristle. You may be thinking, *Hey, I'm in pain, don't talk to me about smiling.* That's fine. The sages and the scientists are on my side. Just stick with me for a few pages and see what happens.

You may recall a meme that trended online a while back: RBF, or Resting Bitch Face. It featured photos of people, usually female celebrities, wearing apparently bored, miffed, or sullen expressions. The owner of the face may well have just been concentrating or taking a break from posturing for cameras, but the trolls, with their customary gallantry, were delighted to pounce and to pronounce their victim a bitch.

This is obviously sexist and obviously dumb. But it does have a context. Research has shown that onlookers will generally interpret photos of resting, unsmiling faces as hostile or otherwise negative, even when the owner of the face intended simple neutrality.* So, as a simple,

---

* First and only footnote: I'm not going to clutter this book with footnotes consisting of long URLs that no one's going to retype and look up. To confirm or look deeper into any of the research I cite, just Google a couple of key words and you'll find the most up-to-date information.

practical tactic of social lubrication if nothing else, smiling is a good idea. It signals to others, *Things are OK—relax*. That's just good manners.

And your smile, or your lack thereof, communicates something to yourself as well. The mind-body connection is a two-way street. As the Vietnamese Zen master Thich Nhat Hanh has said:

> Sometimes your joy is the source of your smile, but sometimes your smile can be the source of your joy.

Does this mean you should plaster a forced, insincere smile across your face when you feel like crap? No—we all know how hollow that fake smile looks and feels. Awakening is about coming out of what's false, not adding to it. But there's a way to make the smile real.

Please start by deliberately assuming your Resting Bitch Face. Even exaggerate it a little, make it harder, bitchier. Notice how that makes you feel. Ugh. Next, try a big, fake smile: pull back the corners of your mouth while you keep the rest of your face immobile, dead. Notice how *that* feels. Double ugh, and it looks stupid.

So let's start again—go back to RBF. This time we're going to use our eyes. The old saying is that the eyes are the windows to the soul, and the neuronal pathway between the eyes and the brain *is* very short. So smile with your eyes. That is, imagine that you're doing with your eyes what your mouth does in a genuine smile: narrowing slightly and letting the warm *feeling* of a smile take over and pull their outer corners back and slightly up. At first, keep your mouth frozen, playing hard-to-get with the smiling eyes, till it can no longer resist and the smile slowly spills or suddenly bursts through the mouth's emotional dam. That breakthrough will in turn feed back to your brain, making you feel smilier still. As that happens, relax: settle back into the smile— whether it's just a soft hint of a smile or a broad grin—as if you're settling back on a big, soft, squishy cushion.

You'll probably find that this whole sequence makes you feel at least a little bit happier, and maybe a lot. You get an instant squirt of endorphins, which produce general positivity, so you fear less, anger less, crave less, and so forth. This method also gives you a warm, genuine, happy smile that you can share with others, thus spreading the wealth and making your home or work environment a more positive place. In fact, Swedish researchers have found that smiling is contagious—it's hard to maintain your RBF when others smile at you. That's one of the reasons why we keep smiling entertainers around. If you can hold the corners of your mouth pulled back and dance at the same time, you can be a Rockette. If you can summon a genuine, endorphin-flooding smile from so deep inside that it's as if the sun's in your heart and you're ready for love, then you're Gene Kelly performing "Singin' in the Rain." (He filmed that sequence while running a high fever. The stuff works.)

The notion that facial expressions can be a cause as well as an effect of emotions is called the *facial feedback hypothesis*, and its roots go back to Darwin. Over the years, it's been tested in various ingenious ways. Recent research has shown that using Botox to immobilize the frowning muscles can reduce depression. I like the study that had participants hold a pen while watching a cartoon and then rate how funny it was. Group A had to hold the pen between their lips, forcing them to frown; Group B held it between their teeth, forcing a smile; and the control group held it in their hand. Group B found the cartoon funnier, demonstrating that even a mechanical, mouth-only smile can give the brain some happy feedback.

There's yet another way to do this that works better than a pen between your teeth. You've probably heard of mantras, sounds whose psychoacoustic qualities can be used to tune our consciousness, the best-known being OM. But here's another, slightly less traditional one. A dear friend once told me, "Dean, always remember—no matter what's happening, you can never have a bad time as long as you just say, Wheeeeeee!" This mantra is most effective if you combine it with the proper *mudra*, or hand gesture: as you exclaim it, throw your hands up and out, like . . . like . . . like a person exclaiming, Wheeeeeee! Do this three times, and then try to feel depressed. I dare you.

If you really want to test the power of the smile, try making up your mind to apply it at least, let's say, half a dozen times a day. You can be on your commute, working at your desk, walking your dog, or doing anything else. When you first wake up in the morning, before you get out of bed, do a smile or two or three to set the tone of the day and short-circuit the habitual negative loops that, till now, might have kicked in. Identify some of the usual stress points of your daily routine, and try applying your smile topically: as you walk up to the podium, when you deal with a difficult client, or just before you jump off the diving board—*whatever* kind of board you have to jump off of. When you talk to people on the phone, whether socially or for business, do it with your warm smile on and you'll probably notice that they respond to you more positively—they can't see you, but they'll feel you. If you combine this with the technique of relaxing at the moment of contact, which we introduced in chapter 3, it will be especially powerful.

After a while, you may find that this way of functioning becomes automatic, so you no longer need to deliberately choose it. Welcome to your new default face—Resting Bliss Face—and your new default mood. Our brain prefers happiness to unhappiness. We only need to cooperate a little, and it will rewire itself for happiness. That's what's happening here.

CHAPTER 7

Snakes on a Plane

A reader in Manchester, England, recently sent me an e-mail. He wrote:

> I once asked a Catholic priest who was on a twelve-step programme, "What's the difference between religion and spirituality?" He replied, "In my opinion, religion is for people who pray to God so as not to go to hell. Spirituality is for people who have already been there and are now looking for a way back home."

If you're reading this book, there's a good chance you've been to hell, or at least some pretty serious heck. Fear, anger, addiction, grief, guilt, confusion, loneliness—something has set your hair on fire. Like the Prodigal Son, most people are happy to party on till one day they've run out of money (or health, or family, or stories, or good looks, or luck), and they hit bottom. The Prodigal Son, having demanded his inheritance early and then burned through it, finds himself in a faraway land, feeding pigs for pennies and envying them for the garbage they eat. Only then does he think of making his way back home.

An updated version of that hair-on-fire moment occurs in 2006's most sublimely dopey film, *Snakes on a Plane*. After the 450 deadly snakes set loose in the cabin have finally attacked one passenger too many, our FBI agent hero, played by Samuel L. Jackson, boils over with exasperation. Preparing to shoot out some windows so the snakes will be sucked out into the thin air, he utters the certified fifty-fifth-greatest movie line of all time. All together now:

I have had it with these motherfucking snakes on this motherfucking plane!

There's something about this line that's irreducibly great. It's like a formula in algebra—you can substitute values to make it work in all sorts of situations:

I have had it with these motherfucking commercials on this motherfucking television!
I have had it with these motherfucking trolls on the motherfucking web!
I have had it with these motherfucking cancer cells on my motherfucking MRI!
I have had it with these motherfucking clowns in the motherfucking Congress!

And more to the point for us:

I have had it with this motherfucking fear (or) rage (or) anxiety (or) addiction in my motherfucking life!

Not everyone has to reach such a dramatic breaking point. The teachings are out there; by now anyone who doesn't live under a rock has at least heard the word *meditation* and knows, at least in some vague way, that it's supposed to smooth out your life. We're past the days when people could routinely dismiss it as some Eastern cult or hippie-trippy fantasy. Now there are meditation classes at the Y and meditation apps for your phone. Some people just quietly realize that their already good lives can be even better. They check out the available resources and go for it—they don't need a bowling ball to fall on their head.

But our old stories, our old models of life, even when they feed our suffering, have the power of momentum going for them. We've invested a lot of practice in them; we know how to do them. So a lot of people need that bowling ball. It may be an illness, the death of a loved one, the end of a marriage, the crash-and-burn of a career, the bottom of an addiction, but they need some kind of pain to catch their attention, some breakdown of their old model of life to make it clear that it no longer works—if it ever really did. One way or another, they need to find themselves at the juncture described by the great bebop comic Lord Buckley:

> They didn't know where they was goin' but they know they
> had to go, 'cause they know where they was wasn't it.

So your fear, your anger, your busted business, your fractured family, your heart attack—whatever crisis has brought you here—has been a blessing, a wake-up call. Yeah, easy for me to say. Depending on how raw your pain is, there's a good chance you don't recognize it as a blessing right now. Fine. It's enough that it spurs you to start looking for a way back home.

The Prodigal Son approaches his father's place, intending to beg for a job alongside the lowest of the servants.

> But while he was still a long way from home his father saw
> him, and his heart went out to him; he ran and hugged his son
> and kissed him.

This is one of the most poignant moments in our literature. We've all screwed up. We've all wasted time, we've all felt confused and perhaps seriously lost, but it's not too late. We just need to take the first stumbling steps back in the general direction of where we came from: the source, the silence at our core, the boundless OK-ness, our true home, our true father. Then *it* comes running to embrace *us*, even when we're still a long way from home.

Till now, we've been dodging this problem or that affliction, like dodging one snake after another. But now we're enlisting boundlessness, the wide-open sky that envelops the little airplane of our life, to suck out all the snakes at once. You have to fasten your seat belt and shoot out a few windows—break through your separation from that sky—but then there's nothing to do but let it happen. You don't do it, it does you. Call it meditation or call it grace or don't call it anything at all, but give it all up to that bigger space that surrounds you.

Fear, grief, rage, bitter disappointment—our various afflictions may look and feel different, but they're all forms of the same primal suffering, which is the sense of isolation, of being alone and cut off, like a wave without an ocean. But there's no such thing as a wave without an ocean. The sages—Buddha, Jesus, Shankara, and people you've never heard of, some of whom you may have passed in the street—are not gods. They're ordinary human beings, who yawn and scratch and pick their teeth just like you, but who have managed to wake up out of isolation and suffering. They've shot out their windows, and their snakes are gone. What they report back is that every one of us can do the same.

PART II

Rest as Awareness

CHAPTER 8

Settling Happens

It's time to introduce our core practice: natural meditation, the wide-open doorway into the space beyond fear. The one recommendation for the smoothest ride is to set aside any assumptions—based on what you may have read, imagined, or previously practiced—about what you're supposed to do or what's supposed to happen when you meditate. This will be simpler and easier than all that. I'd actually love to abolish the word *meditation*, which sounds like some kind of big, exotic task. We'll be hanging out in tasklessness. The Italians have a lovely expression for this: *dolce far niente*, sweet doing-nothing

In case you're thinking, *Wait, I don't know anything about this, I'm just a beginner*, then congratulations—you're starting fresh, without any bad habits to unlearn. If you've been doing other forms of meditation, for now please allow yourself to be a beginner again, with a blank slate. To enter into the kingdom of heaven, we are told, be like a little child. No Advanced Placement credit will be given. Abandon all sophistication, ye who enter here.

Here We Are

Note: I suggest that you read through these instructions a few times in an unhurried way, then set the book aside and practice whatever you remember of them. Don't worry about getting everything "right." As long as you're taking it easy, letting everything be however it is, that's the essence of natural meditation and that *is* right. Also, on the *Fear Less* page of my website, **DeanWords.com**, you can find a streaming audio version of the meditation, narrated by yours truly. After a few sessions, as you connect with the simplicity of the process, you'll probably find your need for external guidance starting to fall away.

For now, please leave your eyes open. Sit comfortably. (If you sat *un*comfortably, you'd be all set for *un*natural meditation.) You might want to shake out your hands a little, then let them flop loosely onto your lap or knees. Anytime during the session that you need to adjust your position, straighten your leg, scratch your elbow, blow your nose, or do anything else to remain comfortable, go ahead.

. . .

So . . . we're sitting comfortably. Now what?

Now there's probably some sense of expectation as you anticipate launching into this new activity—some sense of turning the key in the ignition, feeling the engine start to rumble, and saying, "Here we go!"

But what if we don't start the car? We just roll the top down (yeah, it's a convertible), lean back in our seat, toss the key into the bushes, and say, "Here we *are*!"

Here we are—sitting back, no rumble, nowhere to go, leaving everything as it is, just enjoying the scenery.

. . .

OK, then. As we're sitting back in this lazy way, let's take a look around. What's in that scenery? What's already going on in our experience, without our doing anything about it?

Well, naturally seeing is going on. As we look around, up or down, left or right, the colors and shapes of different objects come in and out of view. No matter what's there, naturally we're aware of it. This is nothing special; it's been happening all our life.

Naturally we're aware of sensations as well. You might feel your back and bottom pressing against the seat, the temperature of the air, or inner sensations of being alert or sleepy, hungry or full.

Awareness of hearing is also going on: perhaps the sounds of passing traffic, birds, a distant airplane, a barking dog.

. . .

Now, please notice whether it takes any *effort* to hear what you hear.

. . .

Nope. No effort. Hearing just arises within our awareness, without our doing anything about it.

Also notice whether you have any *control* over what you hear. Can you choose what sound will arise in the next moment?

. . .

No again. Hearing just happens, arising in our awareness without our effort or control. Notice that the same goes for feeling and seeing. Everything we're aware of arises and changes on its own.

Fine. Now let's close our eyes. That's all—no meditating, please. Just continue in here-we-are mode, only with the eyes closed.

. . .

What's changed? Actually, not much. We still see, even if it's only vague colors or hazy patterns behind our eyelids. Naturally the other senses continue as well, with no effort or control from us.

Perfect.

Since it's all out of our control, let's just rest in the situation as it is, however it is.

. . .

. . .

. . .

Sounds, colors, sensations—notice that all the things we're aware of come and go like breezes in the sky. Only the sky doesn't come and go. And the sky in this case is awareness itself. Just rest in awareness, like open sky, open space, within which everything else comes and goes on its own.

. . .

. . .

. . .

Notice that thoughts and feelings also come and go, arising and changing and vanishing, just like sounds or colors. That's also perfect: just more breezes coming and going in the open sky of awareness. Don't hang on to them and don't try to push them away. Sounds are just sounds, thoughts are just thoughts. The sky has room for every kind of breeze and is not affected by any of them.

. . .

. . .

Sounds, colors, feelings, thoughts—everything comes and goes within our awareness, like breezes coming and going frictionlessly in the open sky. Even a hurricane doesn't damage the sky. So just rest back into this skylike, open awareness, without bothering much about what comes and goes within it.

. . .

. . .

Don't try to focus or concentrate on anything. Don't try to control the mind or feel some special way. Just continue to relax back into this awareness, which is like open space . . . which is always present . . . and within which everything else comes and goes, without our managing or monitoring it.

. . .

. . .

. . .

. . .

Sometimes thoughts about a particular subject may seem very persistent and gripping, even obsessive. That's fine. Don't try to push the thoughts away, and don't hang on to them. Just relax your grip on them and don't worry about whether they continue to hang around.

. . .

. . .

. . .

Anytime you find yourself holding on to a thought or feeling or anything else, or trying to push it away, just relax your grip on it. Whether it goes away or persists doesn't matter. Again and again, just relax your grip and sink back into yourself. Sink back into open, skylike awareness.

. . .

. . .

. . .

. . .

Just rest in awareness. That simple. Marinate in it, soak in it, like soaking in a hot tub.

. . .

. . .

. . .

Now, keep your eyes closed but start easing the body back to a more active state.

. . .

You can change your sitting position, stretch your limbs, perhaps squeeze your hands or gently rub your scalp or eyes. Get the blood circulating again.

. . .

When you feel ready, after about two or three minutes, you can start to slowly open your eyes. Take as much time as you need.

. . .

. . .

. . .

Good.

What Happened?

OK. That's how simple it is: resting in the awareness that's already there.

Nothing more.

Whatever comes and goes—sounds, sensations, feelings, thoughts—just let it all come and go, without trying to do anything about it. Even that word *let* is too much. *Notice* that it comes and goes and that you *can't* do anything about it. You're an innocent bystander, not a participant.

After bystanding like that for a little while, you may have noticed some feeling of relaxation, some settling down into inner silence—maybe for most of the session, maybe just for brief moments here or there. Maybe you're noticing it now in the afterglow. So, what made you relax? Did we give you a nice massage? Did we administer meds? Did we make a large deposit in your savings account? No. Did you do yoga postures or special breathing techniques? No, not that either.

Then what did you do? Well, you started with a very quiet, subtle shift of attention, to notice your own awareness and rest there. But then?

Nothing.

This is the crux of natural meditation, the fundamental principle: *Settling happens by itself.*

Think of leaves falling from a tree: they tell the whole story. A falling leaf will reach the ground in a hundred percent of cases. It may drift to the left or right, it may catch a momentary updraft, it may even get stuck in a lower limb for a while, but in its own good time it will reach the ground, because it's pulled by gravity. Gravity is irresistible and universal, attracting all bodies everywhere. In the case of human consciousness, all people everywhere gravitate toward happiness, fulfillment, peace. We don't mean *happiness* in the superficial sense of just some smiley-face, cheerful mood. We mean . . . you know, that deepest thing, the one we're always really looking for when we go after anything else. In any given moment, our attention is drawn automatically to whatever seems to offer the strongest dose of it. That's why, faster than you can think about it, your gaze is attracted to a good-looking person walking down the street. (Hence the term *attract-ive*.)

Those external sources of happiness and peace—the cookies, the cocktails, the careers, the copulation—are enticing but also unreliable, because they're always coming, going, and changing. They're moving targets. What the sages teach, and what you just glimpsed in our first session, is that the core of our being, our own awareness, is a reliable, unchanging source of happiness and peace. So instead of trying to push our way toward it or push other things out of the way, all we have to do is let ourselves be pulled. Automatically, we're drawn to it and we settle into it.

Rather than a leaf falling to the ground, most people approach meditation like they're pushing a boulder up a mountain—fighting gravity rather than using it, grunting away at whatever task they've set themselves. They'll tell you meditation is hard, and, in a way, they're right. If you work hard at it, it's hard. (Surprise!) But if you take it easy, it's easy. Sooner or later, of course, gravity wins, even for those who struggle against it. But why not sooner?

When a server in a restaurant asks me, "Are you still working on that?" my reply is, "No, I'm still enjoying it." Any tendency to work on this is just a habit you've imported from the tasks and challenges

you confront during the other hours of the day, which legitimately
require work. But every moment you spend just sitting and marinating
in awareness, doing sweet nothing, *dolce far niente*, the old habit loses
some of its grip on you. With dawning clarity, you find that you can
just *be*, and that the graceful ease, the easy grace of just being is available
at all times. To cooperate fully with that dawning, there's just one
crucial thing for you to do: sit down for a little while every day, close
your eyes, and let it happen.

Then that ease starts to permeate your life, percolating through all
its fibers, naturally dissolving and washing out the old gunky deposits
of fear, rage, and self-destructive craving. More and more, you feel OK,
happy and at peace for no particular reason except that that's what you
are at your core, and now your core is coming unburied. Your vision
becomes clearer, so that you see solutions that might have gone overlooked. You do less walking around in circles, less bumping into things,
less making easy things hard. As you awake and break free from the
old distortions, a natural wisdom, bigger than the separate *I* with its
little thoughts, emerges to guide your steps. Speaking in the voice of
that wisdom, the prophet Isaiah described this awakening:

> I will lead the blind by a road they do not know; by paths they
> have not known I will guide them. I will turn the darkness
> before them into light, the rough places into level ground.
> These are the things I will do, and I will not forsake them.

CHAPTER 9

On-Ramps

I think it was in the first grade that we started making projects with colored construction paper, glue, and little red-handled scissors with rounded tips. I remember sitting at the table with the other kids, toiling away, making a long, laborious cut, one tiny snip at a time. Once in a while the teacher would drop by our table with her big, sharp grownup scissors and help move things along. Catching the edge of the paper far back near the pivot point of her blades, and then—*What?!*—leaving the blades wide open, she pushed her scissors forward in one smooth, straight glide. We looked at each other in bug-eyed disbelief.

You've now learned the grown-up way to meditate. Stop toiling away, stay wide open, and it's an easy glide. This approach is so natural, so universal, that it's found in any number of venerable traditions, and has been independently discovered by seekers outside of the traditions. Sometimes folks who weren't even seeking have just stumbled into it. Because there's essentially nothing to it, what's most surprising is that anyone has missed it.

In fact, it's so nothing that sometimes we might want a little bit of something to help us ease into it from, well, everything. When you've been dealing with the busy busy-ness of ordinary life, to just sit down and rest in awareness can seem pretty abrupt. This is why we have certain simple, neutral activities for transitioning smoothly to the ease of just being. Natural meditation, we could say, is like cruising on the freeway on a Sunday morning. The *free way*, the way of freedom: no intersections, no traffic lights, nothing to do but sit back, drop your foot on the gas, and burn up the miles. As you zoom along, there's no more g-force of acceleration; it feels magically like not moving at all. But when you're coming from the slow start-and-stop traffic of the surface streets, you need an on-ramp (or entrance ramp or slip road, as it's called in some places) to ease onto the freeway. Then you can forget about the on-ramp and go merrily on your way.

You've already learned a couple of practices, Resting Bliss Face and breathing through your feet, that can double as excellent on-ramps. In addition, here are some that have been thoroughly tested over the centuries. Once you're seated comfortably, you can use any one you like.

Sound

One of the simplest ways to transition into meditation is to just close your eyes and listen for a while, in a neutral, easygoing way, to the ambient sounds: the wind in the trees, the hum of the fridge, the traffic, the surf, the chatter of the kids in the playground, the clatter of your commuter train—whatever's there. Suppose your head is spinning after a rough day at work, or you've been riding the emotional roller coaster of an unsettled relationship. The neutrality of just listening to the ambient sounds becomes a sort of decompression space before settling within.

Don't try to *do* anything about the sounds. Don't try to vigilantly monitor them (which would be a task); just easily rest your attention there. After a little while, you can ask yourself, *Am I aware of these sounds?* Sure. *Then I'm aware?* Of course. Then fine. Rest right here, in awareness. This approach also dispenses, once and for all, with the idea that sound is the enemy of meditation and needs to be blocked out.

Sound is your friend. In fact, everything is your friend. The whole universe, you'll eventually find, is your friend, but the chirping of the sparrow or the whirring of the electric fan is a good place to start.

I like to minimize meditation toys or paraphernalia (*tchotchkes*, as they're called in Sanskrit), but if you happen to have a bell or chime whose tone you like, preferably one with a nice, long decay (fade), you might want to use that. Strike the bell and listen as it dwindles away— let its pleasing sound catch your attention and then lead you into the silence. Three strikes is a traditional number (three strikes and you're *out*), but you can do anything you like.

You can also use sounds that you generate yourself, including mantras, such as OM, the traditional sounds that are considered particularly conducive to meditative settling down. They generally have a smooth, soothing, mellifluous quality. (*Crepuscular, coruscation, pulchritudinous,* or *ichthyosaurus* would make really bad mantras.) If there's a mantra you're fond of, you can sing or say it aloud, or subvocalize it as a murmur or a whisper, or just have it lightly in your mind. Or you can do a diminuendo: first vocalize the mantra . . . then subvocalize it . . . then lightly think it . . . then vaguely, almost subliminally, feel it . . . then let it fade, in its own time, into silence . . . and just rest there.

I especially like the natural mantra, the one that, no matter what language you speak, you already associate with letting go into OK-ness: *Ahhhhhhh!* When you finally get that piece of popcorn husk out from between your back teeth, when you finish doing your taxes, when you get to the last chapter of the murder mystery and discover that the butler did it, when you have an orgasm, when you find the perfect shoes for your outfit and they're fifty percent off, there's a good chance that you spontaneously say *Ahhhhhhh!* And because the connection between outer and inner works both ways, by using this sound you can evoke letting go. Say it or sing it, think it or sigh it, feel it radiate out in all directions through all your pores. *Ahhhhhhh!*

Simple Breathing

With your mouth closed, take a full breath, a little deeper and slower than usual. Pay attention to the experience of each moment as you breathe all the way in. At the end of the inhalation, pause. Don't think of it as "holding the breath," which sounds like straining. Just fill up with breath and notice that you can rest on the full breath in a perfectly easygoing way, like sitting on a nice, fat cushion. Then keep paying attention as you slowly breathe all the way out, and then pause again at the end of the exhalation, sitting on the cushion of emptiness. Don't force or strain. Rather, note what a delicious privilege it is to breathe. Only people who are alive get to do it. (This offer good for a limited time only.)

Like eating, breathing is necessary for survival, but you can go through your life mindlessly wolfing down your meals, or you can be a gourmet, deeply relishing and gratefully appreciating the gift of fine food. This is gourmet breathing. Take one breath like this, or a few, or go on enjoying deep, conscious breathing for a while. (If you get light-headed, stop—you're probably straining.) After a while, forget about the breath and just rest in awareness.

Again, the inner-outer connection works both ways. People suffering from anxiety or having panic attacks usually take short, shallow breaths through the mouth. By breathing slowly, luxuriously, and through the nose, we cultivate the opposite of panic.

Advanced Breathing

To add some extra oomph to this procedure, slightly constrict the back of your throat so that it makes a mild rasping sound as you breathe in and out, like Darth Vader—a happy, relaxed Darth Vader. Narrowing the air passage slows down your breathing, and, because you can hear and feel the breath more vividly, the experience is richer and gives you more to rest your attention on.

This constriction also stimulates the vagus nerve, or tenth cranial nerve. One of the most extraordinary structures in the human body, it's actually a pair of nerves that reach from the lower brain all the way down to the diaphragm. Stimulating it helps to switch off the sympathetic branch of the nervous system and switch on the parasympathetic branch. This deactivates the fight-or-flight syndrome, where the body is coiled for action in a state of hyperarousal, with the typical symptoms of pounding heart, dry mouth, and sweaty palms. In its place, the vagus nerve activates an opposite response, with slower heart rate and overall mind-body relaxation—variously known as the rest-and-digest, feed-and-breed, or graze-and-gaze syndrome. Studies of veterans with PTSD have shown that this technique can significantly lower their stress markers. Yogis, who call this method *ujjayi* ("victorious") breath, have known about its power for centuries.

You can make this ujjayi/Darth Vader breathing more powerful still by adjusting the relative length of your breaths. Let the breath again be fairly slow, and this time count how many seconds one in-breath takes. Then, after the pause, breathe out extra slowly, so that the out-breath takes about one-and-a-half to two times as long as the in-breath. If, say, you breathe in for a count of six, breathe out for a count of nine to twelve. Then continue like that. Don't strain or feel rigid about getting the count just right on every breath; that would defeat the purpose. No one's giving you a grade.

This style of breathing is particularly beneficial for people who are in (or want to be in) recovery from substance addiction, as well as those suffering from anxiety, fear, confusion, worry, agitation, or any kind of emotional ups and downs, whether chronic or acute. In fact, studies of resting breath rates have shown that subjects with lower levels of those difficult emotions naturally tend to breathe at this ratio, with the out-breath one and a half to two times the length of the in-breath. Sometimes the easiest way to start being a calm, stable, balanced person is to breathe like one.

As you settle into this breathing, let your eyes close. Then you can add another dimension to the experience by imagine-feeling as we did when we breathed through our feet, back in chapter 2. This time, though, imagine-feel your whole body to be porous, like a sponge with extremely fine pores, thousands of them per square inch. As you breathe in and out, slowly and attentively, using the ujjayi constriction if you like, feel the breath pouring in and out through all those fine, fine pores, coming in from all directions and going out in all directions, into infinite space.

Here's another version of that inner seeing-feeling-breathing. Start the in-breath with your attention way down at the very base of your spine. Then, as you breathe in, slowly ride the breath up the spine, all the way to the top of the skull, and then keep going, so that when you rest in the fully inhaled state you're resting the attention in the space just above your head. Then, as you breathe out, ride back down again, so when you rest in the exhaled state you're again at the base of the spine.

The super deluxe variation is to combine this up-and-down-the-spine method with ujjayi breath and the longer-out-than-in ratio. That may take a little getting used to at first, but then you'll find it incredibly powerful. Among other things, you'll find it almost impossible to re-member what you were upset about, or what substance you were craving.

Object-Gazing

Let your gaze rest on something, anything, in front of you: a rock, a flower, the sea or a lake, a spot on the wall or floor, the palms of your hands. If you like looking at a picture of a favorite sacred or enlightened person, that's fine. Don't *stare* at the object, don't try to concentrate on it, don't try not to blink, don't try to analyze it intellectually or relate to it emotionally. Simply rest your gaze there.

Resting your gaze on an object is like setting an apple on the kitchen counter. Once you've placed it there, you don't have to Keep. On. Placing. It. The apple mostly stays there by itself, but if at some point you notice that it's rolled onto the floor, fine: just place it there again. Remember, the object is there to serve you, as a means of easing into meditation. You're not getting paid to serve it by straining for some kind of perfect, unbroken focus.

After a little while, close your eyes, forget about the object, and just rest in silent awareness.

Sky-Gazing

Traditionally popular in Tibet, where the thin, dry atmosphere produces brilliant, crystal-clear skies, this approach is like object-gazing but, well, bigger, more expansive. You can do it while reclining on a deck chair, or lying on your back on the grass or in a hammock, or seated anyplace where you have a fairly unobstructed view of the sky. As with object-gazing, don't try to stare or to resist blinking. Just easily allow your attention, led by your gaze, to rest, mingle, merge, and lose itself in the openness of the sky.

The Tibetans associate the visual openness of the sky with the sonic openness of the mantra *Ahhhhhhh*, and they associate both of them with the ultimate openness of silent awareness. To put it all together, rest your gaze in the sky, take a deep in-breath, then say or sing a long, strong *Ahhhhhhh*, imagining the sound emanating from all your pores, your fingers, your toes, your scalp, your eyeballs, everything, radiating into the open, endless sky. Do this three times, then rest in awareness.

Swaying, Orbiting, Swinging

Swaying works best if you're sitting cross-legged with your back un-supported, rather than on a chair or couch. It's used in traditional Zen meditation, which is done on a *zafu* cushion, sitting with straight but not rigid posture.

Once you're seated, rock your body side to side, like a metronome. Move from the hips, so that the whole spine, up to the head, remains aligned. Start by swinging in a wide arc, and gradually let the arc shorten, till your movement is so subtle that an observer would have trouble telling whether you're still moving or not. Then let the movement grow more subtle still, till you're finally not moving at all. If *you* have trouble telling exactly when you've stopped, that's good.

A variation of this swaying is orbiting. Again sitting with your back unsupported, keep your bottom planted in one spot on your cushion, and orbit around that spot, as if you're drawing an ice-cream cone with your torso. Start with big circles and gradually let them spiral in, be-coming smaller and smaller till they're imperceptible and finally they vanish.

Both of these methods are very effective for getting centered— literally, physically—and for participating bodily in an act of slowing down into stillness. They're also great for children who want to do something meditative. Most kids before the age of about eleven or twelve are too squirmy to sit in silent meditation for more than a minute or two—if at all—but they happily take to physical approaches like these. They also generally work well for people of any age with such conditions as ADD, ADHD, or hypertension.

One more variation is available if you have a hammock. Just flop down into it, shove off with your foot to start it swinging, close your eyes, and thoroughly give yourself up to its motion as it gradually be-comes more subtle. The hammock, by the way, is an excellent example of the principle of meditative practice eloquently laid out by the wise troubadour Sly Stone: "Different strokes for different folks." Some people hate the motion of a hammock and even find that it makes them seasick. Some find that meditating lying down just makes them dull and sleepy. And some find that the hammock's motion is as soothing and comforting as a mother rocking her baby, and that abiding in restful alertness is just as feasible when lying on their backs as when sitting on their bottoms.

Heart Center

Certain meditative systems identify specific locations within the body that are conducive to resting the attention. The heart area is a particularly comfortable and soothing place for many people. We're not talking about the physical organ that pumps blood, but rather the energy center that happens to be in its vicinity. In traditional lore, of course, that's the seat of love, but let's be good scientists and see what our experience tells us.

My experience is that when I'm heartbroken or heartsick, or I have a heavy heart, or my heart is bursting with love or empathy or awe, I notice strong sensations in the middle of my chest that certainly *feel* like the emotional energies those words describe. They're heartfelt. Working with the heart center, unsurprisingly, is indicated for anyone who wants to be more in touch with these feelings. I've found it especially helpful for coming out of anger.

As usual, the method is simple. Sitting with closed eyes, just bring your attention to a place deep inside the chest cavity, like going deep inside a cave. As with the other on-ramps, don't try to force the mind to concentrate or focus. Don't try to give the heart center any particular size or quality. Just rest there. After a little while, you'll probably feel a sense of *ease* centered in the heart, and perhaps a subtle warmth. The

heart center may seem to become very small, or vast, or you may feel
you're dissolving into it—or you may not, all of which is fine. At some
point, forget about the heart center and just rest in awareness.

Do It Yourself

No matter what on-ramp you take, the basic principles are the same.
Use any one that's comfy, use it with a light touch, use it for a little
while, and then forget about it—let it go. There's no need to ritualize
or fetishize the on-ramp. (Do that for a couple of centuries and it's
called a religion.) Just as with a freeway on-ramp, we get on to get off.
The point is to ease into the express lane of just being as soon as possible. When someone tells me, "Yep, I've been meditating on my
mantra for thirty years," I wonder, *Jeez, when are you going to let it go and
enjoy some silence?*

You can also help yourself to a quick dose of any of these methods
during the day, especially at moments when fear or anxiety, anger or
craving well up. When you're jonesing for the drink or drug that you
know you shouldn't have, instead of just suffering, you can, say, melt into
some *Ahhhhhhh*'s instead. When you open up the final exam and feel the
room spinning and your mouth going dry, you can interrupt the stress
cycle by, say, taking a minute to follow a few deep ujjayi breaths in and
out. You'll probably think you can't afford to spend that precious minute
of exam time just breathing, but actually you can't afford *not* to.

There are no rigid rules about this stuff—you'll quickly become
the expert on what's called for at any given moment. You may feel most
at home on one on-ramp for a few days or months, then find yourself
drawn to another. You can't go wrong. The more you keep the whole
project a matter of enjoyment rather than duty, the more happily and
easily you'll stay with it.

Eventually, these transitional activities become less important. With daily sitting practice, your whole life starts to become a cruise on the freeway, the way of freedom. Yes, old challenges persist and new ones arise. Yes, business must be taken care of. But even as you take care of your business, it all somehow becomes smoother, more frictionless, as if that freeway radiates in all directions and has always just been freshly paved. Not all at once but more and more, even the fiercest of challenges and most frantic of scenarios seem to have the fierceness and franticness drained out of them. More and more, they're all seen to take place *within* the skylike silence. And then what is there to ramp onto?

CHAPTER 10

Testimony

But does it work?

It does. You just need to practice for a little while, and you'll see. Meanwhile, hearing other people's testimony can help encourage you to make the investment of sitting down and taking it easy every day. Traveling from place to place to lead workshops, or reading e-mail from people who've incorporated this way of effortlessness into their lives, I often hear myself thinking, *Wow, the stuff really does work!*

Some people's stories are dramatic, like that of the older woman at a workshop in Kansas City, who reported that during our first meditation her chronic tremors suddenly stopped. Some stories are deeply moving, like the e-mail I received from a thirty-year-old in Utah. He recounted a long odyssey of sexual abuse in his childhood, drug and alcohol addiction in his teens, then several years of trying to meditate before hearing me one night in a radio interview, talking about effortlessness. He got one of my audiobooks, then drove around the desert listening to it, occasionally pulling off the road to meditate, and quickly finding the peace and ease he'd been seeking for so long. And some people's stories are written all over them, like the TV producer who sometimes attends our sessions in Santa Monica. Handling complex production logistics, impossibly compressed shooting schedules, and some extremely difficult people, she looked ready to tear her hair out when she first started coming. Now her eyes are bright and calm, her posture relaxed and confident. Nothing need be said.

Let's listen to one person's testimony at some length, and, to make it significant, let's choose a hard case. When I first met him, he was in maximum security at Northern State Prison in Newark, New Jersey, considered the roughest institution in the state.

Prison is a good place to learn things. It's a lot like everywhere else, only more so. There's certainly plenty of fear, anger, anxiety, and addiction to tackle. I love working with prisoners. The Buddha said to practice like your hair is on fire, and theirs is. They understand the gravity of the situation, and their bullshit detectors are very finely tuned.

Our weekly meditation group at Northern State meets in a bare, bunkerlike cinder-block chapel. We sit in a circle of blue plastic chairs, everyone wearing khaki but me. One night in 2005, one of our regulars brought a new guy along, a young blue-eyed Puerto Rican with reddish hair in cornrows, and tattoos up and down his forearms, one of them reading IN ME I TRUST. I'll call him Lucio. His body seemed coiled, as if ready at any moment to fight or bolt, and he looked out through hooded eyes that seemed to say, *What the fuck is all* this?

But he sat and meditated with us, and he came back the next week. Every Thursday night he came back and meditated, and each time I could see his body relax and his eyes soften a little more. He started to ask questions, and to laugh. Out from behind his hard mask emerged a sweet baby face. One night, after about a month, he took me aside at the end of the meeting and said, "I have a question: How do you purify murder?" Before I could answer, he added, "You know, I never trusted anyone, not even my parents, but I trust you." *Uh-oh*, I thought. *I better do this right.*

Over the next five years, Lucio became a leading spirit in the group, always making the discussions lively and fun, and, as his own experience and understanding deepened, always eager to help others understand. When I moved to California and the head chaplain couldn't find a replacement for me, he put Lucio in charge of running the group.

Lucio also started sending me letters. One day I received a photocopy of his brand-new GED certificate, and a proud note telling me that he had earned it after teaching himself to read and write, so that he could read the books that we talked about in the group. Another time I received a lumpy little package. Inside was his hair, in two long braids, and a note asking me to donate it to Locks of Love for a child who had lost his hair to chemo. Seeing the sweet soul that was emerging from under all that armor, I wanted to understand how it had gotten buried in the first place. I asked Lucio if he would write out his story, and he did, over the course of a few letters.

> When I was 7 playing on a corner, when this guy starts fighting with his girl, the guy ends up smacking her, so the big time drug dealer came around and told the guy to take that someplace else before you make the block hot, meaning before the police comes around. So the guy said something slick to the drug dealer, and drug dealer knock out the guy.
>
> A few days later on the same corner, the drug dealer was giving me a dollar so I could go to the store. The guy he knock out jump out of a car and shot the drug dealer more than 10 time. As he laid there, his body jumping around a little bit, blood was pouring out onto the concrete. The blood started to clod up but me only being 7, it look like the fat in pork and bean. The smell of the blood was like a million wet pennys. I ran home before the police came around. At that time, I realize I had blood on me. I

felt so bad because I couldn't help the man who gave me a dollar
every day and told me to stay in school.

Now a week or two later, I'm across the street from the corner
when my cousin throw a bottle at some dude, the guy whip out and
shot my cousin through the leg, the bullet bounce off the sidewalk,
went through my shirt and hit my friend in the spine. At that time
I wanted to hang out with the people who are doing the shooting
because I was scare to get shot. But everybody I was hanging out
with was older then me. So I had to do the same things they was
doing. I start smoking weed and playing around with stealing cars.
Every day, I got jumped or just fight, until one day, you stab
someone and no one want to mess with you anymore.

At the age of ten, ridiculed by other kids because of his shabby
clothes, Lucio dropped out of school and started dealing drugs. Guns
came into his life.

I had a .38 hand gun and loved guns. Every time we got a new
gun we would go to the back yard, shoot them to see if they work.
My cousin wanted me to know what shooting something live felt
like. So he had me killing dogs and things like that. One day I
hear the guns go off in the back yard, so I go back there because I
want to test out the new toys, so I thought. My cousin had this
guy back there, the dude had took some drug or money. He tell
me to shoot him. And I flat out told him no. He grab my left
hand and beat it with the butt of the gun until my hand broke. I
didn't say no to him after that.

Before he turned thirteen, Lucio's mother called the cops on him
and he left the house. He found support for a while from a local church,

but when he realized that the minister was sponging money from his poor congregants to pay for fancy clothes and cars, Lucio was disillusioned. By age fourteen he tried to kill himself twice, and by twenty-one he was locked up.

> *Yes I was full of rage. Now I'm 30 years old. I've been lock up since I was 21. The first 4 years of me being lock up, I'll go to a tier, have a fight, go to the hole. Come back out and if the guy had beat me up when we had the fight, I'll cut or stab him this time.*
>
> *Around 2005, a friend says come check out this group. When I get there I see this white guy saying words I didn't understand and telling us to meditate. After a while, I start to meditate and I love it. But the more I meditate, the more I reflect on all the bad I have done in the past. And I start to feel about all the people I hurt, when I never felt that way because I was full of hate and anger. And I loved feeling hate and anger, because I knew hate and anger would never leave me. Hate and anger would stop love from hurting me.*

At one point I didn't hear from him for several months. Then I got a letter telling me he had been moved to another prison and put in "ad-seg" (administrative segregation, a.k.a. solitary confinement), locked away in a cell above the furnace, where the temperature was constantly around a hundred degrees. So, he figured, it must be time for a meditation retreat. He stripped off his clothes, sat down, and closed his eyes.

> *Now it's going on 6 years and it's been the best 6 years of my life. I have a heart and soul full of love. And even though my past was rough and I made it rougher than it had to be, my past was my hell and inside me I've found heaven.*

Today Lucio is free, in both senses. After a hard first few years facing the challenges of the outside world, he's now working in construction, living with a wonderful woman, and continuing his meditation practice. He's found a church with sincere leadership and a caring congregation, and he has one new tattoo—a big Buddha across his chest.

CHAPTER 11

Being the Ocean

Let's take another dive into natural meditation. As you saw in our first session back in chapter 8, this is not something we work at. We just let gravity take over, and settling happens by itself. It's not about doing, but being. So I'm less like the instructor in your Zumba class ("Now shake it!") and more like the tour guide on your trip to Florence ("See how it's-a nice!"). Since you now have some familiarity with the terrain, this time we'll visit a little longer than before, and we'll notice a few more features. I'll use a few more words, but nothing I say will be giving you anything to do. I'm just pointing out the sights.

As with the earlier meditation, you can first read through the instructions a few times and then set the book aside and practice, or else go to the *Fear Less* page at **DeanWords.com** for a streaming audio version.

So . . . please sit comfortably, with your hands relaxed on your knees or lap.

You're now familiar with several meditative on-ramps, so start with one of those. Take a minute or two to rest your attention on a sound, an object, or the breath, or use any other transitional activity that appeals to you.

. . .

. . .

All right. Now allow your on-ramp activity to drop away. If your eyes are still open, you can close them.

. . .

And here we are.

Nowhere to go, nothing to do.

We're already present.

We're already aware.

Rest in this awareness. That's all we'll be doing.

. . .

Within this awareness, sounds come and go, colors come and go, sensations come and go, thoughts and feelings come and go. It all happens by itself.

Perfect.

. . .

. . .

Let whatever comes come. Let whatever goes go.

See what remains.

. . .

What remains is awareness—the conscious, open space within which everything else comes and goes. Just rest in that. That simple. Nothing else to do.

Just rest in this unmoving awareness, as everything else moves within it.

. . .

. . .

. . .

This unmoving awareness, we could say, is like the ocean. The sensations and thoughts and all the other experiences we're aware of are like ripples and waves. Ripples come and go, waves rise and fall, but the ocean is always resting in its bed. No matter how much turbulence there may be on the surface, the ocean itself is always silent at its depth.

So just rest in this silent, oceanlike, completely ordinary awareness, and let the ripples and waves roll on . . . which they're going to do whether you "let" them or not.

. . .

. . .

. . .

. . .

Notice that this ocean of awareness has plenty of room for whatever kinds of ripples or waves might come along. It doesn't pick and choose. It doesn't matter to awareness whether we see purple or brown behind our eyelids, or whether we hear the patter of the rain or the pounding of a car stereo, or even whether we feel tranquillity or anxiety.

. . .

Even intense emotions don't affect awareness itself: they're simply another experience we're aware *of.* Just remain like the silent ocean, as you already are, within which everything comes and goes on its own . . . unbidden . . . unopposed.

. . .

. . .

. . .

Notice that thoughts are simply one more kind of wave, passing through this ocean of awareness, just like sounds or sensations. There's nothing special about them and nothing to do about them.

. . .

The content of your thoughts doesn't matter. Just as it doesn't matter whether we hear a seagull or a motorcycle, it doesn't matter whether we have thoughts about our love life or our grocery list—or, for that matter, thoughts about our meditation. (*Hey, I'm doing great . . . Hey, I'm doing lousy.*)

Just don't buy into the thoughts. Treat them like they're in a language you don't speak, or just part of the passing scenery. Don't engage

with them and don't try to push them away. If you try to push away
the thoughts, you just wind up wrestling with them, which is another
way of engaging with them.

. . .

. . .

. . .

Anytime you realize you're hanging on to a thought or feeling, or
resisting it, just relax your grip and settle back into this ocean of
awareness.

. . .

. . .

. . .

Whatever's going on, don't much bother about it. What . . . ever.
Just rest in this ocean of awareness, within which everything else comes
and goes on its own.

. . .

. . .

. . .

. . .

There's nothing to focus or concentrate on, nothing to evaluate or
keep track of, nothing to figure out, nothing to strive for. Just remain
as you are. And to remain as you already are, there's nothing to do. Just
remain open and formless as the ocean, always resting in its bed, no
matter what happens on the surface. Nothing more. That simple.

. . .

. . .

. . .

Now . . .

Please easily notice what it is that tells you, in this moment, that you
have a body. What immediate experiences tell you there's a body present?

. . .

Well . . . there are some sensations, such as your breathing or the pressure of your back or bottom against the seat, as well as any aches or pains you may have. There may also be some mental images of the body, but our eyes are closed, so those are just memories—thoughts.

That's about it. Those are things you're aware of. But the you that's aware of them is not an ache or pain, an image or a thought. It just *is*—and yet it's aware.

You are awareness. Everything else is something you're aware *of.* That includes the body.

There's nothing to figure out here. Just notice.

There's nothing to do. Just rest as awareness . . . as you already are.

. . .

. . .

The silent, unmoving ocean of awareness is you. All the waves of motion and change—thoughts, feelings, sensations—pass frictionlessly through you. Just notice this. Leave it as it is, and let it go as it goes.

. . .

. . .

. . .

This oceanlike awareness, you, is the most ordinary thing in the world. It's the most intimate, familiar thing in the world. Don't try to look for it—it's where you're looking *from*, and always have. Don't try to think about it. It's where you're always thinking *from*. Only, for once we're resting in it, resting *as* it, letting go into it, marinating in it.

. . .

. . .

. . .

Notice that this awareness, this *I*, can be aware of different colors and forms, but it has no color or form.

Notice that it's aware of sounds, but it's silent.

Notice that it has no size . . . no shape . . . no density or texture . . . no inside or outside . . . no anything . . . Yet there's something good about it, something satisfying that naturally draws us to rest in it, to rest *as* it.

. . .

. . .

. . .

Just rest as awareness. That simple.

. . .

. . .

. . .

. . .

Now, keep your eyes closed and take a few minutes to gradually rouse the body back to an active state. When you feel ready you can open your eyes.

. . .

. . .

Good.

You're It

OK. Simple, right? All we did was notice that we're aware and then rest as that awareness.

We noticed that awareness is formless and unmoving, like the ocean. It's the *transcendent*, beyond the realm of change. Everything we experience moves within it, like waves, but the ocean is always resting in its bed.

Of course, when we liken awareness to an ocean, or the sky, or anything else, that's just a metaphor. We're not trying to picture an ocean. If such pictures happen to come up, that's fine, but they're just thoughts, like any others. Awareness is that space in which those thoughts, and all thoughts, innocently come and go. You're always already there. Remain as you are and rest there.

It's that simple. We don't try to push away thoughts or anything else. We don't engage with thoughts or anything else. We don't try to feel some special way, and we don't try to "meditate," whatever that means. We don't try to drive—we just kick back in the convertible and enjoy the scenery.

As your tour guide, this time I did point out one important new element in the scenery: the fact that the awareness in which you rest, and the you that rests in awareness, are not two separate things. *You are awareness.* Usually we think of ourselves as a body or mind or role, so this new notion may sound kind of crazy. That's fine. You got a taste of it experientially, and that will keep getting clearer as you keep practicing. But it's really this simple: Who or what is aware of all this stuff—aware of your thoughts, aware of your memories, aware of your perceptions? Who was aware of the pain of scraping your knee when you were five, and the comfort of having Mom put a Band-Aid on it? Who will be aware of the drawing of your last breath? Who's aware of the question mark at the end of this sentence? Why, *you* are! Duh! Who or what else could it be?

The possibility that you're not what you thought you were, but awareness instead, without color or size or name, is a radical, potentially life-changing one which we'll revisit. But for now, please consider this, just hypothetically: If it turns out that what you are is boundless awareness, like the ocean or sky, and that all feelings, including fear, anxiety, anger, and addictive craving, pass through it frictionlessly, like a breeze or a wave, then that goes to the heart of our project. That should *solve* our problem.

But don't take my word for it, or anyone else's. It's much too important. If it's true, sooner or later your own experience will confirm it: come and see. For now, we just tweak our one fundamental meditation instruction, changing "Rest in awareness" to "Rest *as* awareness."

Then everything else happens by itself. As we've seen, the mind and body settle down by themselves, drawn by the gravitational pull of the silent awareness that we are at the depths of our being—by the peace and happiness that are the nature of that perfect, self-sufficient silence. Sometimes the settling and the peace are unmistakably clear, sometimes hazy. Either way it's fine. That's not because sometimes we're doing a better job than other times, since we're not doing any job at all. It's just a natural unfolding that proceeds in its own way, in its own time.

The big picture is that, through daily practice, our conscious contact with that peace and happiness grows stronger and clearer. That's what we've all been looking for all our lives. When we try to conceive of some ultimate, all-pervading, never-ending version of this happiness, we may give it grandiose names. Hardly daring to believe that such a version is possible, we may reserve those terms for religion, songs, myths, or cynical jokes:

Shangri-la, the Holy Grail, the Rainbow Connection, Hakuna Matata.
The peace that passeth all understanding.
Awakening, enlightenment, nirvana.
Heaven, deliverance, grace.

Here's a simple name I like:

Infinite OK-ness.

Whether you're pushing your cart through the supermarket, looking for sweet strawberries and a perfectly ripened avocado . . . or strolling through the liquor store, looking for the beverage that will make you feel good, or at least less bad . . . or scrolling through your dating site looking for the right partner for this lifetime, or at least a frisky hookup with no visible self-inflicted scars . . . in all these cases, and in all *other* cases, what you're really looking for is infinite OK-ness, endless happiness. Not knowing where to find it, you settle for the closest available facsimile.

That's the story of our lives. We're always seeking the juice. That's how we're built—thirsty. Even when the juiciest thing available is just some mild diversion, gravity pulls our attention toward it: it's a reflex. That's why people text and drive, despite knowing better.

What the sages teach—both the ancient sages and the contemporary ones I've been lucky enough to sit with—is that the true juice, the juiciest juice, the transcendental juice that doesn't depend on outer circumstances and therefore never runs dry, is inside you. Whether it's Jesus saying the kingdom of heaven is within you, or the Buddha telling you to look inside and find nirvana, or Socrates saying to know thyself and find the form of the good, it's the same message.

That inner ocean of silent awareness is the fulfillment we've been looking for all along. But if we just suspend our own efforts for a little while, stop flailing around on the surface and creating more turbulence, we sink right into it. Settling happens by itself. If we need to give this a name we can call it meditation—natural meditation. But once we make this little shift of attention, the decision to rest as awareness, all we need to do is hang out. Just be fine with whatever presents itself in each moment, not trying to do anything about anything, and the irresistible, automatic mechanism of attention-to-the-juiciest takes over. That's the kingdom of heaven coming like a thief in the night. That's gravity pulling the leaves to the ground, the *dolce* allowing us to *far niente*. And if it really turns out that this awareness is none other than you, then the *dolce*, the sweetness, what you've been looking for all your life, is the one who's been looking. But, then, you always find things in the last place you look.

Know thyself, indeed.

Tag—you're it.

CHAPTER 12

Every Little Thing

Let's summarize the elements of natural meditation:

- Sit comfortably.
- If desired, take any on-ramp for a little while, then let it go.
- Notice that you're aware, as always.
- Rest as this awareness, which is free and open like space, and leave settling to happen on its own.
- Let all experiences—thoughts, feelings, and sensations—come and go frictionlessly within this awareness-space.
- Anytime you find yourself resisting or holding on to anything, just relax your grip and sink back into spacelike awareness.
- After a while, take a few minutes to ease out slowly.

Or, to summarize our summary, *Relax your grip and rest as awareness.* If you remember nothing else about meditation, remember that and you'll be fine.

That's it. You'll find that this is the single most effective thing you can do to find freedom from fear or anxiety, anger, addictive craving, and, for that matter, grief, loneliness, shame, confusion, or any of the other afflictive emotions. Whether that sounds perfectly plausible to you or totally nuts doesn't matter. You just do it, and little by little, and sometimes a lot, you'll find those old tendencies loosening up and washing away. Every time you sit, the space of boundless OK-ness will reveal itself with some degree of clarity. Sometimes less, sometimes more—that doesn't matter either. In its own time, that OK-ness will infiltrate your whole life. All the supplemental methods and insights we'll introduce later are powerful too, but they'll be most powerful when practiced along with daily, nothin'-doin', natural meditation.

So, to help maintain this practice and answer questions that may crop up as you go along, here are some practical tips and fine points. You may want to return to this chapter from time to time for reference—keep it around like a user's manual. This is where you might expect to find a list of *do*'s and *don't*s, but I don't much like the sound of that. Let's make it a list of *Don't worry*'s. In fact, one excellent, concise, comprehensive, all-purpose meditation instruction is the one from Bob Marley:

> *Don't worry 'bout a thing*
> *'Cause every little thing gonna be all right.*

Don't Worry About the Place

If you have a lovely little garden spot or a pleasant corner of your home where you like to sit, fine. But don't feel limited to meditating there. Because you don't have to sit in a special posture, and because you don't need silence, you can do it anywhere. The world is your meditation cave. Trains, buses, parks, theater seats before your movie begins—they're all in the cave.

Don't Worry About Your Posture

The lotus pose and the other classical sitting postures were developed in parts of the world that historically didn't have a lot of chairs—people were used to sitting on the ground. You can meditate sitting on a couch, chair, train seat, park bench, or anywhere else. In fact, the *Yoga Sutras* of Patañjali, the founding text of the whole yogic tradition, doesn't even mention cross-legged poses or any of the other poses taught in most yoga classes. In prescribing the ideal *asana*, or posture, for meditation, it says, "Asana should be steady and enjoyable." Period. After some experimentation, most people conclude that the best way to keep things steady and enjoyable is to sit *up* and a little bit *back*, neither slouching nor stiff. If you can lie on your back without falling asleep every time, that's fine too.

Further experimentation will also show you that sitting with your arms crossed, or leaning forward with an elbow or two on your knees, creates tension in the body. Sometimes when I lead a group session, no matter how many times I gently suggest, "Just sit back in your seat and let your hands drop loosely to your knees or lap," there'll be one guy—and yes, it's usually a guy—who keeps leaning forward in the Thinker pose, which is indeed an excellent way to stay caught up in thinking. Or there'll be one who keeps his arms defiantly crossed in the Bouncer pose, a great one for taking your macho stand and resisting anything unplanned or unexpected.

If you're used to sitting in a cross-legged position on a cushion, that's great. There's something that can feel really fresh and invigorating about that, conducive to the restful alertness of meditation, *if* you're truly comfortable that way. Otherwise, instead of enjoying the ease of natural settling, you'll be working at maintaining your picture-perfect posture—and no one's taking pictures. It's a bit like those sex manuals with instructions for all the exotic positions that are supposed to bring you and your partner to the heights of orgasmic bliss. It turns out that it's much more important that the two of you just be comfortable and go into it with a relaxed, loving attitude, and perhaps a sense of humor. Same deal here.

Don't Worry About the Time

The first question that many people ask is, "How long should I meditate?" I usually reply, "A while. If you're in a hurry, a little while." Others tell me something like, "I'm up to thirty-five minutes a day, and I'm working on getting to forty." Working indeed. My response is, "Forget about the time." When you're walking on the beach or soaking in a hot tub—basking, lazing, luxuriating—you don't set a timer. When you're dancing your butt off at a club or kicking back with your headphones, losing yourself in your favorite music, you don't grit your teeth and work your way up to forty minutes. One of the best favors you can do yourself is to throw the clock out of your meditation space. Sure, if you need to leave for work or get the kids to school on time you can set a quiet alarm, but otherwise let yourself get lost in timelessness.

The widespread idea that you need to meditate for an hour or more at a stretch to gain any benefit comes from the prevalence of unnatural meditation. If you're fighting the mind's natural gravity, straining to concentrate, you do have to keep at it till you finally get exhausted and gravity takes over—despite your efforts, not because of them. So, instead of fifty minutes of straining followed by ten minutes of letting be, we're going straight to the letting be.

What *is* important is to sit every day, even if it's only for five or ten minutes or even just a minute or two, so that every day you're becoming more at home with the silence that underlies life's dramas and traumas and garden-variety busy-ness. That's the one catch with this stuff: you have to do it. Of course we're all busy, but everyone has a minute or two. Just don't be too lazy to relax: get off your butt and get on your butt. You're never going to "have the time" or "find the time." You have to *take* the time. Your old stresses and fears know that you've got them on the run now, and they don't want to be dislodged from their cozy niche in your psyche. They can invent all sorts of reasonable-sounding excuses for why you couldn't get around to it today, even for one minute.

So the best strategy is to make meditation part of your daily routine, just like brushing your teeth. Have a time when you always sit: right after your morning shower, or on your commute in the bus or train or ride-share, or on your coffee break, or when you get home from work and are unwinding before fixing supper. (People often feel dull or sleepy after a big meal, so before meals may be safer.)

And then don't limit yourself to that one dose. When you're stuck in a waiting room, instead of exacerbating your tedium by checking the time every three minutes, you can close your eyes, duck below the waves, and slip into yummy no-time. As your contact with this space of just being grows, you can pepper your day with little mini-breaks and micro-breaks. When you're, say, at a party, feeling awkward because you don't know people and you're wondering, *What am I doing here?* you can discreetly close your eyes for a second or two and re-experience, *Ah, I'm just being. I'm in the place of always OK-ness.* That's *what I'm doing.*

Don't Worry About Sleeping

When I'm taking questions after a group session and a new meditator raises her hand with a particularly sheepish, apologetic look on her face, I know what's coming: "I fell asleep." There's a widespread notion that falling asleep in meditation is some kind of cardinal sin. Nope—it's fine. The Dalai Lama has even said, "Sleep is the best meditation." If you *consistently* fall asleep in meditation, you should probably look into your sleeping habits at night. But in the unforced, uncontrived situation of natural meditation, we get what we need, and sometimes we need sleep. In fact, because the sleep that comes in meditation is launched from a level of such profound rest, it can be highly concentrated. I'm on planes a lot, leading workshops hither and yon, getting nice and jet-lagged, and I find that nodding out for a few minutes in meditation is deeply healing. In a pinch, it sometimes seems to compensate for a couple of hours of missed sleep.

Don't Worry About Noise

One of the things I love about visiting New York City is meditating on the subway. Is it so I can exercise my yogic superpower of blocking out noise? Nope. It's so I can be reminded, beyond the shadow of a doubt, that noise is fine. Imagine, if you will, a couple of awakened sages—let's say Jesus, the Buddha, and Anandamayi Ma, the Bliss-Permeated Mother—riding the uptown A train. We can almost taste their unbreakable tranquillity, their spontaneous, lighter-than-air sense of infinite OK-ness. But when they get on the train, does that OK-ness evaporate? Do they say, "Gee, I was permeated by bliss till those brakes started squealing"? Of course not. Now, what's the difference between the sages and you? Do they have something going on that you lack? Actually, no. They lack something that you have—your struggle. They just don't resist what's there. Wherever they find themselves, they remain naturally wide open, letting everything pass frictionlessly through them.

Now, we can't necessarily expect to become a 24/7 sage this week, but we're on our way. We start by being a sage for a few minutes a day, during our time of meditation. Your quiet little garden is fine for starters, but don't get stuck in it. Take your practice into the world. Bring on the jackhammers! At first you'll find yourself mentally trying to push the jackhammers away, and that's fine. Sooner or later you'll realize, deeply realize, that you can't. Then you'll give up, and you'll make a life-changing discovery. The great avant-garde composer John Cage, who wrote a fascinating book titled *Silence*, put it this way:

Silence is not acoustic. It is a change of mind, a turning around.

That is, the true silence, the deep silence we're seeking in meditation (the peace we've been seeking all our lives, actually), is not a mere absence of sound waves vibrating in the air and striking our eardrums. If it were, every deaf person would be enlightened. The real silence is the mind's turning within, to the core of our being, awareness itself. It's our always-silent oceanic depth, not some momentary flattening out of the surface waves.

Very simply, noise is not a problem unless you make it a problem. In a way, we're already making it a problem just by labeling it *noise*. Try substituting the more neutral, nonjudgmental word *sound*. Then, when you realize you've been pushing against the sound, just gently let go of that pushing and relax again into your silent, oceanic self.

Don't Worry About Thoughts

Good news! The idea that you have to empty your mind of thoughts is wrong. It's erroneous. It's also false, inaccurate, misguided, unfounded, untrue, unwarranted, deluded, misinformed, fallacious, at fault, all wet, off base, wide of the mark, and barking up the wrong tree.

Did I mention that it's wrong?

Yes, I'm trying to get your attention, because so many people have so much trouble hearing this.

Thoughts are exactly like sounds—just not quite as loud. There's nothing wrong with their being there. With thoughts as with sound, as soon as we stop making them a problem they stop being a problem

When you have the thought *I have to get rid of these thoughts*, guess what that is: a thought. It's *just* a thought, exactly like the ones it thinks need to go. But, as with sound, at first you probably *will* try to get rid of thoughts, and that's fine. You can take ten minutes or ten years, and eventually you'll come to the same conclusion: thoughts will always be there in the mental field, just as sounds are there in the acoustic field and colors are there in the visual field—and that's perfect. Thoughts *must* be there, because you're a human being and not a turnip. In one of his searching essays, Montaigne tried to observe and describe his own mind, finally concluding:

> I cannot keep my subject still. It goes along befuddled and staggering, with a natural drunkenness.

This bears repeating: Mind *is* mental activity. By definition, it can't be still. It's waves. True silence is experienced when you rest in the oceanlike awareness that underlies and embraces the wavy mental field and all other fields. The Buddha didn't succeed in getting rid of his thoughts. He just sat under his tree until he gave up trying, and then, like all the sages, he discovered that he didn't have to get rid of anything.

So the practical application is simple: Don't try to push the thoughts away, but don't buy into them either. Just let them arise on their own and, in time, vanish on their own. When you realize that you're gripping a thought or anything else, simply relax your grip and sink back into the ocean of awareness, the experiencer, yourself.

Don't worry about whether the thought persists. Background thoughts? Ignore them. Foreground thoughts? Relax your grip on them, and they'll fade into the background on their own. Others will come from the background to the foreground, but as long as you're not gripping them it doesn't matter.

It doesn't matter what you think about. It doesn't matter what you think about what you think. It doesn't matter how little or how much you think. All thoughts are a hundred percent irrelevant to resting as awareness: your cleverest thought won't help you and your dumbest thought can't hurt you.

Just don't engage with the thoughts. Listening to your thoughts—buying into them, taking them seriously—is engaging with them. Trying to push them away is engaging with them. Trying to drown them out with a mantra or your breath is engaging with them. Trying to resolve your thoughts is engaging with them. Whether you're wrestling with the meaning of life or trying to remember who played the Professor on *Gilligan's Island*, the feeling is usually, *If I can just get this one thing resolved,* then *I'll be able to settle down.* Hey—what was your must-resolve-now question ten minutes ago?

Anything you try to do with regard to thoughts is engaging with them. And that makes meditation supremely simple. You don't have to work out which kinds of engagement are helpful and which aren't. Just drop the whole thing. Fuhgeddabouddit.

If you live in a city, you're already an expert on how to fuhgeddabouddit: you know how to automatically let the sounds of the traffic go on somewhere in the background of your attention and not bother about them. Your thoughts are just another kind of traffic, and you're not a traffic cop. Yes, sometimes a thought will move to the foreground and seize your attention, but then you can call on another of your expert urban skills. Deal with that demanding thought just as you deal with an aggressive lunatic you encounter ranting on the sidewalk. Don't buy into his rant, but don't try to argue with him or shoo him away; just avoid eye contact and move on.

In fact, not only is it OK that thoughts pop up, it's essential to our project of coming out of fear. It's how we can learn, deep in our bones, deep in our nervous system, that not every thought that comes along has to be believed or even seriously considered. That includes our fearful or angry or obsessive thoughts. In a sense, we're retraining ourselves to just let the thoughts boil away without grabbing the kettle, till they run out of steam and evaporate harmlessly into the air.

Are there thoughts that need to be taken seriously and acted upon? Of course. But not right now. We deal with them after we open our eyes. You've probably heard of *The Power of Now*. This is where we exercise the Power of Later. For the moment, don't try to remember who played the Professor, don't try to complete your shopping list, don't try to work out your business plan, don't try to make sense of your crazy family, don't try to solve your health problems or your romantic problems. When you realize you're halfway through mentally writing an e-mail or psychoanalyzing your sister-in-law, just relax, release your grip on that wave, and go on resting in the ocean.

As the useless thoughts evaporate over time, it becomes clear which are the remaining, useful ones. They're fewer than you might think. In fact, here's a little experiment: Take a pencil and paper, draw a line down the middle, and then, for half an hour, simply watch your thoughts and keep score. Don't try to do anything about them. Just watch the thoughts and keep a tally of how many are useful (*I should have my blue suit cleaned for that job interview*) and how many aren't (*What if I go on that job interview and sound stupid?*). You may be surprised.

Our minds are a wonderful gift. They give us the capacity to contemplate atoms and galaxies, make cathedrals and symphonies, and avoid repeating the blunders of history. But they don't come with an OFF switch. They keep going and going and going, which can be frustrating, especially when we feel caught up in thoughts of worry or rage. But the experience of meditation teaches us that we can ignore our thoughts. They can keep going, but we don't have to go with them. By repeatedly ignoring them, you drain them of their power over you.

You may have heard the popular meditation advice, "Find the space between thoughts." That one messes up a lot of people. It's like saying to find the space between waves—it usually leads to a lot of counter-productive effort. It's more helpful to say, "*Rest* in the space *behind* the thoughts." There's no waiting for that space. It's awareness and it's you, the ocean that's always beneath the waves. Eventually you realize that the thoughts themselves are made out of that space, just as waves are made of ocean water. They can never be an obstacle to it or an interruption of it.

Sometimes you'll suddenly realize, *Oh, I've been so caught up on this long train of thoughts that I forgot I was supposed to be meditating. Now I've got to get off this train and come back.* But while you're caught up in the thoughts, by definition you don't know you're caught up, so there's nothing you can do about it. Then, when the lightbulb moment comes and you *realize* you've *been* caught up, by definition you're no longer caught up, so there's nothing to do about it. And there's nowhere to go back to—you never left. All this quaint drama of getting on and off trains has been happening right *here*, in this awareness (where else could it happen?), and there's never anything to do about awareness but rest in it. The train has not, and never can, carry you anywhere. It's like a toy train on Christmas morning, under the pretty lights, going in circles, round and round the tree.

Sometimes you might even spend an entire session in frenetic, compulsive thinking, never once realizing you were caught up, never coming up for air. Then you might well think, *That was a completely wasted sitting. I'm getting nowhere.* But even this is OK. Many, many people have walked exactly this road before you and have found where it leads. The I'm-getting-nowhere moment is a standard stop along the way. If you just keep showing up, exposing yourself to the gravity, you'll gradually become less caught in the turbulence and do more sinking into the silent depths. It's physics. It can't not happen. Peace will assert itself. It has to.

Which brings us to . . .

Don't Worry About What's Happening

Because the settling down that takes place in meditation happens in a gentle, natural, unforced way, we don't always realize we're settling. Researchers have found that, whether a subject describes her meditation as deep and blissful or antsy and restless, the physiological symptoms of settling, such as changes in brain waves and metabolic functioning, are about the same. We've already seen that we don't control what's happening while we're sitting, and now we can see that we don't even *know* what's happening. We're in the passenger seat—and we're blindfolded. This is great news. It means we may as well relax about the whole thing. Mother Nature's driving and we're just along for the ride.

Sometimes you might have one of those "wasted" sessions, feeling like you've been caught up in one thought after another, or caught up in restlessness, perking away like Mr. Coffee . . . but afterward you have to admit that hey, you feel kind of refreshed. If you happen to have an electroencephalography monitor, a galvanic skin response sensor, and a few other neurophysiologist's instruments handy, they'll show you that, objectively, you settled down. The moral? Don't worry about what's happening. The point of meditation is not just to have a pleasant little eyes-closed excursion. It's about the transformation of day-to-day life. Over the long term we become clearer, more rooted in inner silence, more balanced, less stuck in fear and speculation, more straightforward and confident.

This is why we emphasize taking a minute or three before slowly opening the eyes at the end. Always assume that the physiological settling has been deep, so coming out too fast could actually be a bit of a shock to the system. Sometimes you might even feel like lying down for a while. This is also why, even though we're not setting some rigid length of time to meditate, it's not a good idea to bail out the moment you start to feel antsy or bored. It's working, whether it feels that way or not. The two essential meditation instructions are the same two commands you give your dog:

Sit.

Stay.

Don't Worry About Breathing

If you start a session with deliberate, slow ujjayi breathing, that's fine. After that, though, let the breath, like everything else, take care of itself. Sometimes, if you happen to notice, you'll realize you've barely been breathing at all. Because this reduced respiration is a spontaneous effect of deep rest, it's benign—in fact, it can be powerfully healing. Generally, when you're ill, your doctor will prescribe this or that medicine or therapy but will also recommend bed rest. That, we could say, is because the body heals itself more effectively when its energy is available for self-repair rather than being used for outer activity. In that sense, we can think of meditation as preventive medicine, a daily dose of concentrated deep rest. Many people report health improvements when they start sitting regularly. And in the long term, the rejuvenative nature of this deep rest tends to keep people looking and feeling younger. A prime example is the Dalai Lama, now in his eighties, but with a youthful, even childlike glow on the outside that clearly reflects how he feels on the inside.

Don't Worry About Sensations, Movements, or Moods

Some people occasionally experience a spontaneous body movement during meditation, such as twitching or jerking of an arm or leg, or arching of the back. They may feel sensations such as tingling, lightness, heaviness, heat, cold, spinning, or floating. They may have a sharp intake of breath. Or they may have an unexpected change in mood: a sudden wave of anxiety or excitement or any other emotion, even laughing or crying. These phenomena are all duly noted and explained in the old wisdom traditions: they're part of a clearing process that meditation facilitates. The snakes are being sucked out the windows.

Traumas register in the body. Our language acknowledges this: we say, "Dealing with my child's illness is a big weight on my shoulders," "Renovating this house has become a real headache," "The news from Washington made me sick to my stomach," "My job is a pain in the neck," "My boss is a pain in the ass." Over time, we store these traumas as a sort of neurological imprint or residue. But now, when we settle into the trauma-free zone of just being, the old residues start to loosen up and dissolve. This flushing-out process can express (*ex-press*, press out) as a physical movement, sensation, or mood.

This is a tremendous gift. It's why meditation isn't merely a relaxation break, followed by a return to the same old same old. If we keep falling back into habitual fear or anger, even when we know it's unreasonable, it can be because the deep, persistent imprints of past traumas override rationality. Now that we're clearing the imprints out of our system, we're beginning to find the open space for a life of freedom.

It's very important to understand this. Otherwise, we could think, *Hey, I started meditating to relax, not to twitch or feel anxious.* It's as if sometime in the past a pile of dirt was swept under our rug. Now the cleaning crew has arrived. While they're doing their work we might think, *Wait, the room was nice and clean, but now I'm seeing all this dirt.* That's temporary. If we let the cleaning continue, soon the dirt will be swept away and the room will be *truly* clean.

Some of this cleaning happens every time we sit and rest as awareness—usually very quietly, subtly, without any noticeable moods or sensations or movements, but sometimes with them. It defies analysis. It's impossible (and unnecessary) to know exactly which trauma is being flushed out when. But if, say, you suddenly feel a wave of hot or cold or restlessness or fear, don't decide that meditation has stopped working and it's time to bail. It has started *really* working.

Occasionally the moods and associated thoughts that are kicked up may be so intense that they seem to overwhelm your attention. In that case, easily scan your body from the inside and note the physical aspect of the feeling—perhaps pressure in the head, butterflies in the stomach, tightness in the chest—which may have gone unnoticed till now. The cascade of moods and thoughts will probably continue in the background for a while, but, rather than focusing on them, just go on resting your attention on the physical sensations until, in their own time, they ease up. Unlike moods and thoughts, sensations are just sensations— neutral phenomena, like changing weather—so this tactic facilitates the smooth release of the old imprints while, psychologically, you take a breather in a neutral corner.

My old teacher, the late Maharishi Mahesh Yogi, used to insist that all his students should appreciate this process. In my twenties, I attended as many long retreats with him as I could, whether in the mountains of Colorado or Switzerland, or in off-season beach hotels on the island of Mallorca, sometimes meditating for many hours a day for months at a stretch. (Don't try this at home.) In such a setting, with hundreds of people aboard, we would hear reports in our evening meetings from retreatants going through some very intense catharses: reliving old physical injuries or emotional crises, laughing, crying, sometimes feeling like they were going to sock someone or their heads were going to explode. Maharishi would patiently field all the reports, reminding us again and again that these experiences were just temporary symptoms of neurological clearing. He would chuckle and repeat, like the refrain of a song, "Something good is happening!" And he was right. My whole subsequent life has taken place in the sparkling open space cleared out on those retreats.

Don't Worry About Doing It Right

You *can't* do this right. You also can't do it wrong. You can't do it at all—it does you. Worrying about doing it right is like worrying about whether you're paddling your little canoe the right way as the white water sweeps you downstream. This is not about cultivating a skill. It's about shrugging your shoulders and giving up all notions of skillfulness. What a relief!

Here's another way to look at it:

You might have noticed that it's never any time other than the present moment. (Check and see.) And it's always too late to change the present moment—it's already here, and it's already however it is. So you may as well give up. Just rest in awareness, as it is, now. Marinate in it. Bask in it. What else can you do? Your only other choice is to bang your head against it, like an animal banging its head against the bars of its cage. We know how to do that—whether feebly or fiercely, we've all tried it. Now, instead, for a few minutes a day, choose basking over banging, and see what happens.

Every moment you spend resting in this space of giving up is a moment giving the sympathetic nervous system a break and allowing the parasympathetic system to kick in. That is, it's a moment spent unlearning the cranked-up fight-or-flight state and replacing it with the stay-and-play state, the subside-and-abide state. It's a moment of unconditioning from your old, habitual how-do-I-fix-this hypervigilance and relaxing into if-it-ain't-broke serenity. *Ahhhhhhh!*

Don't Worry About What Other People Tell You

Good-hearted, well-meaning friends may tell you that to *really* meditate you have to sit motionless for an hour, concentrate on x or y object, kill your thoughts, press your tongue against your palate, or whatever. If you find some tip to be consistent with effortless, natural resting, then fine. But otherwise, feel free to nod, smile, thank your friends for their kind advice, then go on your way and forget about it.

A Stroll in the Park

Just think of meditation as less like shoveling coal and more like taking a stroll in the park. How long will you walk? Someone timing you with a stopwatch might report afterward that it was five minutes or fifteen minutes or thirty minutes. But *you* have no stopwatch—you just get lost in the experience. If a dog barks in the distance, you don't complain about it "spoiling your concentration." If a passerby says hello, or if you have to scratch your elbow or blow your nose, you don't fret about that "taking you out of it." You don't concern yourself with whether the experience is as "deep" or as "good" as your previous strolls in the park, or the strolls in the park that other people are taking, or the ones you've read about in books. You certainly don't worry about whether you're good at strolling in the park, or doing it right, or making progress. You just take a stroll in the park.

PART III

Overdrive / Hyperspace

CHAPTER 13

Take a Little Walk with Me

When my kids were young, I had an old, dark green Volvo. With its square, heavy body, it was built for safety, not for speed. But on the dashboard there was a button marked OVERDRIVE. You were only supposed to push it when your engine was winding out in fourth gear, to lower the RPMs for a quieter, more relaxed, more fuel-efficient ride. But my son Day was fascinated with two things—cars and *Star Wars*—and he somehow managed to conflate the overdrive button with the hyperspace control on the Millennium Falcon. As soon as we got buckled up and hit the road he would start urging me, "Put it in overdrive! Put it in overdrive, Pop!" hoping to see the headlights on the Garden State Parkway suddenly draw back like the radiating streams of starlight as Han Solo jumps his craft to light speed.

You now have your craft, the vehicle that will bring you to the dimension beyond fear: natural meditation. If you just keep your foot on the gas—keep sitting down for a few minutes a day—there's no reason it shouldn't get you there, as it has so many before you. But sometimes you may want to goose things along, to punch some overdrive button or other, to make your ride faster or smoother or just more fun.

There are many such buttons: auxiliary methods. Most are simple, some more elaborate. Some are done sitting with eyes closed, some when you're in the thick of things—at your parent's sickbed, or as you confront the other driver's road rage or your own, or as your friend offers you the drink or the joint that you know will send your life careening over the rails (again). These methods can make use of any aspect of your life, from your posture to your sleep to your voice. They're all effective and all optional. And sometimes, when things are lined up right, they'll take you into hyperspace.

So, as you read this section, keep an open, playful, experimental attitude. The best method is the one you'll actually *do*, so try the ones that somehow talk to you—and know that next week or next month different ones may talk to you. Eventually you can make up your own. George Carlin used to do a stand-up routine about driving that I think applies here (and just about everywhere else, actually):

> Fuck it! You paid for the car, use everything! Use the sun visor, even on a cloudy day. Flip it up, flip it down, flip it over to the side like the French people do. Lower the passenger's visor, even if no one is sitting there. Open the ashtray, push in the lighter; who cares if you don't smoke? Turn all the knobs, press all the buttons. Have a lot of fun! Change the mirrors all around! Press the trunk release! Pop the hood open! Put your seat in a ridiculous position!

Walk This Way

If I were a psychotherapist—which I most assuredly am not—I think I wouldn't sit in a room letting my clients talk, stuck in one position while their problems (or perceived problems) ricocheted again and again off the four walls. I would walk with them in the open air, where our forward motion and freedom of movement through space could model forward motion and freedom of movement through life. Together we would take in whatever sights, sounds, and chance encounters happened our way, welcoming the continual incursion of the larger world which rolls on and on, of which the client's problem would be seen as one part. In that context I would let them talk . . . if they still wanted to.

Whether with a therapist or with a sympatico friend or on your own, consider taking your fear, your anxiety, or whatever your issue is, for a walk. In addition to putting your situation in a bigger, less self-concerned context, a 2016 study found that a five-minute walking break once an hour made office workers feel happier and more energetic, with fewer food cravings. Nietzsche said, "All truly great thoughts are conceived by walking," and many writers, artists, inventors, and other creative types have long found that that's when they get their most out-of-left-field inspirations.

Recent studies at Stanford University have confirmed this belief. Students assigned a creative task, such as generating as many innovative uses as possible for a common object, scored from eighty-one to a hundred percent better while walking than while sitting. Not surprisingly, many forward-looking companies, including Apple, Facebook, and Oracle, have started using walking instead of office sit-downs for meetings of two or three people. Research has shown that greater creativity and focus result from a relaxed, collegial, side-by-side stroll. And one of the best things you can do for your marriage or relationship is to walk together as often as possible, side by side, literally seeing things the same way, letting the flow of shared thoughts, feelings, concerns, jokes, and silence be easygoing and spontaneous.

For centuries, walking has been an essential method of the sages. Socrates roamed the sunny streets of Athens with his young followers in tow, stopping here and there to engage the big shots of his day in penetrating dialogues that would deconstruct their bigness. Jesus roamed from town to town with his disciples, as did the Buddha, as did Adi Shankara. Generally the records tell us what they said when then they arrived and the locals gathered for a teaching, but not what they said to their closest students on the road. We can imagine that they often strode along in perfectly contented silence, just walking, enjoying the journey, perhaps throwing out an occasional comment or gesture, subtly facilitating their students' ability to join them in the depths of their own beingness. And we can imagine that sometimes students would air their questions, doubts, fears, and unresolved traumas, and the sages would respond with a spontaneity and intimacy (and humor) which the transcripts that later became scriptures failed to capture. You had to be there.

This rather lofty scenario has a straightforward neurophysiological basis. Walking is a *cross-lateral movement*. As you step with your left leg, your right arm automatically swings forward along with it, and vice versa. Any cross-lateral movement engages both the left and right cerebral hemispheres in coordinated activity, their neurons firing synchronously. This has a rejuvenating effect on brain function, mobilizing and integrating the analytic faculties associated with the left hemisphere

and the intuitive faculties of the right, priming the whole brain for fresh ways of seeing and understanding. (Our first cross-lateral movement is crawling, which helps prime the brain for the infant's dramatic period of rapid learning.)

In fact, a recharging, mental-palate-cleansing technique that you may find useful—especially when you're engaged in long periods of study or work at a computer—is a kind of hyperwalking that you can do without leaving the room. It exaggerates the cross-lateral movement to the point of *midline crossing*, which further enhances the neurological benefits. Standing in one spot, lift your left knee and touch it with your right hand. Return to the starting position, then lift your right knee and touch it with your left hand. Continue to alternate, stepping in place or marching around the room. And to add a more invigorating cardio workout, touch the opposite foot instead of the knee.

For a full-on, hilariously exaggerated version of this exercise, bring your knee as high as you can and across the body's midline. Meanwhile, swing the opposite hand diagonally in front of your torso and past your ear. (I don't think Socrates did this, but it's fun to imagine.) This is a great nervous system warm-up and clear-out, just before, say, taking an exam, negotiating a deal, competing in a sport, or coming onstage to perform. You'll enter

the fray with a sharp but relaxed confidence, not because you or your teacher or coach has pep-talked you into some whipped-up belief that you can succeed, but because you're objectively, neurologically *wired* to succeed.

Walking, incidentally, has a host of additional documented benefits. That shouldn't be a surprise. Obviously, we're built to walk, and, until about fifteen minutes ago in evolutionary time, we all did plenty of it. Walking has been shown to enhance T-cell production and other markers of immune-system health. It aids weight loss, boosts blood glucose control, and lowers blood pressure and triglyceride levels, especially when done right after meals. If you do it in the daytime, the exposure to sunlight helps prevent nearsightedness. Walking can ease depression, and, as indicated by reduced cortisol levels, it lowers stress.

That's dry clinical language, but it points us back to the juicy reality of the kingdom of heaven within, and the sages who walk there. Walking, like sitting, can be meditation, a way of waking up to delicious, empty, open awareness. Increased synchronous activity of the cerebral hemispheres also happens to be a symptom of meditative states—it's literally getting your head together. There are venerable traditions of walking meditation, going back at least twenty-five hundred years to the time of the Buddha. In fact, in the *Anapanasati Sutta*, walking is the first position he lists for meditation, followed by sitting, standing, and lying down.

When I visited Lumbini, the birthplace of the Buddha, I spent time with some monks who practice extremely slow, deliberate walking meditation, taking several minutes to mindfully complete each step. Given all the millions of mindless steps we take in a lifetime, that's a useful exercise to try at least once, paying microscopic attention to the amazingly rich nuances and the sequence of uncountable sub-actions and sub-sub-actions contained in a single step. Some people, watching the monks do this kind of slow walking, might say, "Wow, they must be in some kind of trance." But it's us who are usually in a trance, so hypnotized by our thoughts that we miss the simple, immediate reality of actual experience. Our scenarios of fear and craving are indeed scenarios—little scenes playing out in the theater of the mind. Every moment we spend paying attention to our feet touching the ground is a moment spent breaking out of our trance.

This super-slow walking might become a regular part of your

meditative practice for a little while or a long while, or it might be something to return to as needed, when things get crazy. Or it might not speak to you at all. But even when you're fast-walking down a city street, phone in hand, hurrying from Point A to Point B, you can rest as awareness and know that the passing sights and sounds are just the stuff you're aware of, like the passing thoughts and sensations during sitting meditation. What is the silence through which everything frictionlessly passes? It's *you*, the very awareness in which the question resonates. Rest as that.

When I walk this way, I sometimes hear the words of the old bluesman Robert Lockwood Jr. in his song "Take a Little Walk with Me." He sings about longing, and about getting back to the "same old place."

We're walking back to the same old transcendent place where the sages walked, back beyond trouble and fear, where all the trembling beings long to be, even when they think they're longing for the next dollar or doughnut or spliff or screw, longing for happiness, safety, peace. It's the same old place where we've always been but have (till now) somehow failed to recognize.

How can we arrive where we already are? The song tells us that too: "Come on, *baby*." To enter into the kingdom of heaven be like a baby, a little child, a tabula rasa, without plan or concept. Then there's not much to do—just take a *little* walk, sing a little song, sit a little while. Take any road, but take it easy. It's so simple, closer than close, which is precisely why we keep overlooking it. It's where you are now, at this step, at this step, and now at this step. Walking, sitting, standing, lying down. Just rest in it. Right here.

CHAPTER 14

Drop Your Thoughts

Our next overdrive method is dramatically effective and stupid simple; for some people, it becomes *the* method. You can use it anytime, anywhere. It works in all kinds of situations by taking a principle of eyes-closed meditation and applying it to the eyes-open world:

Drop your thoughts.

You can do this right now. Just put your hands in front of your face, clap them together once sharply, and drop your thoughts. Ready, go:

. . .

That's it. As in meditation, dropping your thoughts doesn't mean trying to push them away or block them out. Just relax your grip on them, and it doesn't matter whether they continue. They're like some blah blah blah commercial playing on your TV in the living room when you've gone off to the kitchen to grab a drink. They're like the buzz buzz buzz of a conversation a dozen yards away at the airport, between people speaking a language you can't even identify. They're just there. Don't bother about them.

Don't try to drop the thoughts forever. Just drop them for right now—say, five seconds' worth of right now—and then you're done.

The moment you relax your grip on the thoughts, their power over you deflates. Remember our experiment with the ball, first walking around gripping it tight and then relaxing our grip. We saw that it doesn't matter whether the ball remains in our hand or rolls off: our hand is now open to the sky, and the ball's presence or absence makes no difference.

Of course, in meditation it's a little easier to write off thoughts. You may get caught up in an extended fantasy about your upcoming vacation, and then it's as if you're there, strolling along the tranquil white beaches of Puerto Vallarta. Or you get caught up in an extended rehash of that argument you had with your partner or parent or child, and *that* becomes your reality. But then you realize, *No, these are just thoughts . . . I'm just sitting here with my eyes closed . . . this is nothing but blah blah.* And once again you relax your grip and sink back into yourself, into simple awareness.

It's fine that this happens. In fact, you *have* to experience getting caught up so you can experience letting go; you have to know clenching to definitively know unclenching. Getting caught, then letting go, then getting caught, then letting go—that's how we ultimately stop getting caught. We finally get desnagged, neurologically rewired to process thoughts with a nonstick mind. Then we preemptively recognize thoughts as just thoughts, and are free of them even as they show up. Being free doesn't mean getting rid. If you have to get rid of something, you're not really free.

But now we're not just sitting with our eyes closed, wandering off into dreamy little reveries. Now we're in the world. Now our thoughts are *real!*

Well, *are* they now?

Are our thoughts a clear window onto the outside world? Or are they more like graffiti spray-painted on the window? Hey, look! There's the first robin of spring, hopping around the lawn in the morning dew, grazing for its breakfast. How adorable, how delightful, how springtime-poetic, how evocative of our nursery rhymes and picture books about Robin Redbreast—unless you happen to be a worm. Then the robin is a terrifying monster. Cue the *Jaws* theme. (David Lynch brilliantly conveys this robin-as-monster vision in *Blue Velvet*.) On the other hand, a crocodile is a terrifying monster—unless you're a baby croc, and then it's Mom.

So those qualities of being adorable or terrifying are not absolute, not inherent in the object. They're our graffitied-on thoughts. For practical purposes, of course we need to know that robins are harmless (to us) but to steer clear of crocs. Many thoughts, though, instead of helping us judge accurately, can stoke our fears and actually bring more danger into the world. *Persistent fears are fed by set ideas.* We've seen political bedlam and actual deaths result from set ideas along the lines of Westerner = Great Satan or brown skin = Muslim = terrorist. We've seen police shootings arise from the idea that black male = big and scary. A recent study by the American Psychological Association found that subjects viewing photographs of black men and white men of identical height and weight thought the black men were taller, heavier, and more muscular than the white men. And the more stereotypically black the men's features were, the more pronounced this bias was, whether the subject viewing the photos was black or white. And white subjects judged the black men as more threatening.

To find a contrasting unbiased, idyllic innocence, we can look to nineteenth-century New England and the woods of Walden Pond, where Henry David Thoreau lived in his hand-built cabin and became America's first great nature writer. As John Cage later wrote:

> Thoreau got up each morning and walked to the woods as though he had never been where he was going to, so that whatever was there came to him like liquid into an empty glass. Many people taking such a walk would have their heads so full

of other ideas that it would be a long time before they were capable of hearing or seeing. Most people are blinded by themselves.

We can't all live in the woods, but we can all do this: be like an empty glass into which experience is poured, stop being blinded by ourselves (by our thoughts, more precisely), and hear and see with sublime clarity. It doesn't matter how many thoughts have been poured into the glass over how many years. It only takes a moment to turn it over and empty it. Just clap your hands in front of your face and drop your thoughts— disengage from them. It's true that a few moments later they start reengaging, but every time we drop them we weaken their power and strengthen our clear vision. In one chapter of *Walden*, Thoreau lists all the different colors of winter ice on different parts of Walden Pond. I had always thought that ice was white. The key word is *thought*.

Name-Dropping

One of the ways we maintain our set ideas is through naming. Different names for the same thing can make you feel differently about it—that's why there are dozens of lawyer jokes but no attorney jokes. Depending on what they want you to think and feel, politicians will talk about undocumented immigrants or illegal aliens, terrorists or freedom fighters, the estate tax or the death tax. Republicans routinely refer to "the Democrat Party," which sounds like something that lives in the sewer. And of course this kind of manipulation is what advertisers do for a living. Car commercials used to reel off the exciting features of the latest model, including rack-and-pinion steering. It turns out that *all* cars have rack-and-pinion steering; it just sounds cool, especially when growled by a macho voice-over artist.

But even more important to see—and see through—is how we manipulate our *own* attitudes with names. A friend of mine was born with one leg a few inches shorter than the other, and whenever he talked about it, he called it his "deformity." I suggested that he try using the less loaded word *anomaly* instead, and that simple shift helped him see how he had made his leg the focal point for feelings of guilt, shame, and inadequacy. William Blake called these attitudes "mind-forged manacles." Because they're forged by the mind, made completely out of thoughts, they have no substance. Once we see what they are, they can no longer hold us.

But we have to see them. Try referring to your parents by their first names instead of calling them Mom and Dad. That can help you see that they are (or were) just people, with their own lives, their own dreams and frustrations, their own virtues and limitations. They're neither gods for you to live up to nor dragons for you to slay nor problems for you to make a lifelong hobby of sorting through with your therapist. They exist on their own, not just as characters in your drama, the hero's parents. To other people they were a son or daughter, a brother or sister, a vague neighbor without any name at all. The less it's all your drama, with its claustrophobic plot and tedious themes, the more relief—the more freedom.

Believing Is Seeing

If we return to the same thought enough times, it becomes a *belief*. Each time we revisit it, it seems more familiar, more apparently substantial and permanent, more as if it's part of the reality outside our heads. Once, during my schoolteaching days, I was sitting in the cafeteria at lunchtime with four or five colleagues. I got up from the table to get some dessert and returned with a big, square piece of chocolate cake, slathered on top with that great, gooey, artificial-flavor-laden cafeteria chocolate frosting. Suzanne, a fellow English teacher, blurted out, "Dean! You don't eat that stuff!" Hmmm. I considered for a moment, then replied, "Well . . . evidently I do." It seems that her concept of who I was—a strict, health-conscious, pure-food-only type, and God knows what else—had collided with the actuality before her eyes, and she chose to go with the concept.

"It's my story and I'm sticking to it": that's our mantra. When it's applied to less benign matters than cake—matters such as race, religion, and that tribe at the other end of the valley that grunts in a different language from ours—it explains a lot of wretched human history. We think we're terrified of people or furious with them when what actually terrifies or infuriates us may just be our own thoughts. Then we start giving the other tribe the skunk eye and sharpening our spears, which confirms *their* worst thoughts about *us*, and soon everyone's biases become self-fulfilling prophecies. Ka-boom!

The irony is that, even when we regard a belief as solid and permanent, it's actually absent more than it's present. Because our beliefs contain no ingredients other than reiterated thoughts (they're gluten-free!), they exist only when we think them. When you're in the state of dreamless sleep, what's your religion? In mid-orgasm, are you a Democrat or a Republican? All your doctrines and ideologies vanish when you sneeze, or focus on your income taxes, or lose yourself in a movie or a novel or a kiss. This is why we *need* such engrossing diversions: if you could really succeed in being a good one hundred percent Muslim or Christian or Socialist or Libertarian or anything else for twenty-four straight hours, your head would probably explode. Of course, we don't realize that our doctrines evaporate every time we stop thinking them, because when they come back they include the thought, *This has been here all this time.* Nice trick. It's a built-in back-story, but it's still just a story.

So, no one has to teach you how to drop thoughts. You've already done it hundreds of times today. Every time you turn to another object of attention, whether it's the breakfast menu or the ringing of your phone or that inaccessible itch between your shoulder blades, you've dropped your other thoughts. All we're doing now is dropping them all, consciously and deliberately, and turning—instead of to another object of attention—to nothing in particular.

Not realizing they already know how to drop their thoughts, people go to great lengths to relieve themselves of that pressure. When I walk past a club on a Saturday night, see all those loaded people on the sidewalk, hear the pounding music, it sure looks like they're trying to blow away their thinking. They have the right idea, but their method is a tad heavy-handed; it wreaks a lot of wear and tear. When you discover how easy it is to just drop your thoughts, you don't have to wait for Saturday night, and you can do it with a feather instead of a jackhammer.

Just drop your thoughts. Boom. Done. Disengaged. A few seconds later you're probably engaged again, but now the thoughts' hold on you is a little weaker because you've punched one more little hole in their illusion of permanence. Perfect. There are many ways to click UNSUB-SCRIBE. You can smack your hands together in front of your face, or, a bit more gently, snap your fingers, or, in the middle of your mental monologue, suddenly exclaim, "Hey!" and look up at the sky: see if you can surprise yourself! You can sigh or exhale deeply, or douse yourself with cold water (more about this one in a later chapter).

Or stick a Post-it message on your bathroom mirror or your computer screen saying DROP YOUR THOUGHTS. Or, in the middle of a thought-fest, suddenly put your attention in the place of nonthought that you inhabit when you sneeze or sleep; it's always available. Or imagine that you win a free vacation on a paradise island (Wheeeeeee!) but you've packed all your old thoughts in your suitcase and the airline loses it (Buh-bye!). One way or another, do it again and again throughout the day. Then, when things get serious and you need to drop your thoughts to save your sanity, it's a reflex: you can find the UNSUBSCRIBE button in the dark.

Eventually, even the thought of dropping your thoughts can be dropped. They're always there when you need them to work with or want them to play with, but they no longer suffocate you. There's more space between your thoughts and more space within them. They're less like cold, congealed bacon fat, more like meringue. You're less weighed down by whatever stories you've been dragging around. Then your interactions with others become less squeezed and distorted—clearer, more straightforward, with more room to be intelligent and kind. Freed from our old self-constructed, claustrophobic labyrinths, we meet in open space.

The Question

Here comes a question to ask yourself. Don't try to think up an answer. Just close your eyes, ask the question, and see what bubbles up. The very first thing that pops up, before your mind gets in the way, may be the deep truth you need to hear. If so, make note of that right away, maybe write it down. Don't feed it to your mind, which will try to analyze it, rationalize it, soften it. Ready? Go.

What are the underlying beliefs that fuel your fear, anxiety, anger, or addiction?

. . .

. . .

OK. If you got some surprising news just now, you may want to walk around with it for a little while.

. . .

To spur further exploration, here are answers that some people find when they do this exercise:

I'm the good child, and I'm responsible for everyone.

I'm the bad child, and will disappoint everyone.

Sooner or later, people always let me down.

I must be intimidating.

I must be desirable.

I have to be my father (or mother).

I have to reject my father (or mother).

There's a catch.

It's every man for himself.

Those were the good old days.

Men are _____.

Women are _____.

No one can tell me what to do.

I deserve more.

I deserve less.

It's never OK to be alone.

If I let my guard down, someone will hurt me.

I don't get to sit at the cool kids' table.

If I'm cynical, I'll be safe.

Life is so unfair.

Life is so confusing.

Life is so predictable.

Being happy is so difficult.

Recognizing such beliefs, and recognizing that they *are* beliefs—
habitually reiterated thoughts masquerading as permanent, objective
realities—is a big first step. Then, even if (for now) they're still there, it's
easier to see through them to the free, open space on the other side.
When they come up, you can clap your hands and drop them for five
seconds. They'll probably still hang around, but, because you've disengaged from them even momentarily, their claws have disengaged from
you. Any time you drop *any* thoughts, you're becoming less susceptible
to the spell of *all* thoughts, including these.

There are a lot of nebbishy loser beliefs on our list, and these are
obviously a burden, but what about the quasi-heroic ones? "The record
shows I took the blows and did it my way." Oy. That can be a lot of
work, for you and the people around you. But, as always, don't take
my word for it. Experiment. If you've lived your whole life with
some belief, try living without it, five seconds at a time. Or if, say, you
believe *I have to be my mother,* for one week assume that you don't, and
then see if your life is more sane and graceful with your old belief or
without it. Beliefs are a lot of dead weight, compared to the lighter-
than-air weightlessness of just being, which is always instantly available
the moment you drop your thoughts. Why keep hauling that big bag
of manure? Where are you hauling it? When do you get to redeem it?
And for what?

If you feel resistance to dropping these thoughts, that's normal—
that's a measure of how identified you are with them, how much, deep
down, it feels as if you'll disappear if they're taken away. But, by the
same token, it's an inverse measure of how much more free and spacious
you'll be without them. Meanwhile, don't panic: it's only for five

seconds, and then you can have them back. And they'll *come* back, wagging their tails behind them. May your biggest problem be that you get stuck in freedom.

Often these things are easier to see in others. Observe your friends. Use your X-ray vision. What are their underlying beliefs, and how are those working out for them? Take a walk, look around at people, see the ones who look happy (in a sustainable way, not just riding a momentary whooshing thrill-coaster), and see the ones who look conflicted and jammed up within themselves. You can see it, if you pay attention. Which ones are stuffed with beliefs and which ones are full of open space?

And if you're really ready to rock 'n' roll, try this:

What if *everything* you think about *everything* is complete bullshit? What if, for five seconds—or maybe five minutes—you can just assume that? All the stuff you think you've figured out about life, politics, diet, music, religion, your so-called self, all of it: utter bullshit. When you take a break from having to believe it's all true all the time, can you feel by contrast what a strain it's been to maintain? Can you feel how infinitely refreshing it is to just drop it all? *Ahhhhhhh!*

Extending the Experiment

There's been a lot of talk lately about men who "mansplain" things to women with an excess of self-confidence (or at least an excess of bluster, posing as self-confidence). Maybe the deeper problem is that, regardless of gender, we all mansplain things to ourselves: the blustering, assertive part of our mind bullies the gentler, more open part. So perhaps we could extend this dropping of thoughts into some experiments in non-explanation. Look at a work of art that puzzles you. Actually, *it* can't puzzle *you*. It's just sitting there, being perfectly whatever it is, while you scratch your head and puzzle at *it*, hurling thoughts at it and trying to get some to stick. Like life, it's only confusing when you think about it. Try dropping all your thoughts about what the object *means* and let it just *be*. And then feel how that gives *you* space to just be.

Then try doing the same thing with that greatest of unexplainables: another person. Look into your partner's eyes, or a close friend or colleague's, notice all the thoughts about him or her that come up, and drop them, drop them, again and again. For once, let the other person just be, and feel the space open up for *you* to just be. If you're in a marriage or relationship, with continued exploration you'll start finding moments to drop together into this thought-free space, peppering your days and nights with them. More and more, you'll find yourselves just being, together: together in the wide-open space of just being.

Do this with your friends, do it with your turtle or fish and the tree across the street. Eventually extend this space to all beings. Perhaps the most fundamental crime, which makes all other crimes possible, is to reduce others to concepts—to squeeze the gorgeous, sprawling complexity of those living, breathing beings into the straitjacket of my thoughts about them. How tragic, to spend all those years with fellow beings who are alive and real behind their eyes, just as we are, and see not them but our own stale thoughts. How much less interesting, how much more dangerous.

Imagine what your life would be like if everyone you know—all your friends and relatives and colleagues—dropped their thoughts a few times a day. Wouldn't their lives be better? Wouldn't yours? Imagine if everyone in the world did it. Wouldn't the world be better? Well, there's one little piece of that world that you can do something about. Gotta start somewhere . . .

Eventually, when you feel fairly at home with this practice, look at the thing that scares you: the closed window if you're claustrophobic, or the spider if you're arachnophobic, and drop your thoughts about it. As you did with your partner, let the spider just be. If you have the thought, *But I'm still shaking, my visceral response has not gone away*, fine: that's another thought. Relax your grip on it, drop it, and let the visceral response be whatever it is.

If rage is your thing, look at the person who enrages you. Maybe that's a matter of closing your eyes and visualizing the a-hole in the white Beemer who tailgated you on the way to work this morning. If it's someone in politics, get his image up on your phone or computer screen, look into his eyes, see all your thoughts come up about how badly he sucks, and then drop them, see them come up again, relax your grip, drop them, drop them. (But don't let that stop you from voting, donating, and marching against him. We're just putting the Zen in *citizen*.)

Meanwhile you've been sitting in meditation, ideally every day. If the approach we've been exploring in this chapter is like scrubbing thoughts loose from the mind, as when you scrub burned rice from the bottom of a pot, then meditation is like letting the pot soak in sudsy water, so all the burned grains can gently loosen up. Together, the two approaches will get the thing clean. As you move on in your life, cooking up new dishes, they don't need to be tainted by the old dregs.

I once interviewed Wolfgang Puck, the famous chef, and I asked him the secret of great cooking. He said, "Start with the best ingredients, and then don't screw them up." No matter what your background, no matter what your circumstances, God or life or the universe has given you the very best ingredients: a human mind and body, capable of navigating through this amazing world full of fellow beings, and capable of opening to boundless OK-ness, perfect simple peace.

And even if you think you've screwed it all up—well, that also is a thought. Smack your hands together and drop it. What's left? Here we are.

CHAPTER 15

The Fire Hose

Sometimes we feel like we need to take a shower on the inside. It may be a passing thing—for a day, a moment—or it may be some ongoing life situation. But something needs to be cleaned out. We might feel as if whatever's at the base of our fear, anger, or addiction has such a stubborn presence within us that it really is *stuff*, an internal substance, a thick, gooey, sticky sludge, and we need some kind of powerful fire hose to flush it out.

The Tibetans have a particularly wide array of specialized meditative tools, including a fire hose called the Vajrasattva practice. The name Vajrasattva (pronounced roughly *vuhj'-ruh suht'-wuh*) can be translated as "Thunderbolt Being," and the practice does clean folks out with the brilliant luminosity and awesome power of a thunderbolt.

Traditionally, it's used for clearing out the "karmic residues" of past wrongdoing, as well as the deep roots of physical illness, negative feelings, personal demons, or anything else that might be gumming up our consciousness, what Buddhists call "emotional defilements and obscurations to enlightenment." Most of the men I work with in prison love this practice; they understand the need for it. One winter, after I'd been working with my group at Northern State for a year or two, we decided to tackle the most elaborate version of Vajrasattva practice, which requires learning a hundred-syllable mantra in Tibetan. One of the most inspiring teaching experiences I've ever had was sitting in the cold cinder-block chapel with my guys, some of whom had never completed grade school and could barely read English, all working diligently to memorize the mantra as I recited each word and they recited it back, gradually stringing it all together, syllable by syllable, line by line.

But let's start with a more accessible, entry-level version.

Sit comfortably, close your eyes, and consider what defilement or obscuration you want to work with. Obscurations are any emotions that block your clear view of the infinite OK-ness of existence, including fear, anger, anxiety, or any other emotion that makes life seem not OK. Defilements are anything with which we feel we've polluted ourselves: broken promises, actions that have caused suffering to ourselves or others ("sins," to use a highly loaded word), and self-destructive habits, including addictions. If you feel there's a "demon" (whatever that might mean to you) at the root of your addiction or of any problem, then that's an emotional reality for you and you can approach it in those terms. In a given session you can focus on purifying one specific thing or all of them in a general way.

Next, consider what role you may have played in creating the obscuration or defilement, or inviting the demon, and commit yourself to stopping doing it. This is crucial. The traditional teaching is that if you truly, sincerely make that commitment, there's nothing that can't be purified.

Next, consider the fact that innumerable others have suffered from the same thing as you, even though their circumstances may have been quite different. Deeply consider this: How many men have abused their wives or partners? How many people have felt enslaved by a drug? How many have realized the horror of having done terrible damage to another that can never be undone? Whatever it is, know that you're not alone in this. And then entertain the wish that, through the practice you're about to undertake, not only you but all other beings might be purified and liberated.

Then, just as you've done before, rest as awareness—simple being, like open space.

After a while, imagine-feel a source of pure, brilliant white light, shining in the space above your head, the color of fresh snow in intense sunlight. Once you have a fairly strong sense of that light, imagine that it begins to pour down in liquid form—pure, brilliant, liquid light, a sort of enlightenment nectar—and it enters through the top of your head. From there it gradually fills your whole body, pervading all your tissues, all the way down to the atomic level. As it does so, it starts to loosen up the stubborn substance of your obscurations or defilements, which you might imagine as thick sludge, noxious smoke, black soot, creepy-crawly vermin—whatever icky form embodies the way your particular emotional ickiness feels.

As the liquid light loosens this stuff up, it continues to pour into you till it fills you to the brim. Now it starts to work like a liquid trash compactor, pushing from top to bottom, forcing all the sludge or vermin out into a space far beneath you, where it's finally neutralized and dissolved. As this is going on, you may feel some strong emotional or energetic aspect of the clearing process. That's fine; just let it all happen. Stay with the process till you feel completely cleared out, as translucent as glass and empty as space, and then once again rest as empty awareness. After a while, ease out of meditation extra-slowly. You may have gone through some heavy catharsis, so really take your time coming out. Lie down if you feel to do so, stretch, perhaps have a drink of water.

That's the basic process. If something in this speaks to you, give it a test drive. See what happens. You may feel to do this once in a while, or to make it a regular part of your meditation practice, at least for now, for as long as it has juice for you.

The Pile Driver

If you want to soup up the process, you can add the short version of the Vajrasattva mantra: OM VAJRASATTVA HUNG (pronounced *om vuhj'-ruh suht'-wuh hoong*). As you start picturing the light above your head, also start chanting the mantra over and over, vehemently, like a pile driver, and feel that the mantra is somehow driving the whole process. Have a sense that the mantra and the light are one, powerfully coursing through all the tissues of your body, pushing out and dissolving all the muck, purifying everything.

Over time, if you find yourself so taken with this practice that you want to do it in the deluxe form, there are many Buddhist books and websites where you can learn the hundred-syllable mantra, as well as a far more elaborate version of the visualization. You can also hear the mantra on the *Fear Less* page of my site.

This Vajrasattva practice, in any of its forms, can be used as widely as you like, in any context calling for purification. In 2001, following the September 11 attacks, a highly revered lama organized a project to have meditators around the world chant a collective total of a billion repetitions of OM VAJRASATTVA HUNG. In Tibetan tradition, it is said that when someone dies, especially someone who has been dedicated to awakening, the best way to help them along is to do the Vajrasattva practice on their behalf—to help them, as it were, clean out the old house they're vacating. By tradition you would do 108 repetitions every day for forty-nine days, visualizing the brilliant light of Vajrasattva going through their body and, at the end, seeing them as completely, translucently clear. To some people this may sound a bit woo-woo, but Tibetan teachings generally have some shrewd psychology structured into them. I've done this practice for some dear ones when they departed, and over the course of the forty-nine days I did feel that some powerful purification was taking place—even if what was being purified was my own grief.

One of those dear ones was my first wife, Maggy. She became something of a Buddhist teacher in her own right, and Vajrasattva practice was her specialty; she used to teach it at retreats for the lamas she assisted, and she loved practicing it. That surprised me, because she generally didn't care much for chanting or anything that smacked of ritual. "With Vajrasattva, I feel like I'm *accomplishing* something," she explained. "I'm getting things clean." Well, she loved doing laundry too, so that made sense.

A few days after Maggy died, one of her students found a cassette tape of her explaining and leading the practice, including the instructions for using it after someone's death. We played it at her funeral, so that she wound up leading us in doing the practice to facilitate her own clear passage. We sprang it on the group without any introduction, but it opened with her saying, "OK, we're really gonna have some fun," followed by her deep, uninhibited laugh, and everyone knew right away who it was.

CHAPTER 16

Working In

In the prisons where I've taught, most of the guys work out. They may do push-ups and chin-ups and, especially, lift weights every chance they get. Of course they're trying to stay fit and vital despite the pasty food and long hours of inactivity. But they're also packing on layers of armor, making their bodies formidable so that, even if they have no desire to mess with anyone, no one will mess with them. Under the circumstances, that's a perfectly sensible strategy. It's one way of using the body to find a more relaxed, fearless way of being.

Still, covering your fear with armor is not the same thing as discovering the space beyond fear, and then living from that space. That's our project, and there are skillful ways to enlist the body to help accomplish it. Working out is fine. We're going to work in.

There are elaborate, traditional systems of working in, such as yoga and tai chi. But not everyone will have the time and motivation to find an outstanding yoga or tai chi teacher, take classes, and follow up with a full routine. So it's good to have something you can do in just a few minutes a day, on your own, no matter where you are. That way, you'll keep working in from the outside, making the body more pliable, confident, and tuned in to the place of frictionless freedom, which you're finding from the inside through meditation. And if you also like to lift weights or do kickboxing or bungee jumping or anything else, that's fine too. It's all good.

The following Six Moves are about as natural and intuitive as the stretching a dog or cat does when it gets up from a nap. Versions of them are found in Asian martial arts and yoga, but let's speak American and give them names we can remember:

Twisting

Rolling

Bumping and grinding

Closing

Turning

Opening

As with tying your shoelaces, it takes a lot of words to describe the whole sequence, but after you've done it a few times you'll see how simple it is.

Important: Don't strain. Never try to force your body into any position. Breathe normally. And move slowly as you come out of one position and go into the next.

Twisting

Stand with your feet slightly more than shoulder width apart, your arms loose at your sides. Keeping your arms and shoulders very loose and relaxed, twist your hips and lower abdomen to the left, then to the

right. Your relaxed arms will flop along, trailing a moment or two behind. Keep twisting left and right, initiating the movement in the hips and lower abs, not the upper body.

As you pick up a little speed, twist as far to each side as you comfortably can, and pause there for half a beat, letting your floppy, loosey-goosey arms swing around you a moment later. As you twist to the left, your right hand should swing around in front of you and then gently slap your lower back on the left side, while your left hand swings around behind you to gently slap your lower back on the right. Then vice versa as you twist to the right. Go back and forth like this for a while.

Physically, this is a quick, do-it-anywhere way to loosen up the whole body. The gentle slapping of your lower back stimulates the kidneys and adrenals—a natural way to get energized before diving into the day's activities. But you're also reprogramming yourself out of the habit of trying to muscle your way through your challenges with your upper body and limbs—carrying your burdens on your shoulders, taking arms against a sea of troubles, elbowing people out of your way, taking the situation in hand. Instead, you're using the greater untapped power that comes, literally, from deeper down.

In my aikido days, I would often find myself straining unsuccessfully to throw my practice partner by using upper body strength. My teacher would come up behind me, gently lay his hands on my shoulders, and say, "Drop your energy to your center." I would relax my shoulders and do the move again, this time from the abdomen and hips, and my partner would go flying across the mat. This exercise can help you engage your daily challenges in the same way I learned to engage my partner. When a challenge arises, pay attention and see if you feel tension rising in your shoulders. Then, just as if the teacher's hands are on them, consciously let the tension go and drop your energy to the abdomen and hips, with a sense of initiating your response from that deeper, stronger, less stress-prone place.

Rolling

Lie down on your back, preferably on a carpet, folded blanket, or yoga mat. Pull your knees up to your chest, or as close to your chest as they'll comfortably go. Roll over onto your left side. Push off with the left elbow and roll onto the right side. Then push off with the right elbow and roll back onto the left. Continue to roll back and forth a few more times. Your head can either be raised or remain on the floor, whichever is more comfortable.

This rolling has a wonderful loosening, softening effect on the whole body. Some people say it makes them feel like a tough steak being tenderized. And, because of the connection between outer and inner, it loosens up and tenderizes your attitude as well.

When you're doing something so childlike and playful, it's hard to take your sad, grownup stories very seriously. It always makes me think of Teri Garr as goofy, sexy Inga in *Young Frankenstein*: "Vould you like to have a roll in ze hay? It's fun! Roll, roll, roll in ze hay! Roll, roll, roll in ze hay!"

Bumping and Grinding

Get on all fours, with your hands directly beneath your shoulders, fingers pointing forward, and your arms and thighs squared off beneath

you, perpendicular to the floor—keep them that way throughout this move. Now round your back toward the ceiling while dropping your head toward the floor and bumping your pelvis forward toward your head. Next, do the opposite: let your back sag, arching toward the floor as your head comes up and your pelvis tilts back. Go back and forth a few times between rounding and sagging, then rest in the original squared-off position.

Next, still keeping the arms and thighs perpendicular to the floor, move your pelvis round and round in a circular grinding motion. Make the circles nice and big, and feel the movement all the way up your spine. Do several circles in one direction, then in the other.

Bumping and grinding quickly loosen the entire back

and particularly free up the booty. One of our language's most insightful mind-body puns is *tight-assed*. Not surprisingly, people often store tension, fear, and inhibition in the areas of the buttocks and crotch, including sexual inhibition (or its flip side, sexual aggression). But thousands of years before Freud, the ancient yogis understood that the powerful energies we think of as sexual are deeply connected to powerful energies that play out in all areas of our lives. In another edifying pun, our *seat* is the seat of forces that we may understand only dimly, yet which can drive our actions with an almost irresistible force. These moves help make the flow of those energies smooth and relaxed, and give you a chance to have a friendly, easygoing, playful relationship with them. What shall we do today, pelvic energy? Make a baby? Build a house? Write a novel? Let's work together.

Closing

From the previous position, keep your hands and knees where they are and simply sit back on your heels, or as close to them as you can, with your forehead on the floor. Again, never strain. Continue to rest in this position. If you prefer, bring your arms back till they're alongside your legs, palms up. Then fully release your arms, elbows, and shoulders, surrendering them to gravity. (For some people, especially large men with lots

of muscle mass, this position will be easier if, as you sit back, you place a cushion between your calves and your thighs.)

In the final position, close your eyes and relax. Feel all the muscles of your back stretching and letting go along both the vertical and horizontal axes simultaneously, as gravity pulls them toward the floor. Emotionally, you're now closed within yourself, cozy, sheltered from all storms. Your heart is tucked away, hidden, protected, like a not-yet-germinated seed within its husk. You're safe.

Stay like this for as long as you like. Don't count the seconds, and don't be mentally moving on to the next activity. For now, be here, safe, timeless.

Turning

Return to the original all-fours position, with the arms and legs perpendicular to the ground. Bring both arms straight out in front of you, palms down, fingers forward. Then extend your left arm under your right armpit, palm up, sliding it along the floor as far as you comfortably can. At the same time, turn your head to the right and rest the left side of your head on the floor. Close your eyes and feel the turning, torquing force that this position exerts, all the way from your hips to the base of your skull. There's something delicious about this—it almost hurts, but it hurts real good. To intensify that effect further, you can inch your left arm a little farther out to the right, and inch your right arm, at about a forty-five-degree angle from your head, farther out to the left. Rest like that for a while, relaxing completely into the position even as you're torqued.

Again, the key is to let go into timelessness. Then do the same thing on the other side. (If you can do this one while sitting back on your heels, you'll get an even better torque.)

In this position, it's as if the seed of your heart begins to germinate. Your arms are like fresh green shoots that the heart-seed sends out into a new, unknown world. That's going to twist and turn you in ways that at first feel unfamiliar and even uncomfortable, but turn out to stimulate growth. Anytime we point, we're directing the mind in some direction. Now we're pointing in two opposite directions at once. By letting your mind follow and vividly *feel* the contradictory energetic trajectories of both arms, you're programming mental flexibility, opening neural pathways that allow us to be at home with paradoxes and contradictions. Life requires that. It's messy and multidirectional and a lot more interesting than the sterile yes–or–no simplifications that our minds try to impose on it.

In *The Wizard of Oz*, this wonderful flexibility is portrayed by the Scarecrow, who, as played by Ray Bolger, convincingly appears to have no bones. The first time Dorothy meets him, she's at a fork in the Yellow Brick Road, asking, "Now which way do we go?" He replies, "Of course, people do go both ways," pointing left with his right arm and right with his left in a gesture that looks a lot like this move.

Opening

Now come up to a sitting position. Extend your legs in front of you, then bend your knees toward the ceiling at about a ninety-degree angle, with your feet flat on the floor about shoulder width apart. Leaning back a little, place your palms on the floor about a foot or so behind your hips (depending on your height), with the arms rotated outward so that your fingers point straight back. Now, keeping your palms, bottom, and feet firmly planted, *pull* against the floor with your feet, as if trying to bring your bottom closer to them. At the same time, close your eyes and arch your back, bringing your shoulders closer together behind you and pushing your chest forward and upward toward the sky, at about a forty-five-degree angle. If you can do so comfortably, let your head drop back. (If you experience vertigo or other distress when you drop your head back, don't.)

In this position, just be. Keep breathing. Feel the arching of your back all along your spine, from your hips to your skull. You'll notice a sort of effervescent tingling in the chest area, as the heart center and the emotional energies that are rooted there open up. Let your heart open wide to the sky, to limitless space, to all beings, all of life. This is the opposite of the sheltered, protected feeling of the closed position, so you might think of it as vulnerable. But it feels so delicious and so strong that you know you're OK—boundlessly OK, OK beyond the horizon. You learn, deep down into your nervous system, that it's safe to open your heart.

Stay like this for a little timeless while. Then let the body go soft, allowing your chin to fall toward your chest and your shoulders to collapse toward each other in front of you. If you like, do a few more alternations of arching and collapsing.

Some people find this to be the most profound yet the easiest of the Six Moves. So if your time or mobility is limited, you might do just this one. You can also do it first thing in the morning, before getting out of bed, as a wake-up stretch and a way to set a heart-opening tone to your day.

Again, never push beyond what's comfortable. And as usual, try things out and see what works for you. Any or all of these moves can be done pretty much anytime, anywhere. You may find them especially helpful before giving your big speech, running your big race, or taking your big exam. Anytime you feel tension or stress in the body—while having a sleepless night or drying out from some substance—these moves can help smooth things out. And as a regular routine, it's great to do them once a day, then go straight into your meditation.

The key to these Six Moves—and to everything, actually—is to just be present within them. Don't be going *through* one move to get it done or get to the next. There is no next. There's never a next. There's only ever *here*, *this*. Be here. Rest in this.

CHAPTER 17

Fear vs. Love

It's one of those Bible verses that you've probably heard even if you've never touched a Bible or set foot in a church:

Perfect love casts out fear.

Well now, that's a challenge—an offer we can't refuse, or at least can't ignore. It's such a simple, sweeping claim that we at least have to check it out. And this notion is not confined to the Bible. It's echoed in the insights of psychiatrists like Elisabeth Kübler-Ross and David Kessler:

There are only two primary emotions, love and fear. . . . We cannot feel these two emotions together, at exactly the same time. They're opposites.

Even Oprah says it, so it must be true:

I believe that every single event in life happens in an opportunity to choose love over fear.

Clearly, all these people are talking about something bigger than relational, romantic love, although it certainly might include it. In the Bible verse, the word translated as "perfect" is, in the original Greek, a form of *teleios*, which means something completed, fully expanded— as in the pirate's telescope, which shares the same root. Love is expansive. Fear is contractive. As "every single event in life" comes along (spectacular sunset over the Rockies, oblivious guy shouting into his phone on the morning commuter train), we can contract to reject it or expand to embrace it: love less and fear more, or love more and fear less.

The question is, how? Is there actually a *way* to choose the expansiveness of love over the contractions of fear when fear is a deeply ingrained habit? As we've said before, fear can rule the mundane, everyday moments of our lives, so that we find it too anxiety-provoking to eat dinner alone in a restaurant or to insist that an ornery customer service rep treat us right. And fear can rule the big moments, when you've just gotten the diagnosis and the adrenaline and terror set in, the ground drops out from under you, the room spins, your heart pounds, your mouth goes dry. Then this love business can sound like just a fluffy, pretty idea, no matter what Oprah says.

Well, it takes some practice, but it can be done. Some very skillful methods have come down through the centuries. One is supposed to have been taught by the Buddha himself, who was forced by circumstances to do deep research into the subject in his early years of solitary meditation in the forests of northern India. People often enjoy the fantasy of escaping the stresses of everyday life to meditate blissfully in some cheerful storybook forest, with a few friendly Disney woodland creatures curled at their feet. But if you've ever sat alone with your eyes closed in a real forest, you know that every thud or creak is a potential bear or wildcat, and the snakes arrive unannounced. (Once, twenty years ago, when I was on a solo retreat in upstate New York, a snake glided over the instep of my bare right foot. I can still feel it.) Later in the Buddha's life, he is said to have taught the fear antidote that had worked for him, calling it *metta bhavana*, lovingkindness meditation.

To practice metta meditation for the first time, it's best to do it when things are relatively calm rather than on red alert. Again, do the fire drill before the fire.

Sit comfortably with your eyes closed for a little while. Perhaps things settle down a bit on their own. Then think:

> *May I be happy.*
> *May I be peaceful.*
> *May I be free from suffering.*
> *May I live with ease.*

> *May you be happy.*
> *May you be peaceful.*
> *May you be free from suffering.*
> *May you live with ease.*

> *May all beings be happy.*
> *May all beings be peaceful.*
> *May all beings be free from suffering.*
> *May all beings live with ease.*

Think this (or, if you prefer, softly speak it) in a deliberate, unhurried way, pausing after each sentence to let it sink in, to be felt. Be present with each sentence as if there's no next sentence (or next anything) to go on to. Don't try to manufacture some artificial loving mood, but, in a natural, straightforward way, be open to the sometimes heartbreaking aspiration of all beings as they strive to be happy and not to suffer. That's all they want—just like you.

Who does the word *you* in the second stanza refer to? Fill in the blank: whoever you choose, or whoever or whatever shows up in your thoughts. If you're meditating in the forest, it could be the bear or snake or whatever unidentified creature just snapped that twig. At home, it could be your child or boss or partner. If you do this practice in a relaxed, easygoing way, you may be surprised at who makes the next appearance: perhaps your unfavorite political figure, or the guy who stole your parking spot this morning, or your daughter's doofus boyfriend. If you've had a difficult romantic breakup, or a loved one has died, or someone has become the perennial turd in the punch bowl of your life, make them the *you*. You'll find some powerful healing here. Don't try to feel loving, and don't worry about what you do feel. Just think the words, let go into the practice, and the results will sneak up on you in their own way and their own time.

The one rule is, whoever appears, no matter what they're like or what they've done, we bless them with the wish for happiness, peace, freedom, and ease. On the way to perfect love, we can't leave anyone out. In this era, when seriously depraved people in positions of great power indulge in truly repugnant behavior, that's not always easy. But blessing people is not the same as endorsing their conduct. As soon as you open your eyes, you can go back to calling them out for their crimes. You can go back to loathing them, if you feel like it. You may not. For what it's worth, you may start to see that if we could really give them peace and happiness, they wouldn't act the way they do.

I-and-I

How does this practice work to break down fear? There are a few levels to it. First, it subtly introduces a revolutionary definition of love: the wish for the happiness of the innumerable beings in the universe, of which we ourselves are one, but only one. This immediately shifts things away from the conventional, usually unexamined, desire-based romantic definition, reinforced by pop song lyrics from Elvis (*I want you, I need you, I love you*) to Rihanna (*I'm no good without you and I can't get enough*). By this definition, metta really can generate love, and, as Kübler-Ross and Kessler point out, you can't love and fear at the same time because they're opposite emotions.

But there's also a deeper, more fundamental truth that starts to open to us. As the contemporary British sage Rupert Spira puts it:

Love is not a feeling; it's lack of an other, of otherness.

Fear depends on a sense of otherness—separateness between the you that appears to threaten me and the I that feels threatened. As soon as I start wishing you happiness, I'm warming up and softening that sense of separation. We've experienced those softer boundaries with the loved ones of our own family. They're actually *not* entirely separate from us but flesh of our flesh—even when they're infuriating—so we feel at home wishing for their happiness. Certainly we may go through days or weeks without acknowledging how deeply we love our loved ones and how earnestly we want them to be happy. That which is most intimate and most dear can most easily be taken for granted. (Nothing is more intimate or dear to us than our own breath, but we don't think about it till something threatens to stop it.) So metta is, among other things, an opportunity to acknowledge this love deeply, inwardly, even when acknowledging it aloud might be awkward.

And now we are, in a way, enlarging our family, finding that same intimate connection with strangers and even with enemies as we have with our loved ones. Outwardly, of course, if you're the boss and you're unjustly raking me over the coals, or if you're the bear and you're trashing my campsite, I still have to do what I commonsensibly have to do. But I can also sit down in the morning or evening and inwardly find our deep connectedness, and that will blunt my fear of you.

You and I are seeking exactly the same peace and ease, even if the paths of our seeking collide. In that sense, you and I *are* family, and the more clearly I experience that, the less I fear you. Our quarrels are all in the family. Our relationship starts to shift from I-and-you to I-and-I, as the Jamaicans say. True non-otherness means there's only one of us here, taking a two-ish shape. We've been grappling with each other, like two wrestling octopuses, but now, as we get our tentacles untangled, we discover that we're really just one big octopus with two heads. Why would I-and-I fight with myself?

The point of all meditative methods is the effects that carry over into day-to-day life. If I can really grow in this sense of non-otherness, then, even as I defend myself from the boss or back away from the bear, acting as the situation demands, I can do it while fearing less, and my freedom from panic will make me more adept at handling the danger with grace and skill. I can relax at the moment of contact. That also means I can be more skillful in helping others. Social activists sometimes worry that meditative practice might be a kind of tranquilizer that makes people apathetic about the plight of the world, but it doesn't work that way. If we think of the activists who have really made the world better—Gandhi, Mandela, Dr. King—it's clear that the great power of their actions, even in the face of almost insurmountable opposition, has come from a place of peace, not stress. A few years ago I attended a celebration of the Dalai Lama's eightieth birthday, and to me the most striking thing he said was:

If you pray for the benefit of all sentient beings with sincerity, then when an opportunity presents itself you must act.

So love casts out fear. The same analysis applies to anxiety and anger. In fact, some preliminary studies indicate that metta practice may measurably improve symptoms of anger, anxiety, depression, and even stress-related inflammation. These findings would not have surprised the Buddha. In touting the benefits of metta practice, he said:

> One sleeps easily, wakes easily, dreams no evil dreams. One is dear to human beings, dear to nonhuman beings. . . . One's mind gains concentration quickly. One's complexion is bright.

If the idea of a meditative practice making your complexion brighter seems far-fetched, think of the times you've seen a friend and said, "Wow, you're glowing," and they replied, "Well, I'm in love." That glow, indicating improved blood flow to the skin, is just the most immediately visible symptom of physical well-being associated with being in love. Other symptoms, studies have shown, include lower blood pressure and lower levels of the stress hormone cortisol. There have even been some indications of improved cancer recovery.

A key symptom is higher levels of oxytocin, the mellow, relaxing "trust hormone" that is produced during childbirth and breastfeeding—the activities of intimate, mother-glow, flesh-of-my-flesh connectedness. Sex can stimulate oxytocin production as well, which is why (when all goes well) sex is accurately called "making love." The Buddha's point about improved concentration also makes sense. Focusing on the task at hand becomes easy and natural when, instead of being distracted by doubts and anxieties, we're performing the task from a place of quietly glowing intimacy, even when the task is trigonometry homework.

When we say, "I'm in love," please note the word *in*. What if, even without another person necessarily being involved, we could be *in* love, like being in a warm bath? (I've seen good actors do this on cue, with the same unmistakable hormonal glow.) Through practices such as metta, we're soaking, marinating in love, and if we soak deep enough we're going to stay damp when we come out. Then others, even subliminally, will pick up the signal and start to soften toward us, whether it's the boss or the bear ("dear to human beings, dear to nonhuman beings"). That makes our immediate environment a friendlier place to live in, where there's objectively less for us to fear—as the Buddha learned in the forest. One lama I studied with, when asked what the benefit of meditation is, replied, "Other people become so much nicer!"

Also notice the psychological shrewdness of the way metta practice is structured. Few of us are saintly enough to devote ourselves to others' happiness if ours is in doubt, so the technique starts with the wish for our own happiness and expands outward from there. As Albert Einstein wrote:

A human being is part of the whole called by us "universe," a part limited in time and space. He experiences himself, his thoughts, and feelings as something separated from the rest— a kind of optical delusion. This delusion is a kind of prison for us, restricting us to our personal desires and to affection for a few persons nearest to us. Our task must be to free ourselves from this prison by widening our circle of compassion to embrace all living creatures and the whole of nature in its beauty.

The third stanza of this metta practice is a staging area where we can start to do just that: embrace all beings. As our circle of compassion grows bigger, our own problems takes up a smaller part of the stage. Paradoxically, we're the one who benefits: the way to liberate oneself from Einstein's "prison," the optical illusion of separation, is through selflessness.

We can only be wrapped up in "I'm scared" or "I'm furious" or "I need a drink" to the extent that we're wrapped up in *I*. The word *escape* is derived from the Latin *ex-cappare*, meaning to slip out of your cape. Think of the separate, personal I as a cape we've been wrapped in, one with a lot of static cling that's always collecting bits of lint and fuzz. We can try to keep picking it off, one bit at a time—an endless task. But if we can manage to slip out of the cape, we're all done.

CHAPTER 18

Cold, Cold Water

There's another procedure you can add to your morning routine that will help start each day fresh, free from old patterns of fear, anger, or anything else that constricts your consciousness. It's quick, simple, and convenient. It would be nice if it were also pleasurable and inviting, like the soaking-in-a-warm-tub ease of meditation, but it's virtually the opposite.

It's simply this: every morning, douse yourself with cold water.

I know, I know, and I'm sorry. But believe it or not, you're going to love this, even if you hate it, and even if—especially if—you hate the cold, like me. (My wife's always opening windows, I'm always closing them. She turns the thermostat down, and when she's not looking I turn it back up.)

You don't have to jump into an icy lake, or even take an entire cold shower. You can enjoy your usual warm shower and then, for a cool rinse-off, nudge the knob from H to C, or at least close enough to C to put you well into your discomfort zone. As the water turns cold, you can start with it streaming onto the top of your head, where you'll feel it the least, then ease the rest of your body into it. After all of our emphasis on easy, comfortable meditation, it may seem surprising that now we're suggesting something so harsh. But this works *because* it's harsh, because you'd always rather not, because you think you can't do it, because when you do it you feel like you're going to die. But you do it anyway, and you *don't* die. That starts the day with a powerful message, delivered directly and physically to your whole body, deeper than the pep talks you give your mind or emotions:

> You may receive other shocks today that you'll think will kill you, but they won't. You may face other challenges today that you'll think you can't handle, but you can.

You've started the day by rising above. Because it didn't kill you, it made you stronger.

And at some point you may notice that this practice reveals a form of survival more profound than the physical. Despite the intensity of the shock, it's just another passing experience, another phenomenon of which we're aware. The experienc*er*—silent, perfect, nonphenomenal awareness—persists, ever the same, before, during, and after this shock or any shock the world may offer, no matter how intense. The Gospels' "Be of good cheer, I have overcome the world" becomes more than just an inspiring declaration. It's a matter-of-fact report on our own status.

In addition to jump-starting your morning on a note of fearlessness, this energizing jolt to the body also serves as a sort of palate-cleanser for the mind and emotions, so they can encounter things afresh. If you've been dwelling on some sticky problem or wallowing in some tired emotional pattern, whether compulsively in the back of your mind or vividly up front, this bracing dose of cold water cuts through all that. It's a benign form of do-it-yourself shock therapy. When that water hits your chest, you can't think or feel much of anything except *Aaaarggghhhhh!* So, at least for that moment, you've dropped the old stuff, the habitual concepts and neuroses. You've interrupted their momentum, so they can't continue unless you pick them up again. You probably *will* pick them up again, but every time you drop them—through meditation, cold shower therapy, smacking your hands together, or anything else—you weaken their hold a little. Eventually you ask yourself, *Why do I keep picking these up?* and you stop.

Among apes and proto-humans, we can assume that only a privileged few had access to hot springs; most had just cold surf or streams or waterfalls. Cold water is what our bodies are evolved to bathe in, and it makes sense that there's a biological rightness to it, with measurable benefits. Studies have shown that cold showers reduce depression—not surprising for a form of shock therapy. In fact, if you're depressive, another tip is to keep a stiff brush in the shower and give your skin a good scrubbing every morning. The nature of depression is to withdraw from the senses, and vigorous stimulation helps to bring you to your senses, literally.

Other studies have shown that cold showering even promotes weight loss through the production of brown fat—a beneficial, non-accumulating type of fat that babies have in abundance and that acts as a kind of metabolic furnace, burning up the white fat that otherwise makes people overweight. As the cold water pours down, feel free to imagine that your accumulated traumas, fears, and stubborn habits are somehow bound up in your congealed white fat, and now you're stimulating your metabolism to burn it all away. (I suspect that one day science will discover some truth to this.)

When you douse yourself in cold water, you're also participating in a grand awakening-tradition that cuts across cultures and eras. For thousands of years, Hindus have bathed in the Ganges. Every morning, they walk down the *ghats* (stairlike stone embankments) on the western shore of the river to do their physical and spiritual cleansing. One of my most indelible memories is of sitting in a little rowboat at the ghats of Varanasi, considered India's holiest city, at sunrise. It's stirring to see thousands of people crowding to the water's edge, the men in bathing suits or white cotton dhotis, the women in colorful saris, some dunking themselves, some scrubbing up with soap, some washing their kids. As the sun rises over the sandbanks on the opposite shore, many people chant the Gayatri Mantra, the ancient invocation to the dawning of the new day and the dawning of enlightenment.

Jesus's awakening seems to have taken place when he was baptized by John in the cold waters of the River Jordan, where the holy spirit descended upon him like a dove. The dove is the symbol of peace, and the more you sit and abide in the utterly silent, utterly peaceful nature of your own essence, baptizing yourself in it every day, the more you'll recognize this story as a description of your own awakening, not just a remote tale about events that happened two thousand years ago. John had been telling everyone that the kingdom of God was at hand, but Jesus, like you, saw that it was even closer than that. It's within you.

CHAPTER 19

In Your Eyes

In chapter 17, we introduced metta meditation as a way of softening up the apparent boundaries between ourselves and others—of casting out fear by being *in love*, soaking *in* the warm tub of non-separateness. That awakening into love is such an important part of our project that it's useful to have more than one method for doing it. So here's another one:

You may have had the good fortune to be around someone who, one way or another, has soaked deep enough in the tub of love that they're sopping wet all the time—someone who radiates the glow of love so brilliantly that it illuminates the place of connectedness for others in a way that's hard to miss. I've seen the Dalai Lama fill whole stadiums with that glow.

In particular, that glow can show in the eyes. Again, the eyes are the windows to the soul, and some eyes seem like crystal clear, unobstructed windows to crystal clear, unobstructed souls. These are eyes that are free of worry, judgment, expectation, need, fear. They look at you from a place that is bottomless, and bottomlessly accepting and loving. They may be the eyes of someone who's widely regarded as an awakened sage, or the eyes of your nana or your kindergarten teacher or your electrician. In India, being in the presence of such a one, seeing and being seen by such eyes, is called *darshan* ("vision"), and people traditionally have gone on long, arduous journeys just to experience the darshan of some great sage. Sometimes even a painting or statue or photograph of such an awakened being can capture and transmit that spark.

Please sit down with a picture of someone who, for you, seems to have the eyes of non-otherness, the eyes of awakened love, whether it's the Dalai Lama, the Blessed Virgin, Jesus, Anandamayi Ma, Einstein, the Buddha, Mister Rogers, or whoever does it for you. Here are two pictures you can use if you like. One is a photo that has deeply inspired many people, of the great twentieth-century Indian sage Sri Ramana Maharshi. The other is a painting of the martyred seventh-century Irish maiden Saint Dymphna. According to legend, after her mother died, her father lost his mind, tried to force Dymphna to marry him, and killed her when she refused. She's the patron saint of those who suffer from mental illness or nervous disorders, and she's supposed to

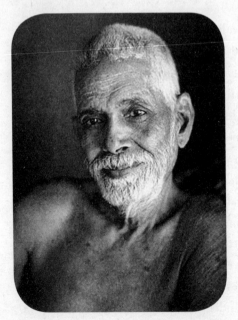

have helped many agitated people find peace. The fact that historically she may never have existed is, of course, completely unimportant. What's important about these pictures is what you find in them, or, rather, *through* them. They're windows—not just to *a* soul but to *the* soul, the non-separate beingness we all share.

Just sit quietly, look into those eyes, and let them look into you . . . all the way in. That's all. Relax and take time to let whatever happens happen. Sometimes, for some people, that may be all the meditation you need.

Seeing with the Eyes of Love

But there's an additional phase of this practice that you can also do. Again, gaze at the picture for a while and let it gaze into you. Then close your eyes and imagine yourself *behind* those infinitely peaceful, accepting, affirming eyes that you've been looking into, but now looking out at the world through them. In your imagination, take a walk wearing those eyes, stroll through your neighborhood or town, see the buildings and trees and animals and people, all so beautiful and lovable just as they are, and they don't even know it.

And then turn the next corner and see *you*, standing or sitting there, perhaps dealing with whatever situation has been stirring up your anger or anxiety or fear. With the natural, unwavering equanimity of those sage's eyes, see that situation, including any people who may be involved. Oh, look: there's you and the project you've been so nervous about tackling. Or, oh, look: there's you and the substance you're trying to quit. Or, oh, look: there's you and your ex and her lawyer. Or, oh, look: there's you and the parent or the sibling or the alienated friend you're trying to get things right with, or have given up on getting things right with. All those beings, all equally your beloved children, flesh of your flesh, just trying to be happy and not suffer. Trying so hard.

Just see them.

Someday you'll have eyes of your own like this, but meanwhile this kind of little stroll, with borrowed sage's eyes, can help you pick up some taste of what it's like, and then recognize your own flashes of genuine love-permeated seeing, darshan, when they come along. And they will. Recently at one of our Tuesday evening meditation sessions, a woman told a story about being in a business meeting and finding herself thinking harsh, judgmental thoughts about the other participants. "But then," she said, "I realized I could drop my judging thoughts. And as soon as I did, I suddenly realized that I loved them all."

That's only natural. As Marianne Williamson put it:

Love is what we were born with. Fear is what we learned here.

Love is not some attitude or mood that we have to construct. It's what's left when we *de*construct our artificial sense of separation, when we clean the dust from our eyes and recognize our long-lost brothers and sisters, our long-lost prodigal sons and daughters, all our long-lost lovers.

CHAPTER 20

Sit Down. Stand Up.

My late first wife, Maggy O'Bryan, was a successful fashion model before we were married. Certainly she was beautiful, but more strikingly she was *glamorous*, which has more to do with attitude than cheekbones: it's a relaxed, elegant, and, above all, confident way of presenting oneself. One day I asked her about it. I had thought of it as a rare commodity, but she laughed and let me in on her secret. "Anyone can be glamorous," she said. "All it takes is great posture and a great haircut."

I can't help you with the haircut, but let's talk about posture.

Posture—the way we hold our bodies—both reflects and is reflected by how we hold ourselves as persons in the world. It can promote either greater ease and confidence or greater constriction and timidity. Once more, the clues are there in our language, when we tell someone to "stand up for yourself" or when we call him a "stand-up guy," or when we tell the truth "straight up," or when the Bible says Job was "an upright man." No matter what you've been through, no matter what you're facing, even if you feel depressed or defeated, you can start to break out of it simply by standing and sitting up straight.

Can it really be that simple? Psychologists have done some compelling research on this point. In one experiment, they had subjects

answer stress-inducing job-interview questions, then complete ques-
tionnaires designed to reveal their emotional state. At the outset, half
the subjects were told to slouch and half were told to sit upright—that's
all. The slouchers scored significantly higher on the fear scale. Those
sitting up straight scored higher on the self-esteem scale, and their
responses to the interview question used much more positive language.

In another study, this time with people who were clinically depressed, again each subject was told to either slouch or sit upright. Then
they were presented with a list of words, some negative, some positive.
When later asked to recall as many of the words as they could, the
upright sitters remembered positive and negative words in equal pro-
portion; the slouchers remembered more of the negative words. The
implications here are stunning. Our entire picture of life is drawn from
what we remember—all the history that we drag behind us and on
which we model our hopes and fears for the future—and it might all
be colored by as simple and dumb an element as how we were sitting
when we formed those memories.

Again, the clue is in our language. We don't just *have* memories,
we *form* them, and apparently, through the mind-body connection, the
form we give them can echo the form of our body. Through the distorting lens of bent posture we create a distorted, bent version of reality,
tainting it with what's called *negative recall bias*. Fortunately, all the
psychologists had to do to elicit the opposite effect was to tell people
to sit up straight.

But sometimes, as a teacher of mine used to say, it's simple but it's
not easy. For one thing, unlike the upright Job, we live in an age of
smartphones. A number of clinicians have studied their effect on
posture, including the New Zealand physiotherapist Steve August, who
has coined a term: the *iHunch* (a.k.a. Tech Neck). People typically
browse, text, and tweet with their heads at a sixty-degree angle, which
adds the equivalent of about fifty pounds of dead weight stressing the

neck and upper back. One result is that dowager's hump—the stooped, forward curve of the upper back often seen on elderly women—is now becoming epidemic among teenagers. And Brazilian researchers have found that this same posture correlates strongly with depression.

In one cleverly designed study, Professor Amy Cuddy and her associates at Harvard Business School sat each subject down alone with either a desktop computer, a laptop computer, a tablet computer, or a smartphone. Each subject was told to use the device for five minutes. When the time was up, instead of telling the subjects they could leave, the researchers left them doing nothing . . . and waited to see how long they would twiddle their thumbs before taking the initiative and asking permission to go. The researchers found that the smaller the device—and, correspondingly, the more severe the iHunch—the longer it took for the subjects to assert themselves. Shrink your body and you shrink your spirit. Sit too long with the iHunch and you have, as it were, less backbone. For Professor Cuddy, there's a very practical takeaway:

> Keep your head up and shoulders back when looking at your phone, even if that means holding it at eye level. You can also try stretching and massaging the two muscle groups that are involved in the iHunch—those between the shoulder blades and the ones along the sides of the neck. This helps reduce scarring and restores elasticity.

But there's a second element that, again, can make this simple prescription not so easy to follow. For many of us, being told to keep our head up and shoulders back summons painful childhood flashbacks of some severe authority figure, perhaps a parent or gym teacher, who chastised and reprimanded us till good posture became a symbol of defeat rather than boldness. (One friend tells me that someday she'll write a memoir about her relationship with her overcritical grandmother, titled *I Stand Corrected*.) The problem, of course, is that the impulse to straighten was imposed from the outside rather than arising naturally from within. This closely echoes what we've learned about meditation: trying to force the body to be straight is a lot like trying to force the mind to be peaceful.

So here's a natural, inner-to-outer approach to posture:

If possible, do this barefoot on the grass or ground. Stand with your feet a comfortable distance apart, about shoulder width, and close your eyes. Now feel the earth through the soles of your feet—it's always there, even when your shoes or fifty floors of office building intervene. Taking plenty of time, feel the gravitational connection between you and the earth. Feel how the earth holds you, and how its gravity reaches up through the soles of your feet . . . through your calves and shins . . . through your knees, thighs, hips . . . through your lower torso . . . through your upper torso . . . through your neck, and all the way up to the top of your head. As you're doing this, let the force of gravity gently pull your head and spine so that they gradually slump forward and your knees and shoulders sag. You're never alone, you're never disconnected—Mother Earth is always holding you to her breast, with the love that we call gravity.

But, as with any loving mother, your connection *to* her also nourishes your growth *from* her. So now, as you continue to feel her gravity, also feel her life-giving fertility—as if you're a tender sapling beginning to firm up and grow into a strong tree. Inch by inch, let that growth straighten your knees . . . your spine . . . your neck . . . and finally your head. Feel your whole body as a tree that has grown straight and tall, firmly rooted to the earth as it rises effortlessly into the open sky—the clear space of limitless possibilities.

Rest in that naturally upright posture for a little while. Notice the firm, confident emotional tone that comes with the firm physical tone.

After a little while, gently open your eyes. Simply stand for a few moments, being tall, then walk around a bit, just enjoying your delicious tallness before easing back into your day-to-day world, with the quiet intention of bringing some sense of this posture back with you.

By repeating the exercise from time to time, you'll become more at home in this naturally strong posture. As a result, when you're in the thick of activity, especially difficult activity—stepping up to the plate or the microphone, standing up to the opposing attorney or candidate, speaking the hard but necessary truth in your family or relationship—it only takes a moment to reestablish yourself in this posture and the strength it confers. Eventually you may not even need to take a moment. The body and spirit *like* to be strong. When you show them how, they'll tend to remain that way. Just as we discovered with smiling, there's a feedback loop here between body and brain. Stronger posture inspires more confident emotional tone, and vice versa.

Seat of Strength

It's also good to do a sitting version of this exercise and become at home in a strong, tall seated posture. This will be useful when you're, say, undergoing a performance review, or even just riding the subway. Whether it's the skeptical HR officer or the sketchy characters on the train, they won't know why but they'll sense that you're coming from a position of strength (literally), and they'll respond with more respect.

You may also find your strong seat asserting itself in your meditation. You've seen that you can settle deeply without the traditional yogic sitting postures. But as your treelike posture becomes second nature, and as, through meditation, your consciousness becomes less cramped, more unfurled, it's as if the body wants to unfurl along with it. You may find yourself spontaneously sitting up and a little back, with your spine relaxed but in alignment, rising straight up from your hips, and your skull floating lightly at the top. Feel free to cooperate with this process and gently encourage it.

At some point you may even find yourself wanting to move your

meditation from your chair to the floor. A simple cross-legged pose is fine. Be sure to put a cushion or two under your hips to raise them about four or five inches above your knees. You'll know you're at the right height when you feel your center of gravity, in your upper ab-domen, settle directly above your hips; you're suddenly in the slot, where sitting straight up and slightly back becomes easy. You can just let your hands rest nat-urally on your knees.

Even better, if your knees and ankles can handle it without strain, is the half lotus pose, with your right heel pulled in at the body's midline, in front of your crotch, and the blade of your left foot resting on your right thigh (or vice versa). As long as your cushion is high enough under your tush and your foot is high enough on your thigh, it's virtually impossible to slouch in the half lotus. It makes sitting straight truly effortless.

In either of these positions, if you find it challenging to your knees at first, only do it for a few minutes. (Also make sure your cushions are stacked high enough, especially if you have long legs.) Then stretch your legs out straight in front of you for a bit, and then recross them the other way. Some people find that, with regular practice, the knees loosen up quickly. Sitting like this, in open space, with no visible means of support, feels good and free and *strong*. It's conducive not only to settled meditation but to a feeling of balance and confidence, a kind of self-sufficient dignity. Enjoy sitting, enjoy being.

CHAPTER 21

Finding Your Fearless Voice

Jerry Seinfeld used to do a bit about this:

> According to most studies, people's number one fear is public
> speaking. Number two is death. Death is number two! Does
> that seem right? That means to the average person, if you have
> to go to a funeral you're better off in the casket than doing the
> eulogy.

Yes, this is comedy, but yes, there have been reputable studies in which
people reported being more afraid of speaking in front of groups than
they are of death, flying, financial problems, snakes, spiders—even
clowns. And yes, Jerry's right. It doesn't make any kind of rational
sense. It's clearly a case of miscalibration of the fear mechanism, and
psychologists don't have a consensus explanation for it.

But the symptoms of speech-fright, if not the causes, are all too
familiar: the tense muscles, the dry mouth, the pounding heart, the
sweating and shaking, the constricted throat and squeaky voice. These
are all indications of fight-or-flight response, in which hyperactivation
of the sympathetic nervous system triggers a flood of adrenaline. As
you now know firsthand, meditation has the opposite effect, activating

the parasympathetic system to cool our jets. So the big first step in becoming a speaker who fears less is simply to keep meditating, ideally every day, allowing relaxation to percolate into all aspects of our lives, including the voice.

Then, just as with the body, we can also work with the voice directly. Even if you're not afflicted with speech-fright, this is good stuff. Since it's meditative in nature, it's delicious to do. And it helps to make and keep your voice delicious-sounding, even into old age. Some voices are open and clear, some are harsh, metallic, or strangled-sounding, especially under strain or fatigue. The stereotypical cackling old lady witch voice ("How about a little fire, Scarecrow?") and wheezy old man grouch voice ("Hey, you kids, get off my lawn!") are just exaggerations of vocal strain, which, over the years, becomes permanent damage. I recently went to a couple of Patti Smith concerts, and it's inspiring to hear the seventy-year-old punk rocker still belting out "Gloria" with the forever-young pipes that match her forever-young spirit.

In the traditional yogic lore, just as the heart center is associated with love, the energy center at the throat is associated not only with speaking and singing but with all creative expression: in the arts, in our projects and enterprises, in life. So relaxing, opening, and awakening our throat energy might help awaken all our powers to express and create.

Speech is a mysterious and miraculous thing. It allows us to connect our invisible thoughts and feelings with the visible world, to *ex-press* them, press them out. Many animals do that with their urinary systems, leaving their pee-mail on trees or in puddles. That's no stranger than the way we use our breath, throat, tongue, and teeth—mechanisms of the respiratory and digestive systems—for the same purpose. Respiration and digestion, like urination, are intimate biological activities. Maybe *that's* why speaking can make us feel timid, even as we tap into its deep power. Whether it's pillow talk with our lover or a political rally of thousands, it's an act of intimacy: we're turning our insides out.

Of course, we've been able to speak to thousands at a time only quite recently. People often assume that Abe Lincoln, with his great moral gravitas, must have been a solemn, voice-of-God bass-baritone. But in that pre-electric age, when politicians gave stump speeches literally standing on tree stumps, Lincoln had a voice made for audibility in large crowds: a high, piercing tenor, sauced with a Kentucky-Indiana twang. The microphone, and later radio and television, opened up political opportunity to a greater range of voices and eventually replaced the old shouting-at-the-crowd Teddy Roosevelt style with the relaxed, seductive, just-you-and-me charm of a John Kennedy or Ronald Reagan.

But the real pioneer of mass intimacy was a singer. Bing Crosby's ultra-relaxed crooning made him the first superstar of the modern media age. At over a hundred million copies, his 1942 "White Christmas" remains the best-selling recording of all time. His warm, effortless tone made GIs fighting Nazis overseas feel they were at home by the fireside, while their lonely wives felt they had a smooth substitute lover in their husbands' absence. Incredibly, by 1948 more than half the recorded music played on radio stations was Crosby's, and in surveys Americans chose him as the most admired man alive, beating Jackie Robinson and the Pope.

Warm and Clear

So vocal relaxation is worth developing. Fortunately, it's not hard to do. We'll start in the morning shower, when the hot steam is already loosening up your vocal apparatus along with the rest of your body (before you switch to cold). Put about a quarter teaspoon of salt in a plastic cup, get in the shower, and stir in about two-thirds of a cup of hot water. Gargle a swig of this, spit it out, and repeat till it's all gone. See if you can *voice* your gargling, so that it sounds a musical note, and then play with that, sliding up and down to higher and lower notes.

It's simple, but yogic lore, medical research, and Nana's folk wisdom all agree that this practice can be highly effective for flushing out viruses and congestion, and for both easing and preventing sore throats, colds, and other upper-respiratory ailments. Of course, this in turn helps make your voice sound clear and open, and it gets the voice box nice and warm, which is the perfect preparation for our next practice.

Long and Low

Now we're going to do a bit of singing. If you're one of those people who insist they can't sing, congratulations—that's about to change. Most such people, when required to sing, unconsciously tighten up their throat and face muscles and barely open their mouths: "I can't sing" becomes a self-fulfilling prophecy. So, still in the shower, start by massaging your mouth and cheeks a little to loosen them up, then open your mouth wide.

No, wider—what feels comically wide to you. Don't be shy, no one's watching.

Now sing the vowel sound *ah*. (No one's listening either.) Start at a comfortable pitch, somewhere around the middle of your range, and inch your way down the scale till you find the lowest note you can sing at full volume. Now sing *ah* on this low note, holding it steady for as long as you can without strain. Repeat with each of the vowel sounds *ay, ee, oh, oo*, as in *play, free, oh, cool*.

It's important not to strain. That would miss the whole point, which is to find your inner Bing Crosby—the relaxed power of your natural, unconstricted voice. Notice that inhaling is like inflating a balloon. Singing and talking are both exhaling, which is like releasing the air from the balloon. Release takes no effort. And practicing this release with our five basic vowels trains you to find that effortlessness in the sounds you use in your speech.

To really tune in to your effortless voice as you do this exercise, imagine-feel that all of space is a field of warm, rich, resonant sound that pervades everything everywhere, including your body, and is vibrating at the frequency of your low note. (Being in the warm, echoey shower makes this easier.) Then, instead of working to *produce* the tone, just breathe in, open wide, surrender into that warm sonic field, and *release* the tone. Let it come *through* you rather than *from* you. As you imagine-feel it vibrating through your whole body, radiating in all directions, resonating into all of space, lose yourself in it and dissolve into that field of vibration.

Musicians call this *long tone* practice, and it develops a sound that stays steady and full, even when things are moving at a gallop. Like a trumpeter playing through the fast movement of a symphony, you can go through a hectic, pressured day at the office and your voice will maintain a relaxed tone that will make everyone respond more positively to you, just as they did with Crosby. More concretely, this practice works the larynx muscles that control the vocal cords. That helps protect your voice against fatigue and damage, and strengthens the low overtones that make your speaking voice sound powerful and confident—less like a mouse, more like a lion.

Here's a version of this long-tone method that's even more effective. Sing the first three notes of "The Star-Spangled Banner": "O-o say." Now do it again, but substitute our first vowel sound for the lyrics: *ah-ah-ah*. And now smooth it out so that, instead of dropping down in three distinct steps, you *ooze* down in one continuous glide from the first note to the last: *ah~ah*. For reasons you don't have to worry about, this is called a *descending perfect fifth*. Experiment till you find the right note to start on, so that the one you slide down to is the lowest note you can sing at full volume. Now sing that same descending fifth with the rest of the vowel sounds: *ay~ay, ee~ee, oh~oh, oo~oo.* (To hear a demonstration, go to the *Fear Less* page at **DeanWords.com**.)

The physics of the perfect fifth—the relationship between the two frequencies—makes it the most stable and harmonious interval in all of music, and it calls forth something deeply stable and harmonious in *us.* It's the strongest musical resolution: it sounds and feels like question-answered, suspense-dispelled, problem-solved, anxiety-relieved, The-End, A-men. It's found in every known scale and every type of music in the world. You can hear it in the first two notes of the *Flintstones* theme, the Bach Minuet in G Major, the *Superman* march, the bass hook of "My Girl," and the Godzilla of soft rock, "Feelings." If you sing it as an *ascending* fifth, from low to high, it's the first two notes of the *Star Wars* theme, the first two "twinkles" of "Twinkle, Twinkle, Little Star," and the first two trumpet blasts of *Also Sprach Zarathustra,* which everyone knows from *2001: A Space Odyssey* and as Elvis's Vegas-era grand entrance music. And all those guitar power chords in hard rock? They're fifths with both notes played together—that's where their power comes from.

But enough musicology. The point is that, by tuning our voice and brain to the fifth, we're tuning to something universal. It's deep in our nature and *everyone's* nature, including every person you'll ever speak to. You're already getting attuned—literally—to your listeners, days or months before you sit down across the desk from them or step up to the lectern. And any time you feel yourself slipping out of attunement, into anxiety or hostility, you can just sing a few effortless, relaxing, expansive fifths right on the spot—under your breath or even mentally, if other people are around.

Singing Free

The most memorable thing my most memorable college professor (Wilder Bentley of San Francisco State) said was, "In a great civilization, everyone sings." Here's one more suggestion for the shower, or the car: After a few minutes of melting into your low note, your warmed-up voice is now ready to romp all over the scale and just sing. Sing playfully. Sing with gusto. Sing free. Sing whatever feels the most fun in that moment, whether it's blues or show tunes, Janis Joplin or Mister Rogers, Beethoven or Chuck Berry telling Beethoven to roll over. Open your mouth wide, way wider than you think makes any sense, and let that be the cue to open your energy that wide. Use the reverb chamber of the shower to encourage your freed-up voice, and use your freed-up voice to spark *enthusiasm* (from the Greek *én-theos*, "having a god within"). Rock and roll into your day.

Time for a story:

When I started teaching some mantra singing to my group at Northern State Prison, I discovered that most of them couldn't carry a tune or keep a simple beat to save their lives. One day I was chatting with my supervisor, "the Rev," a conservative Southern Baptist minister from inner-city Newark, and I mentioned that my guys were about the worst singers I'd ever dealt with. He started getting excited, which he did easily—all his sentences seemed to end with exclamation marks. "My men are the same way! It's awful! When we sing hymns, it's me and two others trying to sing loud enough so the rest can follow!" I told him about the studies I'd been reading on music education and brain development: how playing or singing in a group cultivates the ability to listen, pay attention, and wait your turn; how listening to symphonies may raise academic scores; how music lessons strengthen the neural connections necessary for clear thinking and decision-making.

I said, "When my guys sing, I feel like I'm hearing their disorderly brain function out loud. And those are the same brains they have to use when they try to function in society—so they wind up here." By now the Rev's eyes were very wide. He pointed out the window, to the inmates across the yard in their khaki uniforms. "These men . . . you realize who they are?! They're the first generation to go through the public schools after all the music programs were cut!"

With continued practice, my guys' singing improved. Certainly their lives improved. Many of them are back in society now and leading productive lives. I know the meditation helped, and I think the singing helped too.

Going Public

When you actually get up to speak in front of a group, everything we've been exploring—meditation, posture, breathing, opening up the throat energy—gets a chance to kick in and make you relaxed and confident, with a steady, clear, open voice that makes people feel like agreeing with you. There are only a few things to add to that. Some of it is the standard advice you'll hear from any speaking coach, but now, with the added depth of the practices we've been doing, that same advice will work better: Make eye contact with everyone in the room, project your voice and attention to the back row, keep your hands alive above your waist. Stay hydrated. (Various concoctions are said to keep the voice warm and clear when sipped before or while speaking. I get good results from ginger tea.) Don't pace around, don't lean on a lectern, don't shift your weight from foot to foot—take a strong, balanced, stable stance.

This last point is important. When Abe Lincoln took the stage, wrote one observer, you could lay a silver dollar between his feet at the beginning of his speech, and at the end it would still be in the same spot, unmoved. When you stand your ground physically, you're silently telling your audience—and yourself—that you stand your ground with what you say. Of course, some speaking situations call for movement, but not aimless pacing. "The way to do is to be," says the *Tao Te Ching*, the great Chinese wisdom text. The way to speak is to be—just standing, just being, in the silent moment before the first word, feeling the power of simple presence. Then, rather than groping to create truth and power with your words, let your words flow *from* this place of truth and power.

In this regard, the rooted-tree exercise we did in chapter 20 can be helpful. So can breathing through your feet, our very first exercise. And here's one more approach:

If it's possible, before your audience shows up walk to the spot where you'll be speaking. Otherwise, imagine that you're there. Stand with your eyes closed and your feet about shoulder width apart. Imagine-feel that you're a mountain: massive, immovable, high at the top, huge at the base. Feel how tremendously heavy your base is, and how the solidity of that weight supports you all the way up to the peak. Once you vividly feel this mountainlike solidity, sing some of your descending fifths: as before, slide down, let go, and dissolve into the field of sound vibration which is far bigger than you are, even when you're a mountain. Continuing to sing, slowly open your eyes, feeling how that field of sound lovingly engulfs you and your audience to-gether. *Ah~ahhhhhhh!*

CHAPTER 22

Twelve Steps, Two Thorns

Hi. My name is Dean, and I'm a chocoholic.

I unwrap a bar of dark, high-quality, dark, seventy-seven-percent-cocoa, dark chocolate. (Dark, please.) My pulse quickens as the hormones of arousal rush through my veins. I take the first bite, and it's like a hit of sweet fire going straight to my brain, then lighting up my body from the cranium to the crotch. True, the second bite is never as good as the first . . . but it's still good. So is the third. And the fourth.

The first time I read that chocolate was unknown in Europe till sixteenth-century explorers brought it back from South America, I immediately pictured earlier generations of Europeans, pacing nervously, scratching their forearms, and muttering, "Man, I don't know . . . I feel like something's *missing*."

I cheerfully read about every new study documenting the health benefits of chocolate. If there's information saying it's bad for you, I don't know about that—I've blocked it out.

I have more than one shirt in my closet ruined by chocolate stains.

I eat chocolate alone.

My mother had it worse. Once, she came out from California to visit us in New Jersey a few days before Easter. Maggy and the kids and I had to go somewhere for a couple of hours. Left alone in the house,

Mom started jonesing. By the time we got home, she had tossed the place like a junkie looking for smack, till she found the kids' Easter baskets, in the back of the closet where Maggy had hidden them. Oh yes she did—Mom ate the kids' Easter chocolate.

She may have been a genuine addict. I'm not, not really, or not anymore—most of my compulsions have been mellowed by time and/ or meditation. Sometimes days or weeks go by and chocolate doesn't cross my mind. I can even unwrap a dark chocolate bar and stop before eating the whole thing. Well, sometimes.

I've worked with addicts of all kinds, teaching meditation at rehab centers and prisons as well as to those who show up at my public sessions. What I've seen is that real addiction, whether it's to drink, drugs, food, sex, smoking, gambling, electronic screens, or anything else, is actually the expression of an impulse that's deeply right: the impulse to be whole, connected, complete. Addicts feel isolated, cut off. They feel, in other words, like every other human being this side of full awakening, but they feel it more acutely.

As far as we can tell, animals, plants, and rocks don't feel incomplete. Cows and squirrels seem perfectly content being cows and squirrels, or at least not discontent. The uniqueness of being human is that we're self-reflective enough to sense the limits of our experience. If I'm in *this* city, in *this* room, in *this* body, I'm cut off from everywhere else. Wherever I go, whatever I do, I'm peering out from my little cell through two little peepholes. I know that there's vastly more life going on beyond the walls of my cell and that it's forever inaccessible to me. I'm all by myself in here, I'm missing the party, and it will go on this way till I die. Who locked me in here? Who left me alone? I don't understand. I'm scared.

That's intolerable. Cows are not haunted by the knowledge of their limits or the specter of their death, but I am. Squirrels don't feel abandoned, don't feel baffled by a sense of withheld love, but if I'm a serious addict I do. That may be traceable to an undemonstrative parent or it may be a mystery impervious to years of therapy. But somehow non-addicts, though locked in cells of their own, manage to reach out to one another, to touch hands through the bars in a way that's denied to addicts. Even in a room full of warmly chatting friends, or in a club that's wall-to-wall with dancing strangers, or in bed with the stranger I've gone home with, I'm all alone.

And I'm insecure. Maybe I can attribute that to a volatile or unre-liable parent, or to other elements of childhood uncertainty. But we don't really need bespoke psychological scenarios to explain it. *Life* is uncertain. Careers, families, relationships, health, the fate of the re-public, the fate of the environment—none of it is solid ground. (Where I live, near a couple of earthquake faults, even the ground is not solid ground.)

Other elements are surely involved. But from what I've seen, and from what those who work with addicts every day affirm, there's a lot of truth here. Addictive behavior attempts to address deep-rooted feelings of isolation and uncertainty. The problem is that our drugs of choice get us halfway there. As trauma researcher Vincent Felitti puts it, "It is hard to get enough of something that almost works." The crack or the chocolate *almost* blows my skull open wide enough so that I don't feel stuck inside it. The three after-work martinis *almost* make me numb enough to forget how much I hate my job. The parade of sex partners *almost* resembles intimacy. ("I couldn't feel," sang Leonard Cohen, "so I learned to touch.") The politician's rally, where I pull on my ball cap and chant hateful slogans along with a stadium full of my bros, *almost* makes me feel powerful and free. The OxyContin is *almost* the one good friend that never lets me down—until it destroys my life.

But damn it, why *must* those addictive agents wind up destroying, or at least seriously damaging, our lives? Why can't we just declare them good enough and enjoy them? Here's where we come back to that deeply right impulse toward wholeness. The real wholeness of existence is existence itself, the silent ocean of being we discover in meditation and eventually find everywhere. It's delicious, boundless, all-encompassing, all-resolving *nothing*: no-thing, not a thing. Everything else is *some*thing. Every substitute, even the pretty bad ones, conveys some element of that delicious nothing—that's what keeps us coming back for more. But every substitute, even the pretty good ones, also has ingredients that are something—artificial additives, and that's what does the damage. But from a bigger view, that's a blessing. The side effects of our substitute nirvanas provide a kind of feedback. It's Mother Nature lovingly kicking your ass, as gently as possible but as forcefully as necessary, and saying, "OK, sweetheart, right idea, wrong method. Try again—you'll get it."

The Program

So, the problem of addiction is just the problem of human life, but more so. And therefore, the Rx for addiction is the Rx for human life, but more so. Do more meditation. Smack your hands together and drop your thoughts more times a day. Take more opportunities to relax at the moment of contact. In particular, do more of the practices that have an active, physical element—they can help normalize the addict's out-of-whack body chemistry. Do the Six Moves extra-mindfully, or maybe sign up for hard-core yoga classes. Smile with your Resting Bliss Face even when you feel like throttling anyone who mentions smiling. (Especially then.) Do lots of deep ujjayi breathing. Try bodywork: massage, acupuncture, shiatsu, anything that encourages healthy flow of your body energies and makes you feel too good to want to mess it up with some substance.

It can also be helpful to do the voice exercises and sing energetically. Try the Vajrasattva purification; you'll find that it really is a powerful freaking fire hose for loosening up and blasting out the psychic crud that's at the roots of your disease. You may want to look into *kirtan*, "the soul music of India," which involves energetic group chanting or singing of mantras. There's live kirtan going on now in cities where it was unheard-of not long ago, and many people in recovery have found that there's something about banging on the drum or harmonium and singing your heart out that can be very effective in lifting your energies out of their old addictive rut.

As you know, sooner or later some voice will come along and say, "Hey, how about a little toot? That won't hurt you." Sometimes that voice comes from within you, sometimes it comes through the mouth of some so-called friend. The most insidious version I ever heard of was in New Jersey years ago. A friend of mine who was a heroin addict finally checked himself into a large public rehab institute. There was a guy there, a dealer, who had checked in with a whole supermarket of drugs stashed in his clothes. He sneaked around at night, going from bed to bed and saying, "Hi. I'm the devil. What do you want?" My friend dimed him out, and he was arrested right on the floor. I hope he's still locked up.

Whenever and however that devil voice comes, you have a choice of three responses: "Yes, please" is a good one if you want to destroy your life. "No, never!" is obviously much better, but it has the downside of setting oneself an impossible task: managing the future in the present. When you say that, you're bracing and tensing yourself in the present moment against temptation in all those future moments that aren't here in the room with you. Suddenly you're like the little Dutch boy in the story, with his finger in the dike, holding back the sea, holding back the pressure of all those future moments of possible using.

The AA philosophy understands this, with their approach of one day at a time. But we're going to sharpen it further, to one moment at a time, one now at a time. The third response to the devil is a polite,

"Oh, thank you very much, kind sir, but not right now." Unlike never, now is real. It's the only thing that's real, the only time when we can do anything. You don't have to wrestle with all the years of your future. That creates conflict and strain, which may even make you feel more like you need some substance to help you cope. But just decline the offer right now, in this moment, without worrying about the next. Every time you do that, the thing being offered—and the devil offering it—loses some of its power over you.

Just do that now. And then now. And then now. Eventually the devil will give up and go bother someone else. There's no shortage of customers.

Meanwhile, of course, continue to follow all expert advice—from your doctor, your sponsor, your rehab counselor, your social worker, or whoever's on your team. Don't use anything here as a rationale for saying, "Yee-ha, now I can meditate for ten minutes and suddenly stop doing everything else that's helped me stay sober." Stay on your program, whatever it is. If your program happens to be the Twelve Steps, please note how meditation fits into the sequence. The first ten steps are largely about assessing and mopping up your damage: admitting your powerlessness, acknowledging your shortcomings, making amends. In a sense, that's all clearing the decks for the eleventh step: prayer and meditation to make conscious contact with your higher power—boundlessness, the kingdom within. That, in turn, should lead to the twelfth step, spiritual awakening and carrying the message to others.

This brings us back to a question we skimmed past earlier. Why is it that for some people, the ones who become addicts and alcoholics, the sense of disconnection and insecurity cuts so bone-deep in a way that it doesn't for most civilians? This is just my hunch, but it's supported by what I've seen in a lot of eyes over the years. Even prior to, and deeper than, any childhood traumas that may be involved, I feel that many addicts are born seekers. For whatever unfathomable reasons, they come into the world looking for the transcendent. They have a sense that there should be a source of *infinite* connectedness and security. There's *supposed* to be enlightenment. So the regular, garden-variety, finite forms of connectedness and certainty that are more or less adequate for others—work, family, community, the modest joys of everyday life—don't do it for them. I see these people as intrepid pilgrims on the road of awakening, whose vehicles have broken down on the shoulder. To drive my little triple-A truck and help out with an occasional spare tire or jump-start is a great privilege.

Oceanic Eleven

One of those jump-starts has been my friend Sam. He's got a typical all-American addiction story. He's a smart twenty-seven-year-old and a big bear of a guy, with dark hair in long dreads. He comes from a solid, educated, middle-class family but started smoking weed as a kid when his parents divorced. When he realized that marijuana was not the unmitigated horror show portrayed in the DARE assemblies at school, he figured they must have been exaggerating the dangers of other drugs as well, and he started stealing pain pills from his parents' medicine cabinets. Eventually he was doing half a gram of heroin a day. I ask him about bottoming out, and he says:

> The bottom is when you stop digging. For me it was the night I went to the bar and said, "I'm going to have two drinks—I have to work in the morning." I ended up drinking like ten shots of Crown, five hits of LSD, did some ketamine and heroin, and then popped some Xanax. That is powerlessness. The next thing I remember was my car spinning on the highway. I hit a parked car going sixty-five miles per hour.

Sam totaled his 2013 Kia Soul, walked away without a scratch, and went into rehab. Now in recovery for three years, he's a self-described Twelve Step guy, dedicated to helping others in recovery. Citing the "Big Book" (the authoritative Twelve Step guidebook, officially titled *Alcoholics Anonymous*), he says, "The only reason we go to meetings is so that newcomers can find the fellowship they seek," but he also understands how selflessness benefits oneself: "If you keep being an asshole, you're going to wind up using again." Seeing the need for a more profound way to work the eleventh step, he eventually found his way to one of our Tuesday night sessions. When he opened his eyes at the end of his first meditation, I saw the glow of someone who has dropped straight into the ocean of transcendence with vivid, translucent clarity. Now he regularly brings sober friends and sponsees to our sessions and integrates meditation into his own day-at-a-time sobriety. He describes how that works:

> For me as an addict, waking up is a trigger. So I sit for five or ten minutes, then go to a 7:30 a.m. meeting. I'm content, I'm happy with myself, which was never part of my story. The fear still comes, but it doesn't matter because I'm just an experiencer experiencing this fear. Fear is almost an illusion—it's self playing a trick on what I am. It's nothing to be scared of.

We're fortunate to live in a time when effective meditative methods of awakening are starting to be more widely available. It wasn't always this way. The Big Book was first published in 1939, but by the mid-fifties Bill Wilson, the founder of AA, was concerned that the eleventh step—and therefore the twelfth as well—wasn't really working. Many people in the program had lovely ideas or attitudes about a higher power but no true, direct, conscious contact and thus no authentic spiritual awakening. An idea about the infinite is not the infinite; it's just an idea. In search of an effective methodology, Wilson participated in several supervised LSD sessions with Aldous Huxley and other psychedelic pioneers, and he even flirted with the notion of incorporating psychedelics into the steps.

By now it's clear that, with the help of such substances and under the best of circumstances, some people have life-changing glimpses of the kingdom of heaven within, or at least some of its more scenic suburbs; under the worst of circumstances, they get a tour of the hell realms. It's also clear that the potential for confusion and abuse is enormous. But by now we also have a whole generation or two of psychedelic veterans, including yours truly, who have devoted themselves to deep personal research into substance-free methods for not only paying brief visits to that kingdom but eventually, piece by piece, moving your furniture in and finally living there full-time. (Originally, the twelfth step called for "a spiritual experience." As Bill's insight deepened and he saw that mere transient experiences weren't enough, it was revised to "a spiritual awakening.")

The one catch with meditation, though, is that you have to actually do it. Many AA meetings, like many churches and yoga studios and martial arts dojos, pay lip service to meditation. They may offer some token practice, but they just don't know about the best stuff out there, the most skillful methods of making conscious contact, which people will do every day because they're easy and they work. People in AA pray that beautiful prayer:

> God grant me the serenity to accept the things I
>   cannot change,
> Courage to change the things I can,
> And wisdom to know the difference.

But if the serenity, courage, and wisdom you pray for don't materialize, that's not God's fault. God (or higher power, or boundlessness) has put them all inside you (or *is* them all inside you), and it's up to you to use the slickest means available to open yourself to their outpouring.

One night a young girl, perhaps nineteen years old, came to our Tuesday session. It was her second or third visit. She sat silently through the evening, but just before leaving she took me aside and said quietly, "I'm a heroin addict, in recovery for four months. I wanted to tell you: In the meditation tonight I felt totally peaceful, totally at ease, for the first time since I've been clean. It was so wonderful. It was . . ." She trailed off, at a loss for words. Then she said, "I thought I could never feel that way again without drugs."

Any recovery program that doesn't provide that kind of deep connection to the inner kingdom of heaven will always be incomplete. And one measure of that incompleteness, by the way, is the crowds of recovering addicts and alcoholics you see on break, on the sidewalk outside most AA meetings, smoking America's number one killer drug, cigarettes. (The much-touted opioid epidemic causes fewer than one tenth as many deaths per year.) I suppose one addiction at a time is plenty to deal with, but still, it's a reminder that there's a deeper liberation to be gained than just sobriety.

As it happened, Bill Wilson died of emphysema, brought on by a lifetime of heavy smoking, in 1971. But one cold winter night a few weeks before his death, an old friend of mine from my earliest teaching days visited Bill and a few friends and family members in his Vermont home and taught them a form of deep, natural meditation. He left Bill in his bedroom to meditate on his own for a little while, but when he returned the room was empty. Coming back downstairs he asked, "Has anyone seen Bill?" It turned out that, despite his debilitated state, as soon as Bill opened his eyes he had jumped up, run up and down the back stairs, and then run outside to breathe the crisp winter air. Finally, he burst back into the house, shouting, "This thing works!"

Freedom

Any program—meditation, the Buddha's Eightfold Path, AA's Twelve Steps—is a path to a goal. It's not the goal. The point of meditation is to wake up out of suffering and into freedom; once you're awake, there's no need to sit around with your eyes closed. The Buddha said his teachings were like a raft. When you get to the far shore, nirvana, you're deeply grateful to the raft for getting you there, but it would be silly to carry it around on your back. I've heard Twelve Step people joke, "I used to be addicted to drugs. Now I'm addicted to meetings." True, the downside of staying on the raft too long (dragging around some extra weight) is not as dangerous as the downside of getting off too early (drowning). But even as you work your program, any program, it's important to know that it's provisional.

The Twelve Step program begins with owning your addiction: standing in front of others and saying you're Bill (or whoever) and you're an alcoholic (or whatever). Any good program must end with liberation, where you *dis*own addiction and just live your life. Even to call it "sober living" is to define your life with reference to addiction, which is ultimately a way of holding on to it. Full spiritual awakening, the twelfth step, means awakening out of *all* provisional roles and limiting identities, including "alcoholic" and even "Bill."

The sages of ancient India said that your suffering and delusion are like a thorn that's gotten stuck in your foot. All the methods and insights and programs are like a second thorn that you use to dig out the first thorn. Then you throw both thorns away . . . and just walk.

CHAPTER 23

Meditating with the iPhone 0

I like spiffy gadgets as much as the next guy. My iPhone is an indispensable tool—the Swiss Army knife of modern living—and a lot of fun. I quietly bless the name of Steve Jobs every time the Reminders app saves me from getting a parking ticket or the Maps app saves me from being lost. (In the bad old days I was lost most of the time.) Google Translate is a miracle. Access to pretty much the world's information through a shiny shingle that I carry in my pocket is a miracle. The ability to send words and pictures flying through the ether to my friends anywhere in the world is a miracle.

Of course, the problem with these sleek gizmos (as I'm about the nine hundred millionth person to point out) is that they're portals to endless distraction. I like walking late at night, looking up at the stars and hearing the crickets, feeling the world exhale and grow quiet. The few people I see are usually walking dogs. These days, most of them walk with their heads bent at that telltale sixty-degree angle, faces bathed in that blue-gray glow, oblivious to the night air and the silence. (Their dogs, who happily lack the opposable thumbs necessary to operate electronic devices, enjoy the excursion as they always have . . . unhypnotized.)

Yeah, but what about when it's not a balmy night of stars and crickets? When you're standing in a slow-moving line to get coffee or fill a prescription, what's so horrible about a quick news update or e-mail check or a couple of rounds of *Fruit Ninja*? Well, it's not horrible, and sometimes I'll do that news update myself. But if you're serious about coming out of suffering, it's a missed opportunity.

We seek distraction to escape from the present situation when we think it's not OK. And, of course, standing in that slow line sure seems boring, annoying, not OK. Just look at how bored and annoyed the other people are! But unlike most of them, when it comes to handling that which is boring and annoying, we're professionals. As meditators, we know that its flip side is infinite OK-ness. We've sat with our eyes closed, while the dog across the street barks, our thoughts obsess about how we're going to get our taxes done on time, and that idiotic commercial keeps playing in our head: "1-877-Kars4Kids! Donate your car today!" We feel restless, we're sure we're just wasting our time. But we stay with the meditation. We keep relaxing our grip and resting as awareness . . . and . . . after a while . . . somehow . . . even as all of the above continues in the background . . . settling happens. Then we feel fine for no reason having anything to do with anything, irrespective of the taxes and the dog and the rest of it. Everything (every *thing*) is still exactly as it was, but somehow it's as if we just noticed that our belt has been too tight and now we've loosened it. *Ahhhhhhh!*

Settling into that *ahhhhhhh* in meditation is important, but it's just a prelude to finding it everywhere. If, for a little while, we just be with whatever situation we're in, we'll see, again and again, that we can find that OK-ness in the pharmacy line, in the dentist's chair, on the delayed flight. But if we keep automatically, reflexively distracting ourselves, we never get a chance to find out that it's OK. In fact, we're telling ourselves that it's not OK, and repeatedly reinforcing that notion.

Nowadays, that reinforcement starts early. I see babies in strollers, at the age when they're supposed to be tuning in to human faces and

learning the subtle, unspoken rules of human interaction, staring instead at some game or video on a phone or tablet their parent has
handed them. When I'm at a restaurant and there's a young couple
sitting nearby, if one gets up to go to the bathroom I can count the
seconds till the other whips out a phone to check messages. I rarely get
to double digits. Or they don't even wait till the other leaves. I've seen
couples go through whole meals without eye contact, reverently
bowing their heads to the phones they've parked on the table. My intention here is not to go off on a young-folks-today rant: "Why, when
I was your age, I trudged a mile through the snow to talk to Cousin
Milly with two Dixie Cups and a piece of string." But airports are
becoming an obstacle course, as phone addicts walk head-down
through the crowd, depending on the rest of us to steer around them,
and the number of head-down drivers killing head-down pedestrians
keeps climbing.

Sure, this is not alcoholism or heroin addiction, but it's addiction
nevertheless. It took decades till a tobacco-industry whistle-blower
disclosed that cigarettes were deliberately designed to be an addictive
"nicotine delivery system"; now software developers cheerfully boast
about how addictive they've made their apps. When you look up after
gazing too long at any kind of screen (computer, phone, TV, video
game), please notice whether there's a subtle sort of buzzy, fluttery, achy
feeling behind your eyes and forehead. That's your body reacting to an
overload of the visual and cortical circuits—a sort of electronic
hangover.

As with any hangover, the temptation—the most convenient and
most dangerous way to deal with it—is the hair of the dog that bit you:
just dive right back into your screen, lose yourself in it again, and
you lose consciousness of that annoying hangover sensation. Of course,
you also lose consciousness of everything else in the non-screen world.

Aside from the fact that you're now caught in an addictive cycle, no worries! "As a dog returneth to his vomit," says the Book of Proverbs, "so a fool returneth to his folly."

But (we're told) this is the price of progress. We're living in the Information Age, and craving for information may seem as natural as craving for food. But break down that word, please: *in-formation, in-form-ation.* Engaging with information keeps our consciousness stuck in formation, in the forms of all those words and sounds and pictures, like molten plastic that's poured into molds and left to cool into objects that are now stuck in those shapes. When we get used to that, even though it's cramped and confining, we forget how to live without it. Then, when we're denied access to our screens and our consciousness starts relaxing in the direction of unformed freedom again, we feel uneasy. Without our familiar constrictive boundaries, we can feel like we're going into some kind of free fall. And we are, with the emphasis on the word *free.*

Our natural meditation approach is to use everything in our lives as alarm clocks, to wake ourselves up out of all our addictions and afflictions, into a life of rich experience for ourselves and sensitive responsiveness to others. That includes—that *especially* includes—using the things that seem like obstacles to awakening. So, in the case of the handy, pocket-sized Apple (or Android) Distract-O-Matic, how can we flip this addiction around and turn it into a meditative practice?

Actually, it's simple:

The next time you're in one of those involuntary nothing-happening moments—your date goes off to the bathroom, you're stuck at a red light, you're waiting for an elevator—and you find yourself automatically reaching for your phone . . . *just don't do it.* Yes, I understand how unhelpful that sounds, but hang on: here comes the subtle, skillful part. When you refrain from grabbing your phone, you're going to feel a wave of squirmy anxiety. If there were an app that translated vague feelings into words (and there probably will be soon), it would read out as something like:

> But, but . . . I might be missing something. Maybe something important, or interesting, or fun, or . . . something! Feed me some news, stimulate me with input, give me anything, as long as I don't have to sit here and deal with nothing, because that's unbearable.

Feeling that wave of anxiety is fine. In fact, it's what's going to make this meditation work.

The key is to let the wave happen. Don't try to ignore the feeling. Don't try to suppress it. Don't try to turn it into something else. Instead, experience what that feeling actually *is*: a set of subtle, internal physical sensations, maybe in the chest or abdomen or head. Allow yourself to feel that feeling, as it changes and moves and finally passes through you in its own time, like a wave passing through the ocean. Just don't *ride* the wave. Don't be caught up in it, driven by it, compelled by it to do something . . . like whip out your phone.

Then a small miracle happens. The wave does indeed pass, and you're still here. You didn't follow the compulsion, and your head didn't explode after all. This is called freedom, and this little taste of freedom has exactly the same flavor as the big freedom of nirvana. We discover that the nothing we've been trying so hard to avoid is *delicious* nothing.

You can use the same approach with other kinds of compulsions. When you find yourself getting caught up in the urge to light a cigarette or make a cutting remark that's going to hurt someone, just don't do it—or at least hold off and don't do it right away. Give yourself time to feel that wave of fidgety anxiety, notice what it feels like in the body, let it be there for as long as it needs to, and then let it pass. Don't try to push it away, but don't buy into it. Maybe five minutes later you'll light the cigarette anyway, but if you buy yourself five minutes of freedom you've accomplished something.

If you keep practicing like this, with the cigarettes or the phone or whatever else has been pushing you around, the little patches of freedom will start to connect up. More and more, you'll find yourself living in liberative, wide-open space. You'll start to see how that delicious nothing underlies all moments, even when you're busy with lots of somethings.

We can call this meditating with the iPhone 0. Unlike other iPhones, it doesn't eventually grow stale as we seek our next source of distraction. Liberation never goes out of style. What's now your spiffiest gizmo will one day seem as primitive as a lump of coal in your pocket. But the iPhone 0 is timeless: it will be just as fresh when space colonists use it on the planets of distant galaxies as it was when the ancient yogis used it in the jungles of India.

Enjoy your freedom.

CHAPTER 24

You Should Be Dancing

I hated high school dances. I didn't know the cool moves. I felt awkward and stupid and spotlight-conspicuous in my body. It was my old playground nightmare, now multiplied by surging hormones and hopeless romantic yearnings. I envied the guys with older sisters who would play records or watch *American Bandstand* and make them dance with them. Those guys always looked so slick and confident out on the floor, while I lurked on the sidelines, trying to figure out how they did it.

Figure out. That, of course, was the problem: I was trying to process it through my thinking mind. When I did work up the courage to get out on the floor with a (gulp!) girl, I spent the whole time listening to my mind try to break down what the other kids were doing, explain to my body how to imitate them, evaluate how I was measuring up, and monitor the exact amount of amused scorn with which the girl and every other kid in the gym was surely watching my dorky moves. I was miserable.

A few years later, I discovered how to break out of my misery: weed. By then I was going to college in San Francisco, and some up-and-coming local bands with names like, oh, the Grateful Dead, Jefferson Airplane, Quicksilver Messenger Service, and Big Brother and the

Holding Company kept showing up at the auditoriums and parks, with their pulsing, flowing new sounds. Suddenly it was fine to dance without a partner. With no girl to impress, I could lose myself in the sea of friendly, groovy strangers. Dancing high, dancing with my eyes closed, dancing with myself, I had a big epiphany: Forget how it looks from the outside, just feel it from the inside. Listen to the music, not the thoughts. And listen with the whole body. I could let the music bypass my mind and go straight to my belly, my spine, my pelvis, my arms and legs. The music moved them and I just went along for the ride.

There was one disappointment, at first. I thought marijuana was supposed to *blow my mind*: to bomb that ever-churning thought factory into incapacity. But the thoughts were still there—often, in fact, amplified, as if ricocheting through some kind of funhouse echo chamber. Then, however, the disappointment gave way to another discovery: I could ignore the thoughts. I was too busy listening to the music, and being moved by it, to worry about thoughts. Screw 'em.

Within a few years, my earnest pot-smoking phase came to an end, having served its purpose. I learned to meditate and quickly discovered that it worked basically the same way as dancing high: you close your eyes, you relax, you ignore your thoughts, you let what happens happen. The option of ignoring thoughts, it turned out, was always available, even without herbal assistance. I realized that most thoughts, both in and out of meditation, were just static, and, rather than try to grapple with them or silence them, I could let them sizzle harmlessly in the background, like a skillet of onions frying back in the kitchen while I relaxed at the table, enjoying my pie.

I still love to dance, whether it's late at night in my living room with the lights off, or on a crowded floor while some cornball bar mitzvah band murders "We Are Family." I don't need weed or the Dead or the hippies in Golden Gate Park. I can dance, I can jive, having the time of my life. As far as I know, my moves may still look dorky to anyone watching. But you know that Facebook cliché, "Dance like nobody's watching"? Well, nobody's watching. It turns out no one cares what your moves look like. And if they did, so what? Who cares if they care? That's all just more thoughts. If anything, my dorky moves give other people permission to relax and stop worrying about *their* moves. My ungracefulness helps confer a state of grace. You're welcome.

Dancing like this—closing your eyes, giving up to the music, feeling the moves from the inside rather than watching them from the outside, disempowering your thoughts and fears by simply ignoring them—is meditation as surely as sitting on a cushion is. As it happens, research has shown that dancing has some of the same benefits as sitting meditation, including reduced stress, anxiety, insomnia, and depression, enhanced cognitive abilities, and, crucially, enhanced *neuroplasticity*: the body's ability to keep renewing and rewiring neural pathways, even into old age. That's consistent with the results of a twenty-one-year study of subjects over age seventy-five, led by the Albert Einstein College of Medicine. It found that swimming, bicycling, and golf gave no protection from dementia due to Alzheimer's and other causes; reading or doing crossword puzzles gave some mild protection; but frequent dancing reduced the risk by seventy-six percent.

Of all these findings, the one I've seen demonstrated most dramatically in real life, again and again, is that of breaking through depression. If you're depressed, dancing may be the last thing you want to do, but it's the first thing you have to do. In traditional cultures, no one needed scientists to tell them this. Gabrielle Roth, the great pioneer of healing and opening through dance, wrote:

> In many shamanic societies, if you came to a medicine person complaining of being disheartened, dispirited, or depressed, they would ask one of four questions: When did you stop dancing? When did you stop singing? When did you stop being

enchanted by stories? When did you stop finding comfort in the sweet territory of silence?

The sweet territory of silence is what we less poetically call meditation, but singing, dancing, and storytelling (*my* profession) belong right alongside it. They're all ways of living boldly, of dancing through *life* like nobody's watching.

Dancing is a door to liberation. (Eventually we discover that everything is.) "Some dance to remember, some dance to forget," says a song we've all heard too many times. Here we're doing both, dancing to remember what we are, which is free, and to forget all the old stories that tell us we aren't.

Dare to Be Silly

I used to teach an acting and public speaking course at a top-drawer prep school in New Jersey. Most of the students tightened up at the prospect of being onstage and possibly looking foolish. The solution was to get that out of the way: look *very* foolish and have fun doing it. I showed them Monty Python's great "Ministry of Silly Walks" routine (available online), and then we had our own Silly Walks Contest. That got everyone nice and loose. It's recommended. It's also recommended as a way to deflate your ability to maintain rage or to take yourself too seriously, two things that often go hand in hand. In fact, my personal plan for world peace starts with a huge, festive, internationally televised Silly Walks Olympics. Let's put the Israelis and the Palestinians in the first round.

You can use dance in a similar way. Fears of looking foolish, of being vulnerable, of being hurt, tend to make us frozen in both our range of motion and our range of emotion. To help bust out of those inhibitions and the patterns of physical rigidity that sustain them, you can (in the privacy of your own home, with the shades drawn) run your own Ministry of Silly Dances. Just play. You can start subtle and inflate from there, doing big, exaggerated, clownlike dances portraying big, exaggerated, clownlike emotions. Be the world's worst mime. Of course, you need the right music to egg you on. You can build your own playlists so you can access different moods as needed, but here are a few suggestions to get started:

Joyous: Tune-Yards, "Water Fountain"; Pharrell Williams, "Happy"; Stevie Wonder, "Isn't She Lovely"; Beatles, "Twist and Shout"; Bob Marley, "One Love"; Louis Armstrong, "What a Wonderful World"; Maria Muldaur, "You Ain't Goin' Nowhere"; Bobby McFerrin, "Don't Worry, Be Happy"; Katrina and the Waves, "Walking on Sunshine."

Melancholy: Tori Amos, "Crucify," "Silent All These Years"; David Darling, "Darkwood"; Patsy Cline, "I Fall to Pieces," "Crazy"; Chris Isaak, "Can't Do a Thing to Stop Me," "Wicked Game"; Roy Orbison, "Crying"; John Coltrane, "Soul Eyes"; Yo-Yo Ma, "Crouching Tiger, Hidden Dragon: Silk Road"; Rolling Stones, "Angie," "Wild Horses"; Jeff Buckley, "Hallelujah"; Beck, "Lost Cause"; Gram Parsons, "Love Hurts"; UB40, "Red Red Wine."

Sexy: Prince, "Kiss"; Marvin Gaye, "Let's Get It On"; Donna Summer, "Love to Love You Baby"; Right Said Fred, "I'm Too Sexy"; Barry White, "I'm Gonna Love You Just a Little Bit More, Baby"; Rick James, "Give It to Me"; Toni Braxton, "Art of Love"; Isley Brothers "Between the Sheets."

Triumphant: Tchaikovsky, "1812 Overture (Finale)"; Vangelis, "Chariots of Fire Theme."

Furious: Public Image Ltd., "Public Image"; David Bowie, "Rebel Rebel"; Queen, "Stone Cold Crazy"; Patti Smith, "Rock n' Roll Nigger"; Nirvana, "Smells Like Teen Spirit," "Lithium"; Sex Pistols, "Anarchy in the U.K."; Verdi, "Dies Irae."

Tranquil: Arvo Pärt, "Spiegel im Spiegel"; Deuter, "Nada Himalaya"; Moby, "Novio."

Tense: David Bowie, "Fashion," "Heroes," "Station to Station"; Rolling Stones, "Gimme Shelter"; Led Zepplin "Kashmir," "When the Levee Breaks," "Immigrant Song."

Menacing: Velvet Underground, "Venus in Furs."

Loving: Elvis Presley, "Love Me Tender"; Stevie Wonder, "As"; Beatles, "And I Love Her," "In My Life"; Chaka Khan, "Ain't Nobody"; Turtles, "Happy Together"; Ry Cooder, "Maria Elena"; Jefferson Airplane, "Today"; Jackie Wilson, "Your Love Keeps Lifting Me Higher," MC Yogi, "Only Love Is Real."

Expansive: Beth Orton, "Don't Wanna Know 'Bout Evil"; Coldplay, "Clocks"; Moby, "Everloving"; Samuel Barber, "Agnus Dei"; Beatles, "Here Comes the Sun"; Jefferson Airplane, "Embryonic Journey," "D.C.B.A.–25"; Beck, "Wow"; Björk, "Thunderbolt"; Byrds, "Eight Miles High"; George Harrison, "Marwa Blues."

(My own favorite moods are loving and expansive, and for that my one indispensable, desert island album is *Music for Yoga and Other Joys* by Jai Uttal and Ben Leinbach.)

As you find your own unrestrained, unstructured solo dancing spirit, it can be extra-fun to bring that spirit to dancing with a partner. This requires you to be awake in the moment, to respond sensitively to your partner and become fluent in nonverbal communication. (That dementia study found that the maximum protection comes from social dancing.)

If you're married or in a relationship and you really want it to work, my top three recommendations are to sit in meditation every day, walk together as often as possible, and dance together at least, say, once a week. Every relationship tends to develop unresolved weirdo energy pockets—places in your interactions where unexpressed anger, resentment, or misunderstanding accumulate and fester. Sometimes talking about these pockets is helpful. But sometimes it isn't, and sometimes it even makes them worse. Time to twist and shout, work it on out.

Nietzsche was probably thinking of the familiar Judeo-Christian image of God as a burly king, planted on his heavy throne, when he wrote, "I would believe only in a God who could dance." In India, they have lots of gods who both dance and sit. The outstanding example is Shiva, who is the Lord of Meditators, seated immovably on his tiger skin high in the snowy Himalayas, as well as the Lord of Dance, with crazy swinging dreadlocks, ecstatically rock 'n' rolling the universe through its cycles of creation and dissolution. These two seeming opposites—stern, steadfast meditator and dancing fool—are understood to be one, and Shiva, like all the gods, is understood to represent the unfolding of your own deepest self. (Hindus chant, *Shivoham, Shivoham*: "I am Shiva, I am Shiva!") If you sit and steep in enough inner silence, or if you dance with enough rapture, you dissolve the dream that you're a finite little organism and wake up as the infinite.

CHAPTER 25

Who Needs Sleep?

Insomnia sucks. If you've had it, you know all about the frustrating hours spent wide awake. You also know about the tantalizing minutes in the hypnagogic state, a.k.a. pre-sleep limbo. This is the transitional "falling" phase that most people pass through briefly on their way to "asleep," but which insomniacs may repeatedly dip in and out of, achingly close to the garden of sweet oblivion, only to be pushed out the garden gate again and again.

For what it's worth, if fear, worry, anger, substance withdrawal, or any other agitated state has been roiling your sleep, at least know that you have it better than some people. Men I've worked with in prison, fearing to drop their vigilance long enough to be assaulted, never allow themselves to fall completely into a deep sleep and never sleep on their stomachs.

Still, insomnia, whether occasional or chronic, is a drag. Because you're agitated, you can't sleep; because you can't sleep, you get more agitated; and round and round you go. Fortunately, the meditative toolbox contains some methods that can help you break out of this cycle. As it happens, I got my genes from two parents who were both lousy sleepers, so this is another area where I've had a strong personal stake in thoroughly testing the tools. Once again, my bad luck is your good luck.

If you've been practicing our core method of sitting in natural meditation with some regularity, your sleep may have already improved. By spending even a few minutes a day settled in a mellow, low-adrenaline state of parasympathetic activation, you're teaching your body how good that feels. Your body learns the way there, so that anytime it's given a chance—like being tucked into a comfy bed—it will tend to return on its own.

There are also specialized nighttime methods for helping the process along, but first let's attend to some practical matters. If you suspect that some kind of medical problem is involved, of course consult your health care provider. Fortunately, more doctors these days are getting tuned in to nonmedicinal, no-side-effects therapies. They may suggest anything from a glass of warm milk at bedtime to a stiff dose of melatonin or honokiol. If the underlying problem is sleep apnea, they may even recommend playing the didgeridoo—studies have shown its therapeutic effectiveness in restoring proper breathing.

Most experts warn against reading in bed, to avoid its stimulating effect. But these things are not one-size-fits-all. Some people find that reading in bed can knock them out real nice if they get it tuned just right—for example, by using dim light and reading material that's just engaging enough to distract them from compulsive thought patterns but just boring enough to gently bludgeon them into oblivion. (I've had a lot of luck with certain books of the Old Testament. Thank you, Gideons, for all those hotel room Bibles.)

Electronic screens of all kinds are considered a no-no as well, but if your reading light keeps your bed partner awake, you may have to resort to reading from your phone or tablet. (These days there's a helpful feature called Night Shift, which changes the screen's display from the stimulating blue end of the light spectrum to the more sedating red end.) Or you can switch off the screen and listen to an audiobook, preferably a nice boring one narrated in a droning monotone. LibriVox .org offers a lot of free downloadable audiobooks, many of them obscure texts of ancient history, all read by amateur narrators with, let's just say, varying levels of skill.

Attitude Adjustment

Once, when I was on a five-month-long retreat with Maharishi in Mallorca, a retreatant complained, "I can't sleep because I'm afraid of ghosts." Maharishi replied, "No, you're afraid of ghosts because you can't sleep."

That's a potent insight. Your obsessive thoughts, whether they're about ghosts or politics or your love life or your finances, may be a by-product of your insomnia, not the cause. Then the root cause is neurological, energetic: some congestion or overstimulation of energy interrupts our sleep, which in turn provokes thoughts. That's why two people with, say, the same financial problem, or the same person with the same financial problem on two different nights, might not suffer the same insomnia.

This means you won't fix your insomnia by thinking your way through the problem of the moment—so you may as well give up trying. Just as you do when you sit to meditate, you can invoke the Power of Later. Decide that you're not going to decide anything in bed: you're not going to solve the world's problems or your own while the sun is down. You've probably had the experience of tossing and turning while seeking solutions, and either coming up empty or coming up with something that seemed brilliant at three a.m. but not so much in the morning light. So just assume up front that all your bedtime thoughts are nothing but chatter, and, just as in meditation, don't try to halt the thought train but don't hop aboard either.

There's a second attitudinal intervention you can invoke that's even more surprising: It doesn't matter whether you sleep. It turns out that what we need is not sleep per se. It's the deep peace of inner silence that refreshes and rejuvenates us—what Macbeth calls the "balm of hurt minds." For most people, the only place where they encounter such peace is in sleep. But as meditators we're learning, with growing clarity, that we can access the peace of our own being in any situation. For those whose clarity approaches a hundred percent, sleep may even become optional. At a Tibetan Buddhist ashram where I once spent some time, a renowned lama came to teach. In anticipation of his arrival, a beautiful bedroom was prepared, decorated with Tibetan religious art and furnished with an extra-comfy bed, topped by a soft bedspread once used by the Dalai Lama. But all the effort went for naught. It turned out that this lama never used a bed. He just sat in the meditation hall for a little while each night and then went about his business.

Even for those of us who still use beds, just knowing that it doesn't absolutely matter whether or not we sleep can be profoundly liberating. We can relax through the night with one meditative method or another and know we'll feel rested in the morning. Ironically, once we let go of worrying about sleeping and get out of that vicious circle, there's a good chance we'll fall asleep.

Here are some methods that can help you either sleep or be fine with not sleeping. First three old friends, then some new ones.

Rest as Awareness

Our core method of effortless resting as awareness makes a perfect nighttime meditation for many people, but not all. As you've experienced, meditation produces a state of *restful alertness*. For most people, the restful aspect will predominate enough so that, if you do it at night when you're fatigued, you'll fall asleep. For a few people, the alertness will dominate and prevent sleep. That's fine if you feel ready to go the way of the lama and not bother with sleep, but otherwise one of the following methods will be a better choice.

Feet First

Another old friend, breathing through your feet, is always good. As you've probably found, this method is especially helpful when you feel that your head is buzzing with thoughts. If that's the situation at bedtime, you can just get horizontal, breathe at a natural rhythm while imagine-feeling that you're breathing through your feet, and let things settle in their own time. If you find yourself repeatedly almost-but-not-quite falling asleep, just stay with (or keep gently returning to) this method, cruising feet first through pre-sleep limbo for as long as necessary.

Drop Your Thoughts

By now you know how to drop your thoughts: not trying to block or suppress them, just loosening your grip, letting go of your engagement with them, and relaxing back into your silent self. As usual, five seconds or so at a time is plenty. When you feel enveloped by obsessive nighttime thinking, repeatedly punching five-second holes in it will weaken its power. You can also use this method in combination with others, such as . . .

Left Breath

When your mental-energetic engine is running hot, a simple way to cool it down and welcome sleep, passed on by yogic lore, is to breathe through the left nostril. Simply hold your right thumb against the right side of your nose so it closes your right nostril, and breathe normally, or also use the ujjayi constriction as described in chapter 9. The variation in which the out-breath takes one-and-a-half to two times as long as the in-breath may be particularly helpful.

In a slightly more elaborate version, after each in-breath you open the right nostril by releasing the thumb; simultaneously close the left nostril with the third and fourth fingers, then breathe out through the right nostril. Continue switching back and forth, breathing in through the left and out through the right. In yogic terms you're filling the body with the cooling, sedating left breath-stream and emptying out the heating, arousing right breath-stream.

Which Picture?

The hypnagogic state of pre-sleep limbo is often a very visual landscape. As we sink below the level of the verbal and conceptual content that dominates our minds during the day, it's replaced by random images and short cartoony sequences that pop up but then dissolve, kicking us back up to the waking, thinking level. If we can just stay with the visuals, we can ride them into sleep.

So this method generally works best if you're already a little drowsy. As you lie there, very quietly float the question, *Ummm, which picture are we on?* (The *Ummm* is important.) It has to be done delicately—you can't make it happen—but, given a chance, the visuals will take over on their own. Anytime you find yourself back in the verbal–conceptual, float the question again, and once again the visuals will come to the foreground while the words and thoughts fade to the background.

Another version is to supply your own picture. Visualize something that, for you, evokes silence or peace—say, a mountain or a tropical lagoon. Every time you realize you've gone off onto other thoughts, come back to this image. Here's a trippy one: Picture yourself, just as you are, lying in the bed, but fast asleep, totally out. At some point, the sleeping you in the picture and the you that's picturing it merge.

Deep Fifths

Recall our practice of singing descending fifths, discussed in chapter 21. For this bedtime version, we sing that same downward slide, but mentally—just hear it in your mind's ear. The "dark" vowel sounds, such as *oh* or *oo* as in *flow* or *blue*, are more sleep-friendly than the brighter sounds, like *ee*. And now, because you're not using your voice, you're not subject to its limitations, so you can extend the low note indefinitely. Mentally keep hearing it, way beyond the point where you would run out of breath, going steadily on and on without break. And again, because we're only singing mentally, you can go as low as you like, octaves below your actual vocal range.

Thought Bubbles

When you feel overwhelmed by the thoughts crowding your attention, you can imagine that each one is inside a comic strip thought bubble. Don't try to get rid of the thought; just put a fun thought bubble around it. If a dozen thoughts are crowding around, vying for your attention, fine, visualize them inside a dozen thought bubbles. Don't try to be specific about what the thoughts are or keep track of which one has gone where. Perhaps the thoughts are about work problems or political arguments or sexual fantasies, but whatever they are, now they're all tucked into fun thought bubbles, merrily bobbing and softly colliding in the air around you.

Then, in the middle of all the other bubbles, visualize one that's empty—a bubble full of silence. Let it hang around over your head for a while. Then, if you're still awake, climb into it, lie back, and float, weightless. As you float along, let this silent, empty bubble slowly expand, gradually absorbing and neutralizing all the others, dissolving them into itself like the Blob, growing bigger and bigger as it happily feeds on their energy. (Yum yum, eat 'em up!) Then let it absorb you too. Finally, let it melt into space, the silent space of awareness, and rest in that.

The ancient sages, by the way, clearly did not practice this method, but I like to think that they would have, had there been comic strips in their time. It's fun to imagine what their favorite strips might have been. I think the Buddha could have been a serious fan of *Peanuts*, with its poignant representation of human suffering and futility—the kite that always gets stuck in the tree, the baseball team that always loses, the football that Lucy always snatches away. I can see the Buddha smiling gently, shaking his head, and murmuring, "You're a good man, Charlie Brown." Socrates, the probing gadfly of Athens, would probably be a *Garfield* man, just because, like Socrates, Garfield is annoying.

Space-Gazing

Lie down, get comfortable, close your eyes, give things a few minutes to settle, and then gaze into space. Yes, it's dark, and yes, your eyes are closed, but that doesn't matter. There's still some sense of space in front of you. Gaze into that space, like gazing out a window into the night sky.

As usual, there's no effort in this. Don't try to visualize anything clearly, and don't stare, just gaze. As soon as you think of it, it's already happening by itself.

As you gaze, the experience may change. At times the space may seem dark, or light, or dark speckled with light, or indefinable. It may seem flat at first, but then grow deeper, three-dimensional. And after a while, as you continue to gaze, the space may seem to have endless depth. Sometimes it might even seem like you're zooming into Han Solo's hyperspace. In any case, it's always perfect just as it is, however it is.

If your mind is very active with complex thoughts or emotional turmoil, it may at first resist this gazing into space and keep careening off in other directions. But be gently persistent, coming back again and again to this sense of space till your attention locks into it.

If you're still awake after a while, notice that, since you're not gazing with your physical eyes, you're not limited to their narrow scope. So now widen your scope so that you're gazing into space in all directions, through your whole head.

And now notice that you can widen your scope even further, so that you're gazing out through your whole body, 360 degrees.

After a while, let your body dissolve into that space, so that nothing remains but space. Rest in this space, *as* this space.

Occasionally you may notice what feel like areas of energetic congestion or overstimulation here or there (a disturbance in the Force), trying to pull you back into the body. Just allow these areas to dissolve and dissipate into the space.

With practice, you may find that you can skip the preliminary steps and just lie down, close your eyes, and go straight into omnidirectional hyperspace. Gaze, dissolve, be.

CHAPTER 26

Notice the Sensations

Here's something you can try the next time you brush your teeth:

Stand at the sink and brush as usual, but close your eyes and notice the tactile sensations of brushing: the shifting pressure and texture of the bristles against your gums, the swishing of toothpaste and water and saliva in your mouth, the darting of your tongue as it dodges the brush. Be as fully aware of these sensations as you can.

Be like a scientist who is studying the experience of tactile sensations. To isolate the sensations, consider that if you were a newborn infant you would have no corresponding visual images of teeth, gums, tongue, brush. You would have no mental concept that these sensations were part of some process for accomplishing some purpose. You would have no memory of having started the process in some now-vanished time ("past") and no anticipation of finishing it in some not-yet-arrived time ("future"). And you certainly wouldn't be lost in planning and speculating about your upcoming day. You would be immersed in pure, simple sensations, unassociated with anything else. Exactly those pure sensations are present now, as you brush your teeth. They simply need to be noticed in isolation from the other stuff. The visual images, concepts, memories, and speculations are *thoughts*, which are there along with the sensations, but distinct from them. Please notice all this as clearly as you can.

You're practicing one form of what Adi Shankara and other sages of ancient India called *viveka*: discrimination, the skill of distinguishing between different experiences that are commonly blurred together, in this case sensations and thoughts. As simple as it is, this power of discrimination usually goes untapped. And as the sages discovered, it's a surprising key to liberation from fear and everything else that afflicts us.

As you continue to brush your teeth with your eyes closed, now notice the *sounds* of the process, again as pure sensation, in this case auditory sensations, pure hearing, innocent of any association, as an infant would hear them. The tactile sensations persist, but they automatically fade to the background of attention when these auditory sensations move to the foreground.

Now notice the pure sensations of the *taste* of toothpaste, mixed with saliva and water, independent of the concepts of "toothpaste," "saliva," or "water." Those concepts may be present, but it doesn't matter. They're thoughts, and they're separate. Just taste, like an infant, as if for the first time.

And now, still standing at the sink with your eyes closed, notice your emotional tone, such as boredom or excitement, joy or dread. Note that that is also a kind of sensation. It might seem to be clearly located in some part of the body such as the chest, abdomen, or head, or it might be more generally distributed, but it's a sensation with a subtle but specific texture of its own. We call emotions *feelings* because they feel certain ways: joy feels different from depression. As you continue to brush your teeth, the feelings are not the conceptual explanations of *why* you might feel happy (*I hear my kids laughing in the hallway as they get ready for school*) or depressed (*Gotta go to my stupid job*). Those are thoughts. When a thought arises, certainly it's experienced, but that's different from the experience of the feeling or sensation that the thought is about. A thought, we could say, is like the sign outside the zoo that says ZOO. The sign and the zoo are both things, but different things. Discriminate.

And now open your eyes and see what's in the mirror. Do you see a face? Actually, no. Seeing purely, as an infant sees, you experience only visual sensations: colors and shapes. Our identification of one region of the colors and shapes as "shower curtain" and another region as "face," or "my face," or "me" is a thought. The thought is certainly present along with the seeing but, again, distinct from it. Also note that, because vision is the dominant, default sense for humans, as smelling is for dogs, the moment we open our eyes all the other senses tend to fade into the background of attention. This is why people close their eyes almost involuntarily to savor music, or a kiss, or an orgasm.

OK. Let's take a break. Rinse out your toothbrush and go on to whatever's next. But now that you've done this kind of close looking, you may start to notice that, whether you're taking a shower or making breakfast or driving to work, no matter what you experience, *how* you experience is the same. There's a rich array of sensations, including those we call feelings, and there are thoughts. They're all in a perpetual dance: arising, changing, vanishing, advancing to the foreground or withdrawing to the background.

While driving to work, at any given moment you might find your attention dominated by the rush of visual sensations as the scenery whips past, or by the auditory sensations of the radio news, the thoughts those sounds convey, and the feelings those thoughts stir up. Suddenly your attention might go to the sensations of anger when another driver cuts you off, or the sensations of impatience when traffic backs up, or of worry when you're afraid you'll be late to work. You might become so engaged in thoughts about your job that your external senses fade to the background—till a sudden auditory sensation (*Screech of brakes!*)

triggers an adrenaline-fueled feeling (*Shit!*) and a thought (*What's going on?*). Then your job-thoughts withdraw, the visual sensations come rushing to the foreground, and you hit your brake, all in a fraction of a second.

Sometime later, while you're, say, shopping for groceries, see if you can remember the experience of brushing your teeth. *Re-member* means to reassemble, to put a bunch of members, or components, back together (as opposed to *dis-member*). But those components—the tactile sensations, the sounds, the sights, the flavors, the feelings and thoughts—are no longer present for assembly, and the present is the only place where we can have an experience. What *is* available in the present, and therefore experienceable, is a bunch of thoughts *about* the past experience, which we call memories. We assemble those into a kind of thought-model of the original experience, the way we assemble a plastic model of an airplane. Notice, experience, discriminate.

So What?

Why bother? What does all this noticing and discriminating do for us?

First, anything that you focus on with this kind of clarity comes to be experienced more vividly. If you're a musician or a serious music lover, you know that you hear music with a kind of three-dimensional detail that most people miss. If you're an architect or contractor, when you walk into a house you see the hundreds of large and small design decisions that have been made, the craftsmanship and the hours of work that have shaped the materials into a building. My years of moonlighting as a film critic, and then marrying and learning from a film editor, have made watching great movies extraordinarily rich.

The greatest movie-symphony-skyscraper is life itself: regular, ordinary, mundane, moment-to-moment experience, whether you're paragliding in Oahu or changing tires in Trenton. That's fortunate, because present experience, moment-to-moment life, is the only show in town. If you miss the richness of that show, you've missed the whole thing. Intuitively, everyone knows that, and the terror of missing out on life is what drives people to *addiction to intensity*: the need for ever-crazier parties, ever-kinkier porn, louder explosions in each movie sequel, a bigger body count in each video game, a more skull-splitting rush from the next drug. Man, that's a lot of work, and with so much collateral damage.

But the more you wake up to the vividness of brushing your teeth—or feeding your baby, or playing your guitar, or *tuning* your guitar—the more you recognize that this moment, and this one, and this one, with whatever's going on in it, is plenty for anyone. No moment is deficient. The five loaves and two fishes of any given moment turn out to be a banquet. Addiction to intensity, in whatever forms it may have manifested in your life, naturally starts losing its power over you. That doesn't mean your life becomes bland or dull. Quite the opposite—it was our old dullness of perception, our bland, blind oblivion to the silent marvel of a seagull's flight across the sky or a raindrop's course down a window, that made us a slave to each new extra-shiny object or extra-fervid rush.

This seeing with an infant's eyes is what Jesus called being like a little child to enter the kingdom of heaven, which he also said is spread upon the earth, mysteriously overlooked by most people. This is being born again, again and again, ever-fresh in the ever-now. It's a natural result of regular meditation. You may have noticed that sometimes, when you open your eyes at the end of a session, the colors in the room seem somehow deeper, the shadows more delicately nuanced, the sounds from the street more vividly sculpted. And as we go through our day, this kind of attention to sensations that we've just practiced can help put that awakening process into overdrive.

If you're lucky enough to have an actual little child around, he or

she can remind you how it's done. Here's my younger grandson, age fourteen months, on his first visit to the aquarium, lost in the shimmering, inexplicable miracle before his eyes. And here's a nice touch: he's so thoroughly enraptured that he's oblivious to the hand of Mother, always there even when unseen, holding him up so he can be thoroughly enraptured.

Part of what keeps our perception fresh is simply discriminating between sensations and thoughts. It's our thoughts that tell us, *Oh, I know what this is. This is just the tire store in Trenton*, or, *This is just the same old walk to work I took yesterday*, or, *This is the just same old wife I've been sleeping with for twenty years*. "Just" is a concept, an anti-spice that the mind sprinkles into the soup of reality to make it bland. So is "same old." In actual experience there is only now. If there's only now, there's no old and there's no same-old: Same as what? It's thought that superimposes time onto timeless actuality, and thus creates boredom and staleness and the need for bigger and better rushes. As Ram Dass said, "Boredom is just lack of attention."

It all comes back to *Ehi-passiko*, "Come and see." Go into your kitchen and take one blueberry out of the container or one orange out of the bowl or one spoon out of the drawer. See it? Now spend five minutes *really* seeing it. Imagine that, after five minutes, you'll have to return it to the container with all the other blueberries, we'll mix them up, and then we'll pay you a million bucks if you can pick yours out again. Imagine you're an artist who has to paint a gigantic, billboard-sized photorealistic painting of this blueberry. See it now? By simply seeing what's before our eyes, unclouded by the dulling power of abstracting, generalizing thought, we fulfill the prophecy of William Blake:

> If the doors of perception were cleansed, every thing would appear to man as it is, Infinite. For man has closed himself up, till he sees all things thro' narrow chinks of his cavern.

Won't Be Fooled Again

This noting has another consequence as well. Although we're savoring things more deeply now, at the same time we're less gripped by them. The gripping quality of experience is a sort of special effect, like the CGI aliens in movies. Through our practice of discrimination, we deconstruct the way we previously smooshed together different components of experience and see how the effect is created. We're no longer fooled.

Take, for example, what some people call *lust*. The very word, from the Greatest Hits list of deadly sins, evokes both the fascination and the fear that sexual desire exerts. It's the world's oldest story: young man sees fine-looking honey, his head spins, and suddenly all he knows is, "I must have that woman!" It all happens in a second or two, so let's go to slo-mo and break it down.

First there's an experience of visual sensations: shapes, colors, motion. Then the mind interprets them as "woman"—a thought—and suggests a closer look to scan her characteristics, such as coloring and texture, size, shape, proportions. A few nanoseconds later, it compares the results of the scan to information stored in a database of characteristics that have been filed under ATTRACTIVE or UNATTRACTIVE. Although some of the stored data points reflect personal history, most of it is derived from open-source cultural shareware, which may vary by region and era (see: BUTTOCK SIZE). If the readout says the woman is attractive, a flood of sensations and physical responses—warm, tingly, bulging—is triggered. There may also be a flood of images of fantasized sexual activities, co-starring the woman and our hero. Those are thoughts.

But despite this elaborate process, our young man is too caught up in it, too tightly gripped by it, to have any sense that he's engaged in a process at all. All he knows is, if he doesn't penetrate this woman's body with his own, he'll die. He's hooked.

Anything that hooks us like that, whether it's drink or drugs or Ben & Jerry's, works by a similar process. Your homework, should you decide to accept it, is to identify whatever craving chronically hooks you, and then, the next time it starts to kick in, observe that craving with the same scientist's eye that we've now brought to lusting and to brushing our teeth. Break down the components. Don't try to suppress the feelings that arise; that usually backfires. Simply observe the whole thing as it happens. Don't try to do anything about any of it. Just *see* the process, and something starts to shift.

You may still feel caught—for now—but you'll notice that you're less tightly caught. The mere act of seeing creates more *space* around the images and feelings, more freedom to either smoke or not smoke the cigarette, to either eat or not eat the cookie. You can also ask yourself, *OK, then, I'm caught by the craving—what does the caughtness itself consist of?* Can you reach out your finger and touch it? Is it a feeling? A thought? Check it out. You may find that the more you look for it, the more you can't find it, like chasing a rainbow. The caughtness that ruled your behavior so imperiously can't stand to be looked at, and evaporates before your gaze.

So then . . . you're caught up in fear of cancer? You're caught up in rage at your partner? You're caught up in eating that quart of ice cream, and you know you're not going to stop till it's gone, no matter how sick it makes you? Whatever it is, once again break it down. Observe the process the way we just observed lust, broken down into components. Discriminate between one thing and another. See that thoughts are *just* thoughts. An image is just an image. Sensations, even very intense ones, are just sensations. So, when the forbidden fruit entices you or the forbidding task frightens you, don't panic. If you do panic, notice that panic also is just a sensation. What does *it* feel like? Eventually, we find that nothing is overwhelming. The fact that you're observing the process of being caught means that at least part of you isn't caught.

Breaking these things down also gives us more space to discriminate between feeling and thought. Often people say "I'm afraid of *x*," "I'm angry about *y*," or "I'm despondent about *z*," and, while they might have had that actual feeling five minutes or five years ago, it has since passed, while the thoughts *about* the feeling and the situation that gave rise to it continue. In these cases, which are very common, being free of anger or fear or despondency is easy; it's just a matter of noticing that you already are. Thoughts are thoughts, feelings are feelings.

It's all just thoughts and sensations, and they're all shifting and changing. What doesn't shift and change? You, the awareness that experiences it all. Just relax at the moment of contact and melt back into yourself, awareness. The sensations move through awareness like waves on the surface of the sea. The silent depths of the sea remain, as ever, undisturbed. Notice that. Thoughts are thoughts, feelings are feelings, being is being.

This is the real viveka. You stub your toe, you win the lottery, your favorite TV show is canceled, your book is optioned for a major motion picture, your toddler learns to hug you, that itchy patch is diagnosed as psoriasis . . . and what part of all that is you? That's right, none of it. That's all the observed, and you're the observer.

Now, this is the place where people insist, often vehemently, "Wait, that's *my* toe, and it hurts! That's *my* toddler, and I love him! Don't tell me to be detached from them!" But I'm not telling you that. *Detachment* is a word I never, ever use, as it's guaranteed to cause confusion—it's almost invariably interpreted to mean suppression of natural feelings. Don't suppress anything. Don't fixate on anything. Notice everything. Have every human experience, every human feeling. Sooner or later, you'll notice that all those experiences are phenomena, made of one hundred percent thoughts and sensations. None of them can overwhelm *you*, because you are not a sensation or a thought, but that which experiences them all: nonphenomenal awareness.

As soon as there's even one really clear moment of this noticing in your life, the root of fear, anxiety, anger, and addiction has been cut, and sooner or later they all must wither and die. If you want it to be sooner, sit regularly, and then, when you open your eyes and return to your daily routine, leave a little room for discrimination. You still experience everything, all phenomena, from *a* to *z*. But what is it that's beyond and behind that whole alphabet? Don't try to see it, hear it, think it, or feel it—it's where you've been seeing, hearing, thinking, feeling *from* in every moment of your life. All the stuff is fleeting, impermanent. You're not stuff. Just notice.

CHAPTER 27

Same Boat

You've heard the same bloodcurdling scream in many different movies—possibly hundreds of them. It was originally voiced in a sound booth by actor-singer Sheb Wooley in 1951, and looped into the film *Distant Drums* as the death cry of a guy wading through the beautiful Florida Everglades who's suddenly pulled under by an alligator. Two years later, it was recycled for *The Charge at Feather River*: a Private Wilhelm is sitting on his horse, filling his pipe, minding his own business, when he's suddenly felled by an arrow.

Ever since, this sound cue has been known by film aficionados as the Wilhelm scream. It's a simple 1.5-second male scream, but there's something about it that's unimprovably hair-raising as the final, desperate cry of a man suddenly caught in the jaws of violent death. At last count, it's been used in over 350 films, including *Titanic*, *Transformers*, the *Star Wars* series, *Reservoir Dogs*, and *Kung Fu Panda*. After more than sixty years, the Wilhelm scream has become a bit of a running in-joke among filmmakers and in droll YouTube compilations. But, hmmmm: Different movies, same scream. Different plot lines, same pain. Different characters, same suffering. Maybe there's a clue for us here about how our own suffering works.

When you feel really lost in fear, anxiety, or any other kind of affliction, it feels like you're in it all alone—as if you're the only person in the world struggling with this thing. You're locked inside your drug habit or your angry marriage or whatever cell you're in, and, just to make your sentence even harsher, your confinement is solitary. But this same one scream pouring out of hundreds of different mouths suggests that we're not alone after all. Perhaps we can loosen the bonds of our suffering by breaking free of the sense that we're suffering alone.

As usual, the Tibetans have worked out the nuts and bolts of the methodology, in this case with an ingenious type of meditative technique called *tonglen*, "sending and receiving," of which there are many different forms. Tonglen is a serious power tool that can cut through some serious pain by dropping all evasion and saying, "Bring it on." It's recommended only for people who are relatively stable emotionally, and who have enough meditation practice under their belt to feel some familiarity with inner silence. If you don't feel ready, save this one for another time.

We'll start with our core practice of natural meditation. As usual, sit comfortably, use breath or sound or any other on-ramp for a few minutes as desired, then rest naturally as awareness, marinating in the silent, spacious nature of your own being.

. . .

. . .

After a while, bring to mind whichever affliction you want to address in this session, such as fear, anger, addictive craving, confusion, loneliness, grief, or despair. For this session, let's say you're dealing with despair. Naturally, the thought-story of the circumstances connected with your despair is probably present: the loss of a loved one, living with a debilitating illness, losing the best job you'll ever have, coming to terms with infertility. Don't try to push the story away, but don't make it your primary focus. As we've seen, emotions are felt as sensations in the body. Let yourself feel the sensations of despair deeply, vividly, completely. Stay with that. For once, don't hold back. The sensations may stay the same or change. You may feel fairly placid behind the feelings, experiencing them from the place of untouched silence, or you may feel as if you're being pushed over an emotional waterfall. Whatever happens is perfect.

. . .

Now please consider that countless other beings have experienced exactly the same feeling of despair as you. Right now, and stretching thousands of years into the past and future, billions of others have stood where you now stand. How extraordinary! So many different people, in so many different lands and ages, families and walks of life, languages and religions and circumstances, yet the feeling is exactly the same.

As you do that, notice the sense of the presence of all those other beings. You can imagine-feel them before you and all around you, but actually this is more than an act of imagination. They're really out there. Palpably feel the bond, the connection created by the despair shared in common by all those beings, you among them.

. . .

And now, in fact, take their despair upon yourself. Through your connectedness with all those innumerable wounded, despairing beings, let it all come to you. Open yourself to receive all the despair in the universe, drawing it away from the others and into your heart center, deep in the middle of your chest. You may feel strong fear or resistance to doing so, and that's fine—that fear is part of what you're working through.

Imagine-feel that your heart center is surrounded by a hard, dry crust. This is the sense of being a separate, isolated self. As you draw all that immeasurable despair into your heart center, now let its intense energy *crack* open that hard crust.

And now, out through the cracks, an intense, pure white light begins to shine, breaking through the crust like a chick breaking out of the egg. The crust is hard, but the light keeps breaking through till it all falls away. This is the light of pure beingness, awakening, healing, love, non-separateness. Let it radiate throughout your body, cleansing and healing you of all your despair. Then let it radiate out from you, out through all your pores, in all directions into all of space, filling the universe, bathing and illuminating all beings, healing them of their despair and of everything else that needs healing.

. . .

Finally, allow this visualization to dissolve, and just rest in the awareness within which it's been taking place: the open, free, spacelike awareness of your own being.

As always, take plenty of time coming out.

. . .

. . .

As with other techniques we've done, once you've practiced this tonglen while sitting on the cushion, you can take it on the road. For example, if you're watching a performer onstage or a colleague (maybe even a rival) giving a presentation and failing miserably, embarrassingly—"dying," as they say—you can do what we usually do in such circumstances: harden yourself, close yourself off from their misery. We do this, of course, because we've suffered some version of the same misery, or have imagined and dreaded it. We're reacting with fear rather than responding from love. We cringe, roll our eyes, and close ourselves to the performer's suffering because we intuitively know that we will otherwise feel it as our own. That strategy, the usual human strategy, has the upside of saving us from some temporary pain but the downside of reinforcing our isolation, our sense of ourself as a separate being, cut off from the universe and our fellow beings.

So, if you're game, try the opposite strategy. Open yourself to the pain of the dying performer. Take it all away from him, let it all flow to you, let it burst open the hard shell of separateness around your heart, and out through the cracks let the blinding light of illumination radiate, healing the performer, the audience, you, and all beings throughout the universe. This all happens on the inside, of course. On the outside, you can just smile and clap politely at the end.

By the way, there's no noble sacrifice in what we're doing here, no cosmic martyrdom in taking the suffering of others upon ourselves. It's all part of our own program for living beyond suffering. We're actually sort of like people who tap into their neighbors' Wi-Fi networks. We're borrowing the suffering-energy of others to free ourselves, selfishly using it to pierce the illusion of a separate self.

And actually, even without our having any method or strategy at all, sometimes life will do this for us. There's a beautiful little throwaway scene early in the first *Rocky* film where our hero, frustrated with his life as a failed boxer and small-time thug, comes to the gym the day after a fight. There he has a testy exchange with an attendant, Mike, played by five-foot-tall Jimmy Gambina.

MIKE: You oughtta take a rest.
ROCKY: No, my back is hurtin'.
MIKE: Your back?
ROCKY (suddenly angry): My back is hurtin'! You deaf?
MIKE: No, I'm short.

There it is. Some of us are deaf, some of us are short, some are scared, some are depressed, some feel like failures. Everyone's got their problem, but no one's alone. Everyone's got their problem, *so* no one's alone. That includes all the people who you think have their acts together, unlike you. For different reasons, we're all in this same boat, with the same scream. There's a wonderful brother-sisterhood in this, which will melt our isolation if we let it.

CHAPTER 28

Decide, Begin, Persist

Fear of making decisions—of choosing a path and getting on with one's life—is one of the most insidious forms of fear. Some people are stymied by one particular challenge, perhaps a fork in the career road or relationship road. For others, the problem is chronic. In either case, they feel stuck, paralyzed. Sylvia Plath captures the sense of this predicament in *The Bell Jar*:

> I saw myself sitting in the crotch of this fig tree, starving to death, just because I couldn't make up my mind which of the figs I would choose. I wanted each and every one of them, but choosing one meant losing all the rest, and, as I sat there, unable to decide, the figs began to wrinkle and go black, and, one by one, they plopped to the ground at my feet.

For some people, it's even worse. They feel frozen by the prospect of potential dangers as well as delights, terrified that any fig they choose might contain a razor blade. It's as if, from the spot where you now stand, you can move in innumerable directions, each leading to unknowable rewards or disasters, which will land you in a new spot, from which you can then move in innumerable directions . . . The more you think about it, the more dizzying it becomes.

And there's the problem: *the more you think about it.* Can you reach out your hand and touch all those branching possibilities? You can't, because they exist only as thoughts. They have no substance. There's only one of those things that you'll actually do, only one possibility to which you'll give substance when you follow it out of this moment. And here's what people who are stuck don't understand: Thinking is usually involved in *preparing* to choose that branch, but the actual moment of choosing is a moment of *dropping* thought. *Decide* comes from the Latin *decidere,* "to cut off," that is, to cut off the thinking process. You whip out your saber and in one instant—*whissshhh whissshhh whissshhhttt!!!*—lop off all those proliferating branches but one.

That doesn't mean the thoughts have to stop. We've learned that from meditation, and from our practice of clapping our hands and dropping our thoughts. We just drop our engagement with them, and then it doesn't matter whether they go on or not. My high school Spanish teacher once said that if you want to drive a Spanish-speaker crazy, you let him rant for several minutes about whatever's agitating him, then shrug, smile sweetly, and say *No importa*: "It doesn't matter." At the moment of decision, that's how to treat the thoughts, and that's exactly what we've been practicing in our meditation: relaxing our grip on them, sinking back into the silence that always underlies them, and letting them go on or not go on without us. This doesn't mean we act impulsively. In the run-up to the decisive moment, extensive research, thought, and debate may well be called for; being lazy about doing your homework rarely turns out well. But when that moment arrives, the way out of stagnation is to act decisively from that same silence we've already learned to rest in.

At the school where I used to teach, I sometimes sat in with the jazz band. (I was a so-so saxophone player.) One night after a concert in which our best players did some slick, out-there improvisation, the head of the music department—an old-fashioned European gentleman with a vaguely Franco-German accent—came up to congratulate us. He conducted the brass band, and his musical concerns focused on getting all the tubas to line up their oom-pahs in strict 4/4 time. "There's just one thing I don't understand," he said. "How do you know what to play?"

Well, you don't know it by thinking. Again, there's thinking involved in the preparation, the whole jazz education of scales and rhythms. But the more you practice them, the less you think about them and the more freely you can use them. I once asked the jazz band director what the secret of improvising was. He said, "You think of something . . . and then you don't play it."

For the real masters of jazz, or anything else, it all flows from nonthought, from silence. Mike Nichols, the director of such brilliant films as *The Graduate*, *Who's Afraid of Virginia Woolf?*, and *Angels in America*, started his career performing completely unscripted improv comedy, and he never lost its spirit:

> This is the thing that I carried into directing. . . . Not naming something, not deciding what to do, being brave and going out empty is the only way, and it's both terrifying and thrilling.

This is what makes all spontaneity exhilarating: the rabbit-out-of-a-hat surprises of great basketball, the careening riff of a stand-up comic working off the audience, the quiet flow of moments with a friend or lover with whom you don't have to weigh your words. Nothing snags. Everything pours forth from the place of silence that is the place of freedom.

Riffing Through Life

Any life can be lived from that place. What if you're not a musician or a comedian but an accountant? That's fine. The free-flowing quality of your actions may not be as obvious from the outside, but you feel it from the inside. The same easeful, frictionless action-from-freedom is possible no matter what path you walk.

I've known Jay (as I'll call him here) since our twenties, when we both started off as penniless meditation teachers. At some point he stumbled into the world of oil trading and found out he was good at it. Now he's semiretired and works at home, trading only his own account. I've watched him at work, sitting in the quiet room that he calls the Bat Cave, with three big computer monitors on the desk in front of him and a laptop on his left, tracking the price of oil, watching the curve creep incrementally across his screens, knowing that there are thousands of other traders—sharp, ruthless—simultaneously doing the same thing. They've all digested the same political, financial, geological, and meteorological information, and they're all breathing together in the silence, feeling out each other's minds, waiting for the moment just before the moment when everyone else clicks their mouse and the price dips or spikes. If you can click a millisecond before the others, you win.

But you can't do it by thinking. You have to feel it. It's like being a samurai in a showdown, and drawing your sword just as your opponent blinks. *Whissshhh whissshhh whissshhhttt!!!* Once Jay went to the bathroom and came back to find out he'd lost a million dollars. Unless you're a serious samurai (and have some serious cash reserves, it's true), you can't do that, get back up, and attack again. And every day, like the samurai of old, he prepares for battle by sitting in meditation. "It's not that I'm not scared," he says. "I am. But I know that everyone else is scared. And I'm coming from a place that's just a little bit below the fear, a little bit quieter. On a good day, that gives me the edge."

Jay also collects art, and it works the same way. You learn as much as possible, think as much as necessary, then drop your thoughts and feel. Not feel as in *emote*, although that may happen too, but feel in the way the blind students I used to work with in college could feel the presence of a mailbox on the sidewalk, by the subtle cushion of air around it and the way the traffic noise deflects around it. In finding art that winds up bringing him deepening enjoyment over the years (and, incidentally, increasing value), Jay has only one rule: *Don't think*. "Whether you're recognizing an artwork or a turn in the market," he tells me, "it's the same muscle."

It's also that same muscle whether you teach school or build houses or coach soccer or do massage therapy. When thoughts try to hijack the intuitive process, just relax your grip and drop them. You know how. Somewhere, in the deep silence of your feeling-wisdom, the thing you're working on gets rejiggered, and the right answer gets spontaneously spat out. But let's face it, sometimes the intuition muscle doesn't come through. In that case, the middle path is usually a good bet. When in doubt, pick Door Number Two.

But what about really hard choices—life choices? The *New Yorker* writer Adam Gopnik describes the surprising advice he received from a professor in his college days:

> Trying to decide whether to major in psychology or art history, I had gone to his office to see what he thought. He squinted and lowered his head. "Is this a *hard* choice for you?" he demanded. "Yes!" I cried. "Oh," he said, springing back up cheerfully. "In that case, it doesn't matter. If it's a hard decision, then there's always lots to be said on both sides, so either choice is likely to be good in its way. Hard choices are always unimportant."

For people who are stuck, it can feel like they're on first base, agonizing over whether to steal second. *What if I get thrown out? What if that loses us the game? I can't choose.* But not to choose is to choose. If you don't run to second, you've chosen to stay on first, and that might also lose the game. The word *choose* comes from a root meaning "to taste." You ignore your clamoring thoughts, taste-feel-sense the totality of the moment, and then either run or don't. There's a Zen saying:

If you walk, walk. If you sit, sit. Whatever you do, don't wobble.

Once you decide, let it go. Either hold that stock or sell it. If you sell, you *can* keep checking the price every day and feeling bad about the money you're not making every time it goes up. Or, if you hold, you can berate yourself every time it goes down. But would it help?

I'm Excited!

So decide and begin. If feelings of anxiety and thoughts of failure are there, they're there. They're just feelings and thoughts. By now you know how to disengage from the thoughts and just feel the sensations. Acting from silence doesn't mean trying to silence your anxiety.

In fact, you can use your anxious feelings as fuel, by reinterpreting them. Professor Alison Wood Brooks of Harvard Business School, realizing that anxiety and excitement are both arousal states, designed a study where subjects were plunged into anxiety-inducing situations: taking a math test, doing public speaking, or singing karaoke. (The chosen tune, poor dears, was "Don't Stop Believing.") Just before starting, half of the subjects were instructed to say simply, "I'm excited!" They did significantly better on all three tasks. They had the same experience of arousal-related physiological symptoms: the rapid heartbeat, the dry mouth, all our old fight-or-flight friends. All they needed to shift was their view: *Hey, I'm just excited*. Of course, with your cooler-running engine tuned up by daily meditation (and helped perhaps by engine additives such as occasional ujjayi breathing), you get less jerked around by arousal states in the first place. But when they do happen, *I'm excited!* is a clever way to reframe them.

But what about when you're overloaded with too much to do and you find yourself rushing madly? That's a primo time to make mistakes, which then can cost you more time—not to mention money, misunderstanding, and heartache. How do you keep your balanced, cool approach when you're rushing? What you do is, recognize the difference between rushing, which involves a grim, frantic, blind energy, and simply moving fast. Never rush. Just move fast.

Here's an experiment to point out the difference and fix it clearly in your mind and your muscle memory. First, do an exaggerated impersonation of someone rushing across the room. You'll find yourself putting your head down, like a snorting bull, and pumping your arms as you make your charge. Notice your emotional tone, which is probably also bull-like. Good.

Now do an exaggerated impersonation of someone strolling casually across the room, with all the time in the world. You hold your head up high, regally. You're free to look around with ease and confidence, surveying your kingdom as you pass through it, seeing the big picture as well as small details, and perhaps even leaning back slightly, while your servants—your legs—bear you along on your mobile throne. Notice your regal emotional tone.

Now repeat exactly that same regal stroll, but move your legs fast. Keep leaning back with royal dignity, owning everything you see. Let your servant legs do all the hustling for you.

And now consider how you can apply the same principles to other activities besides walking. Never rush. Just move fast.

Perseverance Furthers

Once you decide and begin, keep going. Persist. Over the years, one of my major stumbling blocks as a writer has been that, when I sit down and begin a new project, I find myself thinking, *I'm writing shit! This project seemed like a good idea when I was just thinking about it, but now that I'm setting down words, I see that it's shit.* In the early days, I'd often get discouraged at that point and quit. But eventually I started getting contracts and deadlines, so that I had no choice—I had to keep going. I slowly learned that writing shit at the beginning is fine: you have to write your way *through* it to get to the good stuff. That's why God made the delete key. My friend Jodi is a psychiatric social worker, and when I told her about my writing experiences she immediately lit up. "The same thing happens in my sessions!" she said. "I'll go through forty-five minutes with a client, thinking, *This session is shit, we're getting nowhere.* Then, in the last five minutes, the client opens up and it's gold."

So, whatever your project is, assume up front that there will be stretches along the way, possibly long ones, where it will seem completely hopeless. Fine. That's when you find out whether you're an *amateur* (from Latin *amator*, "lover"), someone who does whatever they do only when it's a fun hobby that's easy to love, or a professional, who keeps going when it sucks. As Hunter Thompson put it, "When the going gets weird, the weird turn pro."

The *I Ching*, or *Book of Changes*, one of China's classic wisdom texts, considers the cycles of human life and experience, and analyzes them into sixty-four basic patterns, with advice for dealing with each one. But one admonition keeps recurring: "No blame. Perseverance furthers." Don't get bogged down assigning blame to a situation or another person or yourself. Blame is lame. You can't move pedal-to-the-metal forward if you keep staring at the rearview for the culprits that have supposedly held you back.

Case in point: Django Reinhardt, the first great jazz guitarist and arguably the greatest of all time. His recordings with the Quintette du Hot Club de France in the thirties are some of the most joyously inventive music you'll ever hear. His solos sound like they're being played by a cool, happy angel with at least twelve or fourteen flying fingers. But, in fact, Django had only eight that worked. Early in his career, he was trapped in a fire in the Gypsy caravan where he lived. Half of his body was burned, the doctors wanted to amputate his leg, and two fingers of his left hand were paralyzed. Slowly and painfully, he had to relearn how to play his instrument. There's some rare film footage online in which you can see him playing, his left hand darting up and down the fretboard, making all that sublime music with just two fingers and a thumb. Oh, and he spent much of the forties dodging the Nazis, who were busy trying to exterminate all the Gypsies in France. That's how you do it.

Perseverance furthers. That's almost comically circular: keeping going keeps things going, moving on moves you on. But perhaps that circularity

is the point. Life has its own momentum. The ocean of existence has its own tides and currents, and they move with a majestic wholeness and harmony. It's only when we imagine that we're an isolated little wave that we puzzle over our role in the ocean. Should I crest now? Am I too close to the wave ahead of me? Does this foam make my butt look big? The more we practice consciously letting go into that ocean (from which we've never been separate), the less we worry about deciding, beginning, or persisting. It's less and less a matter of I interacting with life. It's life flowing through all its own parts, including the bit formerly known as *I*.

Godspeed

When people embark on a journey or a project, it's a nice old-fashioned tradition to wish them *Godspeed*. But as my friend Albert once pointed out to me, that means God's speed, not your speed. Things will unfold according to the big picture, not the little picture concocted by your little thoughts. You don't always need a definitive timetable or map. Here's a story a friend told me:

> Dave and I had been in a relationship for two years, and we could feel we were getting close to the crossroads where people commit or break up. There were so many things right about us together, but also a few big things that were wrong. I was truly torn, and so was he, and we were both becoming exhausted by the feeling of getting up every morning and stepping onto an emotional roller coaster.
>
> One day I was having lunch with a girlfriend, and she innocently asked, "So, what's happening with you and Dave?" In that moment I felt the whole thing welling up inside me, and my voice caught in a sob: "I don't *know!*" I think I shocked her—she became very quiet. But then I got very quiet too, and very calm. I suddenly saw that it was what it was. In time the right choice would become clear, and the future would be what it would be. Together or apart, Dave and I would be in the next moment and then the one after that, and we'd both still be breathing. And that drained a lot of the drama out of it. I

kind of looked around, shrugged my shoulders, and said—
matter-of-factly, as if she had just asked me what time it
was—"I don't know."

Not knowing is fine, as long as you're fine with not knowing. As with
so many things, the angst is not inherent in the situation. Much of it
comes from knocking your head *against* the situation.

But doesn't not knowing mean we're disoriented? Sure: *dis-oriented*,
no longer facing east, free to go in new directions. Doesn't not knowing
mean we're *lost*? Sure, but is that always a bad thing? "Let's Get Lost"
is a cool-jazz standard with some lovely, droll lyrics. Check out the
Chet Baker version, especially the happy, relaxed way he invites us to
"defrost" and to get crossed off other people's invitation lists. To defrost
out of the old behaviors and expectations in which you've been frozen,
to get crossed off the stale lists of who's who and what's what and
if-then . . . that might be really refreshing. As we've seen, most people
have a lot of fixed ideas, whether they're about who they are and where
they're going, or about politics, religion, or anything else. The thing
about fixed ideas is that you can have as many as you like, but then
you're stuck with them. They may make you feel strong, but they're
really a sign of fear. They're like a heavy suit of armor, in which you
now have to trudge rigidly along, and which keeps new experiences
from touching you.

When we cast off the moorings of where we've been and what we
thought we knew, we can set sail to discover the New World of what
is. That's how it works, whether you're going on to the next relationship, the next job, or the next moment. If you're on a real journey,
when you arrive at your destination it will be a surprise. Somewhere
midway you must get lost to your old understandings—disoriented,
disembobbled (as my wife says), so that wherever you finally come out
is a place you could not have conceived when you went in. Just say, *Huh?*

The more we take the notion of an individual driver out of the picture, the more we find that life drives itself. And actually, physics bears this out. Mechanical engineers who study the dynamics of bicycles talk about a phenomenon known as "ghost riding." For reasons that are still not fully understood, all bicycles are essentially self-balancing. If you push one fast enough, it will just keep going and going. Whenever it starts to fall to one side or the other, it compensates by steering in the direction of the fall and straightens itself up. So when we learn to ride a bike, we're really learning to get quiet enough to feel the subtleties of its self-steering dynamics and get out of their way. Then we just cooperate and let steering happen.

Everything, it turns out, is like that. The physics that steers the bike steers the universe. We're just along for the ride, rolling along on this bicycle of life, as free as open space—ghost riders in the sky.

J. D. Salinger says it a different way. He has his hero-sage, Seymour Glass, age ten, watching from a distance as his brother Buddy plays curb marbles on a quiet New York City street at twilight. After seeing him miss his shot repeatedly, he finally says, "Can you try not aiming so much?"

CHAPTER 29

The Buddy System

When I was about four or five, growing up on Long Island, I saw on the local TV channel an old cartoon that left a deep impression. *The Sunshine Makers* dates from 1935, and it has that weird-dream quality of many thirties cartoons, with their choruses of identical, rubbery-limbed creatures in perpetual motion, dancing and squawking to the accompaniment of a tinny orchestra. But this one tells a story that seemed to me like an ancient, mythic message. It's about a tribe of joyful forest gnomes who wake up each morning, happily worship the rising sun, and harvest its light with a giant magnifying lens. They distill it into milk bottles and then, like the milkmen of my childhood, deliver it to the doorsteps of the sleeping community. As they work they sing in gnomish falsetto, and their song has echoed in my mind for over fifty years:

> *Sunshine, sunshine,*
> *I just love the good old golden sunshine.*

Then we meet a second tribe: skinny, white-faced, black-haired, needle-nosed Marilyn Manson types in top hats, who live in a bleak land of dead trees, vultures, and a toxic pond crawling with vermin. They chant:

> We're happy—when we're—sad.
> We're always—feeling—bad.

These agents of gloom attack the happy gnomes, and soon there's an all-out war, goths vs. hippies. But the gnomes bombard the enemy with cannonades of bottled sunshine, miraculously turning them into creatures of joy, lit from within with sunshine, and transforming their wasteland into a paradisal garden. The cartoon ends with everyone dancing together in a climactic hoedown of love, singing:

> And now the world is bright and fair
> Because there's sunshine everywhere.

A few years ago I discovered that *The Sunshine Makers* was on YouTube. Watching it again so many years later, I realized that, all along, it had been my mission statement. Here was my life's work, laid out for me in seven minutes: to open up and let the sunshine in, and find ways to share it with others.

Anyone who has tasted that sunshine can share it, and this doesn't have to take the form of "teaching" per se. As you find yourself living more and more from the space of freedom, leaving your old fears and worries and stresses farther behind, the contrast between your own situation and that of people still mired in suffering becomes more poignant. As your own happiness grows steadier and therefore of less concern, you have more bandwidth available to concern yourself with the happiness of others. There's nothing especially noble or exalted about this. It's as natural as breathing in and out.

In Judaism, this dedication to the happiness of others is called *tikkun olam*, "healing the world." In Christianity it's *agape*, or *caritas*, a word that is translated as both "charity" and "love." For Muslims it's *rahmah*, usually translated as "mercy" but derived from the word for "womb"— it's the nurturing love that recognizes all others as our children. For Buddhists it's *bodhicitta*, "enlightened mind," implying that opening to others is inherent in opening to enlightenment. As the Buddhist sage Shantideva advised:

> One should always look straight at sentient beings as if drinking them in with the eyes, thinking, "Relying on them alone, I shall attain buddhahood."

In AA, this equivalence of liberation and sharing is the twelfth step: "spiritual awakening" and "carrying the message." But again, carrying the message doesn't always mean teaching it or preaching it. We carry the message most powerfully by being it. You've probably met people who, just by walking into a room, make you feel happier, less confused, more loved and loving. To become one of those—now, that's a worthwhile aspiration, and that's where you're headed.

Every day, we encounter people who are suffering, whether mildly or intensely. We may pass them in the street or nurse them through a crisis. Perhaps they've just gone through a breakup, they've just lost a loved one, they have an untreatable illness, they're worried about their finances, they're distraught about their kids. As they tell us their story, it's natural that we find ourselves searching for wise words. What can we say that will help them fear less, suffer less? That's a compassionate impulse, but sometimes words are beside the point. The search for words is an act of thinking. Deeper than thinking is feeling, and deeper than feeling is being. Often the most skillful strategy and the greatest gift is to just be fully present for people—to be a wide-open space of lovingly neutral listening, into which they can pour their story, or with which they can abide in silence as well.

Be the Therapy Dog

You had some practice back in Part I being the sweetest dog in the world and listening compassionately to your human self. You can also do that for others. Hear your friend the way that that good dog hears, with complete, ears-up attention and simple, unthinking love. As a therapy dog, you're not required to make sense of it. Sometimes all we hear is radio ga ga, radio goo goo, radio ga ga. Just absorb the ga ga, goo goo into the skylike space of your own beingness, without trying to formulate understanding or speech. Don't worry—when something needs to be said, the words will be there in the moment, coming up from that peaceful, silent depth and conveying its power.

Being there for others is what pulls together all your methods. There's a saying that, to truly learn anything, you must teach it. That also applies to this kind of essentially silent teaching, this core-deep *reaching*. By putting yourself into situations where your witness to the silence is required—at the sickbed, at the deathbed, on the phone with your sibling who's anxious about her health, at lunch with your colleague who's worried about being fired—you're called upon to use all your skills of awakening, from alert, upright posture to relaxed voice to noticing the sensations so you're not overwhelmed by the intensity of the narrative. It doesn't mean you try to do half a dozen methods at once. It means that, in the crucible of the world where suffering beings need our help, all the apparently disparate methods are digested, integrated, incorporated, and seen to be just one method, and, finally, no method. Methods just reveal what you most deeply are. Then you be that, and drop all method.

This approach of coming from silence is especially useful when the other person is babbling in confusion, ranting in anger, free-associating in anxiety, wailing in grief. Don't try to stop your friend's tears. That outpouring of emotion doesn't need your words. It just needs to pour out. Let it pour, but don't be caught up in it yourself. As Maharishi used to say, "When the cyclone hits, lie low."

When your speech is required, often the most helpful (and humble) form it can take is questions, rather than answers. But some questions work better than others. When someone is, say, grieving a death, friends will often call or visit and open with a warm, commiserative, "How *are* you?" Despite the sincere intention, this is usually too sweeping a question. A more skillful one is, "How are you *today*?" That brings things more down to earth, to the livable unit of one day at a time. Even better, if your friend is ready to hear it, is to live one *moment* at a time. That cuts through the notion that we're carrying our burden of suffering 24/7, without letup. Sometimes opportunities arise for you to bring this to your friend's attention, the equivalent of clapping your hands together in front of their eyes: *Drop it!*

And sometimes life does the clapping for us. One day many years ago, I was standing on a sidewalk in downtown Elizabeth, New Jersey, with my friend Rick. That morning we had heard the news of some terrible incident of war or terrorism in which many children had been slaughtered. Rick couldn't comprehend what kind of world could let that happen to little children, and as we spoke about it he began to cry. Just then, down the sidewalk on the other side of the street, smiling the warmest, most radiant smile imaginable, came walking, or, rather, gliding, one of the most astonishingly beautiful, astonishingly sexy, women I—or, believe me, anyone—had ever seen. We fell silent, and, for a moment, we were delivered from our world-anguish by this goddess visitation. Then Rick looked at me and laughed sheepishly: busted! You can say that we were crass, that our compassion was too shallow to withstand the first shapely distraction to come along. But I would argue that this was not merely a distraction but a reprieve, one on the house, a gift that we would be wrong not to accept graciously. And then, back to caring for the world.

Miles Ahead

Herbie Hancock, the great jazz keyboardist, tells a story about a concert he played with Miles Davis in Stuttgart in the early sixties. They had a big, enthusiastic crowd, the whole ensemble consisted of top-flight musicians, and they were having a great night, clicking on all cylinders. Then, in the middle of playing "So What?," one of Miles's signature compositions, Herbie suddenly played a wrong chord—not just a little bit wrong, but glaringly, unimaginably, catastrophically wrong. It was such a disaster that he stopped playing and clapped his hands to the sides of his head, frozen in horror.

Then Miles did something extraordinary. Without missing a beat—literally—he played the notes that made Herbie's wrong chord right. He made it part of the tune, wove it in seamlessly, so that instead of being an all-is-lost, kill-me-now debacle, the chord became a daring foray into way-out-there tonalities, opening an exciting new space for Miles and his trumpet to explore. "So what?" indeed.

There's a lesson here in how to practice rahmah, caritas, tikkun olam:

Here we are. Someone—maybe another, maybe you—has screwed up, and now there's a calamity on our hands. This is the moment we're in, these are the chords that have been played. There are no do-overs. We have to, as they say in golf, play it as it lies. We might get so fixated on the calamitous nature of the situation that we're paralyzed, hands to the sides of our heads. We might rage against the perpetrator. If we're the perp ourselves, and we're not true grownups, we might try to shift the blame to someone else.

But blame is lame. Perseverance furthers. We persevere by playing the notes that make the wrong chords right. On a good day, when we handle things deftly, the disaster becomes an opportunity to expand our melodic range into new territory. This is what I love about Siri when she's performing her GPS function. She doesn't berate me for missing a turn. She just quietly reroutes my trip and, from where I am now, no matter how I got here, she takes me forward. If I can sit back and relax into my seat, rather than berating myself, I can enjoy some new scenery.

And by the way, everything that happens actually *is* part of the tune—the subtle tune of the universe, the harmony of the spheres. Playing the notes that make all the seemingly wrong stuff right is ultimately not a matter of inventing them but of finding them, hearing them, and letting them play you.

Buddies

Once in a while, you might find yourself in a situation where a friend is ripe for more than just help with the immediate, acute crisis. They're ready to hear the teaching, to see the curtains part on the big picture of life: the skylike space of unchanging, transcendent, silent OK-ness, ever untouched by the winds of change, and always easily accessible just by resting as awareness. For at least that moment, they have ears to hear. No one can push them to that moment, just as no one could have pushed you to this one. That's why evangelizing doesn't work. But again, by *being* it rather than preaching it, you've become the example and the lighthouse. Over time, your friends will notice that you no longer get caught in fear or rage, dependency or despondency, and they'll ask why. Then you can explain things in simple terms and offer whatever resources—books, methods, teachers—you think they might connect with. Meanwhile, you can be sensitive, alert for the opening, for when and how this person will be able to hear. That's skillful compassion.

If each one of us does that at least once—each one reach one—then eventually the light spreads to everyone. Then the world is bright and fair, because there's sunshine everywhere.

In practice, of course—in the non-cartoon world—it's a more subtle, gradual, shifting process than that. There aren't perfect children of light, straightening out utter children of darkness. We're all unique, complicated mixtures on the outside, and simple, pure beingness on the inside, with our own shifting inner tides of forgetting and remembering what's what. That's why we're all on the buddy system with this stuff: all the same spacelike awareness, embodied and embuddied in different forms. When I remind you of your true nature I'm talking to myself. Next time, you'll remind me.

PART IV

View

CHAPTER 30

That Guy

In our project of finding the dimension beyond fear and learning how to live from there, we've so far focused mostly on practice, method, technique—stuff that you do, even if it's done effortlessly. But the great meditative traditions also stress a second essential element: *view*, or *insight*. This doesn't mean "opinion," or "idea." The terms are used more literally: view as in, "From this mountaintop, my view of our town is more panoramic," insight as in *seeing into* the way things are. Sometimes nothing needs to change about what is; we just need a shift in perspective to see it more clearly *as* it is.

One day a man comes home to find that there's a tiger in his living room. Naturally, he's distressed: his pulse races, his blood pressure spikes, his mind reels. He can try any number of tactics to deal with the tiger: tippy-toe carefully around it, beat pots and pans to shoo it out the door, start Googling TIGER EXTERMINATORS NEAR ME. While he waits for the exterminator to show up, he might take medication to settle his blood pressure or even meditate to calm his mind. But then his wife comes home and says, "Hi, honey. Do you like my new paper tiger? Isn't it lifelike?" Suddenly, without the aid of meditation, medication, or extermination, his mind and his blood pressure settle down (although he may ask his wife to please text ahead next time). The exact same experience of tiger shape and tiger colors is still coming through his eyes, but his view has shifted. All is well—and, the man realizes, it always has been.

Life, say the awakened sages, is a paper tiger.

This shift cuts through needless suffering. It's not that we find a new solution to our problem (a new, improved tiger gun); it's that we see there never was a problem. You may have noticed that sometimes, when you open your eyes at the end of a meditation session, everything seems somehow simpler, less chaotic, less problematic than it was going in. Nothing has changed about the outer situation, and you haven't spent your meditation finding ingenious solutions to your problems. You may have spent it *trying* to find solutions. That's OK. Everyone does, for a while, but then you give up and your focus relaxes into a more panoramic, big-sky mode, where the same life situations—the same pixels, we could say—resolve themselves into more coherent, more spacious, less oppressive ways of being seen.

Usually this glow of everything-OK-just-as-it-is fades after some minutes or hours, but as our explorations mature it stays with us more and more. We begin to realize that it's not just some peculiar side effect of meditative relaxation, like a microdose of some euphoric drug. We intuitively know that this delicious simplicity is more real than all the tangled drama we formerly superimposed upon it. It's self-evident. There's nothing magic about it. The real black magic, the real sleight of hand, was our old, narrow, problem-filled view. What's sorcery is not that our fear vanishes, but that a paper tiger could ever have frightened us.

"Come and see," said the Buddha. It finally turns out to be that simple. Emily Dickinson said that what we need, rather than "Revelation," is "unfurnished eyes."

That is, our redemption from fear and suffering won't come when at last an angel arrives and whispers some cosmic revelation in our ear, or when we find just the right page of the right scripture or self-help book, or when we have the super-orgasmic-psychedelic meditation experience we've been fantasizing about. All we need to do is relax our focus to see past the old confusion, the clutter of conceptual furniture that's been obstructing our unfurnished view. As Sri Nisargadatta said:

> Don't try to understand. It's enough that you don't misunderstand.

We don't need some kind of super-eyes—just clear, naked, unfurnished eyes.

The True Guru

In our meditation group in Northern State Prison I'm officially the teacher, but I've learned at least as much as I've taught, especially about view. One night, sometime in our first year or two, we were meeting as usual in the cinder-block chapel, about fifteen of us in our circle of blue plastic chairs, and the conversation turned to dealing skillfully with corrections officers—COs, or cops, as they're usually called. Roy, a moon-faced, fortyish Filipino with long, straight black hair pulled back in a ponytail, said, "Well, hey, I'm lucky to be here in the meeting tonight. The cop on my tier is That Guy. He thinks we're doing devil worship here, and sometimes he doesn't 'get around' to letting me out."

"Wait, wait," I said. "What do you mean, 'That Guy'?"

Roy was a talented artist who taught drawing and painting classes in the education wing, so he was used to explaining things patiently. "That Guy, as in, 'Everything would be fine if it wasn't for That Guy.' Sometimes That Guy is a cop trying to prove how big his dick is, so you keep your eyes down and stay clear of him as much as you can. Sometimes it's someone back home that keeps making your life complicated—could be your wife. Sometimes it's your cellie, which is tough. That's day in and day out. If he smokes, or plays his radio all day, or won't stop talking, you're stuck with it."

Other members of the group started jumping in with stories of intolerable cellmates, past and present. Jimmy, a white-haired former bantamweight boxer who was easily agitated, started in on his current cellie. "It's not just that he talks so *much*. Everything he says is *stupid*. He thinks he's an expert on everything, and he goes on and on, yammering about any subject he thinks of, just making stuff up, and he has no idea he's doing it. He's too stupid to know he's stupid."

> ME: "OK, OK. I hear you. But I want to get back to something Roy said. 'Everything would be fine if it wasn't for That Guy.' Is that true?"
>
> JIMMY: "Well, yeah, life would be much better if my guy just went away. I wouldn't have to keep controlling my urge to sock him."
>
> ME: "Have any of you ever had a situation where That Guy did go away? . . . Yeah? And then what happens?"

Silence. Then Roy broke into a broad grin. "Then someone else becomes That Guy." Everybody laughed.

I said, "Maybe it's like those name tags that people wear at conventions. *Hello, I'm Fred.* There's one that says *Hello, I'm That Guy*, and it just keeps getting passed around. But what can we do with this? Is there a way to use That Guy as part of our practice?"

We kicked the idea around a little, and then I had another thought. "Do you know what the Dalai Lama says about his guru?" Our group had been studying Tibetan Buddhism and everyone was familiar with Tibet's modern history: the Chinese Communist invasion of Tibet ordered by Mao Zedong, whose troops tortured and killed a million

Tibetans, destroyed ninety-eight percent of the temples, and forced the young Dalai Lama to flee into exile. "Whenever someone asks the Dalai Lama who is *his* lama, his guru, you know what he says? Mao Zedong."

Mao, I explained—Mao, the brutal invader—was the one who taught him to be patient and compassionate, to bear the unbearable by finding the silent place inside that remains always untouched, but then keep getting up every morning and work to make things better. For the Dalai Lama, Mao Zedong is That Guy. And That Guy, we decided, whoever he or she is, is always your guru.

This insight, that your nemesis is your true guru, is a steep teaching. If it's too steep for you right now, fine: turn the page, maybe come back to it next month or next year. Everything's optional. But because it's steep, exploring it can take you very high very fast. Your moody, unreasonable supervisor, your crooked business partner, your vindictive ex, your addicted child, your neurotic sibling, your narcissistic parent . . . whaddya got? Whoever it is that makes you say, "*This* can't be OK. If only it weren't for *this* I'd be in the clear"—that's your teacher. Sometimes it might not be a person but a situation: if only it weren't for this job, or this joblessness, or this toothache, or this cancer. Hard as it might be, if you can take a step back and get a big-picture view, you might realize that somehow life is so perfectly choreographed that at every point you get exactly the teacher you need.

And what is it that all these teachers—or the one Teacher in all these different guises—is teaching you? That your OK-ness doesn't depend on anything. Sometimes, especially if you're stubborn, your guru, That Guy, uses tough-love tactics and makes things so uncomfortable on the surface that you're forced to seek the depths. He provides exactly the thing you fear or hate, the one you're sure you can't be OK with, so that you have to be with it and find out you're still OK because you're OK-ness itself. Terrified of snakes? Here's a snake.

In the Buddhist and Hindu cultures, the lama or guru is given the

highest reverence. He or she ranks right along with your parents as one
to whom you are unrepayably indebted, for whom you can never feel
enough gratitude. To us egalitarian Westerners, it can seem strange to
see people prostrate themselves before their teachers or touch their feet
in greeting, but to traditional Easterners it's natural. Someone once asked
one of my teachers why he bowed down to a picture of his own teacher,
and he replied, "I don't bow down, I *fall* down."

So—are you ready? Can you take on that reverent gratitude and
direct it toward your loudmouth uncle who spouts obnoxious, ignorant
political opinions at every family gathering? Or toward the oblivious
driver going forty-five in the left lane of the freeway when you're in a
desperate hurry? Or the colleague in your office who keeps screwing
up projects and shifting the blame to you? Or the competing author
whose shallow, repetitive, ghostwritten, best-selling books keep pushing
yours off the shelves? Clearly, this is a big shift in view. But because it's
view, not method, there's nothing you have to do about it. Don't prostrate yourself at your bloviating uncle's feet, don't try to repress your
anger at your ex, don't strain to maintain a fabricated grin-and-bear-it
attitude, and don't try to explain your new, improved spiritual perspective to That Guy. Just know that, like it or not, life has served up
the teacher you require. You can't unhear this. The seed of this
knowledge has already been planted. See what happens.

In time, you'll probably see that this knowledge pulls the rug out
from under much of your fear and anger. How can you fear the precious
teacher who is giving you just what you need? How can you be angry
with him? And if you can't be angry with That Guy, your very nemesis,
how can you be angry with lesser culprits? They're just your guru's
teaching assistants. As anger starts to slip away, leaving clarity in its
place, you see what a waste of life energy it was. The Dalai Lama has
said that while you toss and turn, losing sleep over the wrongs

committed against you, the wrongdoer is sleeping like a baby, having long since forgotten the whole thing.

In close tandem with anger, this shift also pulls the rug out from under blame. Yes, blame is lame, but blame is not the same as responsibility. If you're running, say, an office or a classroom or a household, it's often important to ascertain that Wendy was responsible for leaving the stove on or Max was responsible for feeding Twizzlers to the hamster, so that you can help them correct their behavior. But those are matter-of-fact situational assessments, followed by appropriate adjustments. Blame, on the other hand, has a jagged emotional charge whose function is to make people feel bad about themselves. Christians wisely say to hate the sin and love the sinner: blame is designed to judge and convict the sinner, to say or imply, "Oh, Wendy, what did you do *this* time?" or, "Max, you're such a screw-up!"

By the way, don't try to tell other people that blame is lame and therefore they shouldn't blame you. This is for you to know. In fact, in many situations (office politics, family politics), because most people are so caught up in dodging blame at all costs, being loose enough to accept some can give you great power. At the right time, an unexpected, deftly applied, "Oh, gee, my bad!" can suddenly take the air out of a lot of unnecessary drama.

I learned a lot about blame from my mother, who was warm and charming in many ways but whose swift, fiery judgments made her an excellent guru in this department. I remember driving with her one rainy day, and hearing her shout curses at the driver in front of us whenever his car hit a puddle and (naturally) splashed ours. One Thanksgiving Day, she drove to the in-laws' house where the dinner was to take place. She had a bad knee, so arrangements had been made to leave her an empty parking spot in the driveway, near the front door. But someone had not gotten the word, and when she arrived there was no spot for her. She parked halfway down the block, limped to the house with her sweet potato casserole in hand, and entered shouting, "Who's the *idiot* that took my parking spot?" That Thanksgiving dinner ended before it began.

In meditation, That Guy becomes the barking dog or the nagging thoughts. Until it's the next thing. From this perspective, meditation is a form of training for being at peace with That Guy. Sit, close the eyes, take some comfy on-ramp, rest as awareness . . . *ahhhhhhh!* . . . and then . . .

BEEEEEEEP BEEEEEEEP BEEEEEEEP BEEEEEEEP BEEEEEEEP BEEEEEEEP BEEEEEEEP BEEEEEEEP . . .

Shit! How can I be at peace with that effing car alarm? Whose car is that? When are they gonna outlaw those effing things? Where's my baseball bat—I'm gonna go massage his windshield. Eventually, you may settle for waiting for it to stop (and *then* you'll be at peace), but if you're lucky it keeps going through your whole meditation. Or it stops, but then someone in the next room starts yakking on their phone. *Why is she shouting? Why doesn't she close the door?* Fine. Go ahead, keep blaming stuff, trying to get it to stop with willpower (how has that worked out for you so far?), till you finally see that there's no end to things you can blame for making you not OK. That Guy is a shape-shifter, like the sea god Proteus, who, as you try to hold him still, changes from lion to leopard to pig to tree to water.

Judge Not

As blame and judgment lift, something perhaps unexpected begins to take their place: *compassion*, "feeling with." When we stop judging our chosen That Guys as bad guys in black hats, and, for that matter, stop venerating our chosen These Guys as good guys in white hats, then everyone is left hatless—just guys. Then we can start to see them as they are: At their core? Pure, spotless beingness, just like us. The rest? An impossibly complex product of chains of cause and effect, reaching back to the nutritional content of the breakfast they ate this morning . . . to their last seven years of hating their crummy job . . . to their sweet marriage . . . to the little girl in the sandbox who broke their heart in kindergarten . . . to the DNA they got from their parents . . . yadda yadda yadda . . . back to the Big Bang. Also just like us. Every one of us tender, vulnerable, confused, just trying to figure it all out. Every one of us someone's little baby, toddling off on our own, trying to find that love again, bumping into things, making messes.

That's another thing I've learned about in prison. At my very first session at Northern State, on a cold night in January 2005, three guys showed up. Two of them seemed bored and distracted, probably medicated, and not sure what they were doing there. They stopped coming after another week or two. The third, whom I'll call Duffy, kept showing up. He had been practicing Zen at another prison before coming to Northern. He was in his late thirties, sharp, funny, well read, serious about his practice. I found out later that he wrote poetry and did hospice work for dying prisoners, sometimes sitting up for days at a time, holding their hands, changing their diapers. Afterward, as I walked across the parking lot, I started wondering what he was doing in a maximum-security prison. He must have been one of those nonviolent drug offenders you hear about, who sell a little pot to a narc after the narc lures them into a school zone to jack up their sentence by another ten years.

When I got home, I went straight to my laptop and logged onto the New Jersey Department of Corrections website. I knew that each inmate has his own page, with mug shot, rap sheet, aliases, and parole date. I did a search, and up came Duffy's page. "Admission date: December 1990. Parole eligibility date: December 2020. Offenses: Robbery. Aggravated assault. Murder."

I decided not to look up anyone else's page. They didn't know the worst thing I'd ever done, and I didn't want to know theirs. My job was to encourage their highest aspiration. Their lowest moment was not my business.

Still, though, the question remained in the back of my mind: How did smart, sensitive, articulate Duffy, with no economic disadvantage or racial prejudice to struggle against, wind up doing thirty years for murder? One night, about four years later, the guys got me telling a few stories of my hitchhiking adventures in the sixties—some of them comical, some of them hair-raising. At the end of the session, as guys filed out the door and retrieved their ID cards from the lobby officer, Duffy caught up with me and said, "Yeah, the first time I went hitchhiking out of Florida was when I was fifteen and ran away from home. That was right after my dad raped both of my sisters."

Oh.

My feet kept walking, but my mind reeled as I digested this information. Suddenly I didn't need to know any more details, any of the steps between Point A, the sin of the father, and Point Z, the utter waste of life that was Duffy's incarceration. I felt the tidelike force with which his whole life had been impelled to this bleak spot. Tears sprang to my eyes. Fuck. Some people never have a chance.

"Good stories," said Duffy. He picked up his ID and walked into the night.

CHAPTER 31

The Exploded Moment

Please try this:

Press the tips of your thumb and forefinger together. You don't have to press hard.

Experience that pressure. This is not a thought or an abstraction, but an experience. Completely simple, completely ordinary.

Now stop pressing.

Now press again, but do it three seconds ago.

Can't?

Then try doing it three seconds in the future.

No?

If some wise guy waits three seconds and then triumphantly presses his digits together, has he succeeded in doing it in the future? Um, no. As they say, the future lies ahead . . . and always will.

All action, experience, feeling, thought—everything—happens in the present. All happening happens in the present. Everything but the present is absent.

You can never experience the past or the future. Our wise guy might say, "Sure I can experience the past. In fact, right now I can remember what I had for breakfast this morning." But the key words are "right now." What we call *memory* is a thought, and it's experienced in the present, like all thoughts and all other experiences. It's a thought *about* the past, and it can come in assorted flavors—that is, with assorted linked feelings, such as regret or nostalgia. We can also have thoughts about the future, called *expectation*, and they can come in such flavors as hope or dread. In fact, we can have a thought about anything we want, but there's only one time we can have it, and that's now. Beyond that we're trying to steal time that doesn't exist. We're the world's worst bandits.

There's a piece of advice that's so popular it's become a spiritual cliché: "Be here now." That's unassailable, but it can also be misleading: it sounds as if other options are available, as if you have a choice. Sure, be here now . . . where the hell else can you be?

Even to say, "You can never experience the past or the future," is misleading. It sounds as if there are these two places, called *past* and *future*, lurking somewhere that happens to be inaccessible to us, just around some fourth-dimensional blind corner; if only we looked through the right kind of wormhole with the right kind of super-periscope, we could see them. But there are no such places, except in thought, which is present. And once we've seen through the myth of those two places, our old, unexamined sense of *present* as a third place—the place between those other two places—also starts to evaporate.

Then what's left? Just . . . *this*. Here we are. There's no good word for this. Our language has evolved over the centuries to describe the world of time, but beyond that it breaks down. We can say *timelessness*, but it's a shame that we have to describe what *is* in terms of what isn't— it's like naming your precious child Not-a-Monster. But more important than naming is seeing. When we clearly see the insubstantiality of the past, then the regret and nostalgia (and pain, resentment, confusion, etc.) that once bred there begin to lose their power over us. When we clearly see the insubstantiality of the future, then the hope and dread (and anxiety, apprehension, etc.) that once bred there begin to lose their power over us. They have nowhere to breed. We see that clearly, and we're in the clear.

Of course, when people say, "Be here now," they really mean it's easy to get so caught up in memories and expectations that it's *as if* they're reality, and then we miss the real reality, like a person caught in a dream. Dreaming the future, we can get lost in feverish, anxiety-laden dramas that never transpire. Dreaming the past, we can become embroiled in angry fights with people (our parents, say) who are no longer even alive. A few years ago, at a workshop I led in Northern California, one participant suddenly realized that a trauma she had regarded as the fundamental hurt of her life, something she had re-membered a friend doing to her decades earlier and which she had carried as an open wound ever since, was a complete misunderstanding. It never happened.

A related bit of well-worn advice is, "Live in the moment." Again, that's the right idea, but it also slips a joker into the deck: the concept of a *moment*, a unit, a little particle of time, and the concept of time as a bunch of those particles, arranged in a long, long line. All those time-lines of history and geography you drew back in grade school bolstered this concept. But there ain't no such animal. There's only the timeless *this*. (Go back and check as many times as necessary, putting the tips of your thumb and forefinger together, or doing anything else.) As it happens, the word *moment* shares its roots with *momentum*, which implies some driving force that impels constant movement through that long line of particles. Sharing the root as well is *momentous*, which implies importance, or weight, and the fishy proposition that some moments are weightier than others. So, while living in the moment is certainly better (truer, more liberating) than living in dreams of past and future, it would be better yet to explode the whole concept: blow up those nonexistent particles and live in the clear, open space that's left.

When we don't, then life is like that long road trip to Disneyland with your kids in the backseat. "Are we there yet? Are we there yet? *Now* are we there yet?" By being caught in momentum, in urgent movement toward a future moment that will be more momentous than this one, the kids create their own suffering. Most adults do this less noisily, but they still do it. Up in the driver's seat, although you see that the traffic to the Disneyland entrance is backed up, you may still be caught in the urge to keep your momentum going and arrive sooner than later. Then you suffer that familiar straining-at-the-harness feeling—*mmnhhhh!*—as you grip the wheel and lean forward, as if trying to push the traffic out of the way with your body. That doesn't work. But now suppose you glance over to the next lane and see a bus driver who does this every day, for whom arriving five minutes earlier or later is not so momentous. He's stuck in exactly the same traffic as you are, but he's not stuck in the same suffering. Once again, the key is clear noticing. When you notice yourself straining forward, and know clearly that it doesn't move the traffic faster but it does make the (imaginary) time move slower, you can breathe out and drop the whole thing.

On that road trip, by the way, you've just experienced firsthand the core of the Buddha's teaching, the Four Noble Truths:

- Truth Number One: Human life is subject to suffering. (Check. Obvious.)
- Truth Number Two: We create our own suffering by mentally straining against the harness of circumstances, trying to magically turn what isn't into what is. (Not so obvious.)
- Truth Number Three: When we stop trying to do the impossible (see Number Two), we relax into reality, and then suffering evaporates. (*Whew!* That's a relief!)

- Truth Number Four: Stabilizing that *Whew!* of relief so that it becomes perpetual takes some practice: clear seeing, regular meditation, and sensible, ethical conduct so you don't get bogged down in a lot of distracting drama.

Unsurprisingly, some of the champions of applying this teaching in the real world have been Tibetan Buddhist monks. I've met a few who were tortured when the Chinese Communists overran Tibet. One of them described how he and his colleagues were bound by the wrists, the other ends of the ropes attached to pulleys on the ceiling and pulled tight, so that the monks had to stand for hours on tiptoe, with their arms stretched above their heads. Of course that's going to be excruciatingly painful, no matter what. But as the saying goes, "Pain is mandatory, suffering is optional." Your kids in the backseat suffered, even though they had no pain. These monks had plenty of pain, but their suffering was, if not absent, certainly much less than it would be for most people. Having practiced seeing through time, they knew how to abide in timelessness, rather than keep amplifying their misery by straining against circumstances, fantasizing about the momentous moment of their release, and asking, "Are we there yet?" Only when there's time, duration, is there suffering to be endured. (The monks also practiced loving their torturers.)

As always, it's good to do the fire drill before the fire, as these monks had. Then, when our own potentially torturous circumstances come along—the broken leg, the broken career, the broken romance—we know how to minimize our suffering by exploding the moments into timelessness. And that ability is strengthened every time we meditate. The movement that's most deeply implicated in generating the appearance of time is the movement of thought. In meditation, we simply relax beneath that movement, like sinking below the waves into the silent ocean water that's always just a few feet below the surface, even as the waves roll on. When we rest as awareness, we're resting in timelessness, growing more familiar with it so we can more readily notice it once we open our eyes.

Most people notice timelessness only in exceptional situations—when they finally have the first kiss with the long-sought lover, or they have their astonishingly in-the-flow, happening-all-by-itself performance onstage, or they play their peak in-the-zone, can't-miss-the-basket game. They will often say, "Time stood still," and they're almost right. There actually was no time to stand still, or to stand anywhere. There's nowhere for it to stand. They just briefly noticed the timeless *this* that always is. There was a parting of the clouds, and they said, "Oh, look, the sky has appeared." But the sky's always there, and now we're learning to sense and enjoy its presence, no matter the weather.

In his sonnet "On First Looking into Chapman's Homer," John Keats evokes the cloud-parting, time-stopping, mind-silencing quality of such experiences, likening them to the first view of a planet or an ocean:

> *Then felt I like some watcher of the skies*
> *When a new planet swims into his ken;*
> *Or like stout Cortez when with wondering eyes*
> *He stared at the Pacific—and all his men*
> *Looked at each other with a wild surmise—*
> *Silent, upon a peak in Darien.*

CHAPTER 32

Bruegel to the Rescue

We can find cues to our clearer view wherever we look. How about Rembrandt? You've probably seen his portraits before, with their startling inner depth, but now that we've been exploring our own inner depths let's take another look and see what they can show us about the place beyond fear.

Rembrandt's *Self-Portrait with Beret* was painted around 1655, after success, wealth, and happy marriage had given way to widowhood, sexual scandal, legal nightmares, sickening betrayal, and the constant threat of bankruptcy. Here he's about fifty but looks older and wearier. Every blotch, sag, and jowl is unsparingly rendered, as are the permanent furrows of concentration between his eyebrows. This is the face of one who has seen much (seeing is his job), endured much, made mistakes. We see Rembrandt's fine sensitivity and fierce intelligence, as well as his fatigue, his deep sadness, his battered pride.

But behind that there's a stiffening of the spine that we can almost feel, a stubborn resolve to persevere. And behind *that* is the painting's deepest magic: the light of the transcendent, boundless beingness, shining through it all. You can't miss it. Earlier artists were limited to showing divinity shining through idealized saints and prettied-up royals. (Court painters were the cosmetic surgeons of their day.) But

the rise of humanism freed Rembrandt to show the divinity of ordinariness— the soul glowing through jowls and sags, the peace that passeth all understanding illuminating a face that's a battleground of folly and hard-won wisdom. This is us, blotches and all, nirvana and all. And therefore this is also an object of meditation. Spend a few minutes looking into those eyes and watch everything open up: the heroic striving as well as that which is beyond all strife, peering as deep into us as we peer into it.

In fact, it was during Rembrandt's lifetime that our modern concept of the autonomous individual, with unique struggles and gifts, emerged. Rembrandt was born only a few years after Shakespeare created Hamlet—the first fully fleshed-out, complex, modern individual in literature, at the head of a long line of striving, often self-destructive rebels, geniuses, and maniacs, from Faust and Ahab to Hester Prynne and Scarlett O'Hara. But along the way, the drama of the individual's storm and stress has often overshadowed the transcendent spark behind it all, the spark we see in Rembrandt's eyes. Even for us ordinary non-geniuses, this history has informed our sense of ourselves and our lives. We can feel as if we're flying solo in a one-seater plane, encountering heavy turbulence, without a star to guide us. The missing star is Rembrandt's spark, which we're now recovering through our meditative practice. That's a big part of the solution.

Another part of the solution is Pieter Bruegel the Elder, whose finest works are also objects of meditation. Bruegel painted some two generations before Rembrandt, and rather than piercing close-ups he specialized in long shots of crowded landscapes. In his *Children's Games*, we see the edge of a town that appears for some reason to have been taken over by a great swarm of more than a hundred unsupervised children of various ages, from toddlers to teenagers. They do handstands and somersaults, play tiddlywinks and mumblety-peg, give noogies, wear grotesque masks, mother their dolls, stage mock religious processions, and blow up pig-bladder balls. (Also, one kid is taking a poo and another is happily poking at a pile of poo with a stick. Good times.)

As with Rembrandt, the more you look at a Bruegel, the more you see. But rather than going deep into one individual, here our vision spreads wide into the group. Every face and garment, every hoop and soap bubble is carefully wrought, in exquisite detail. Each person is microscopically fascinating, but no person is *the* person, the center of interest. Each is an inseparable part of the whole: there's a visual rhythm that runs through the crowd, like the rhythm of ripples on a lake. They're individuals, but there's a subtle something-the-same uniting them all. The composition is like a "Where's Waldo?" puzzle without a Waldo. The star of the show is no one and therefore everyone, nowhere and therefore everywhere.

The Rembrandt vision gives us the Great Man theory, where history is driven by a few extraordinary Napoleons. Bruegel's vision fits the more modern view of a world shaped by huge, ragged tides of collective economic and social behavior. Rembrandt is protagonist-driven Hollywood movies where the action hero becomes our vicarious ego, saving the world single-handed. Sitting in the darkened theater, we lose ourselves in him, feeling his triumphs and his pain as our reality, unlike the abstract, fun pain he inflicts on the bad guys. For two hours, Tom Cruise or Dwayne Johnson is our self, and all the others are, well, others, and therefore expendable.

Bruegel balances that out. He brings the *Downton Abbey* or *Game of Thrones* vision: sprawling episodic TV drama with big ensemble casts, compelling us to spread a wider net of identity and empathy. Everybody's real, everybody's important, everybody hurts sometimes, and no one has the pressure of being the singular center of the universe. Sure, you're unique—just like everybody else. Yeah, you're important—like every other leaf on this tree. This view drains the desperate urgency out of our drama. We're all others. Or, all together, we're I-and-I-and-I-and-I. *E pluribus unum.*

Perhaps the most important line in the Bible, in Luke 17:21, has two competing English translations, hinging on the interpretation of the Greek preposition *entos*: "The kingdom of God is within you" vs. "The kingdom of God is among you." Rembrandt gives us "within," Bruegel gives us "among." Go deep within yourself, using the close-up, macro lens, and lose yourself in the zone, the inner kingdom of open space that transcends all problems and limits. Or walk among the others, using the wide-angle lens, and discover that you remain in that zone even in the wide world, in communion with your fellow pedestrians, dreamily zoning along with you whether they notice or not.

There's nothing we have to do about any of this. This is view, not method. Once we see that the sovereign, isolated, gloriously doomed little self is a paper tiger, all the self's fears and woes start to unravel. That unraveling takes some time, but there is a simple way to goose it along:

Don't take things personally.

When you're stuck at the red light, it's only a red light from the point of view of the protagonist you've consented to be, the one I that's been plucked out from seven billion. If you give up the mantle of I, or just learn to wear it lightly, you can share I-and-I-ness with the drivers on the cross street, for whom the light is green. Why dig deeper into your irritation and impatience when you can joyously zoom along with them instead? Shantideva says:

All the happiness in this world arises from wishing joy for others. All the unhappiness in this world comes from wishing joy for oneself.

You can't fixate on Poor Me unless you're fixating on Me. Depressed? Discouraged? Go work in a soup kitchen, pull weeds in the community garden, tutor kids in reading skills. It doesn't have to be dramatic: try to get every clerk and barista and bus driver you deal with today to smile.

This other-orientation, selflessness in both senses of the word, is the great secret of parenthood. Now that, out of the seven billion so-called others in the world, there's one that you care more about than yourself—one that, without hesitation, you'd dive in front of a truck to save—you're shedding the straitjacket of small selfhood. This is what makes parenthood a spiritual path. In the same way, it can make marriage or friendship or *any* form of love a spiritual path. It may start out as, "What's in it for Me?" but if you stay on the path, somewhere along the line Me starts to soften and melt, while you weren't looking because you were too busy caring for the other. And as Me melts, so does worrying about Me and fearing for Me.

CHAPTER 33

Nothing Sticks

In the old days in Tibet, certain sages would wear a small round mirror made of polished metal, called a *melong*, hanging around their necks. In their business of helping people free themselves from suffering, this was the one visual aid they wanted handy at all times. When a seeker of wisdom came to a sage's hut from a nearby village, the sage might invite him to sit and they would meditate together. Afterward the sage might hold up the melong and say something like this:

"What color is the mirror? Look: When I hold this apple in front of it, the mirror appears red. Now, when I hold this hunk of barley bread in front of it, the mirror appears black. So what color is the mirror?"

"Well," the seeker might reply, "first it's red, then it's black. Later it could be other colors."

"But in that case," says the sage, "can we really say that those are the mirror's colors? If the mirror only shows black when the bread is near, then we can't really say the black color belongs to the mirror. So . . . what color is the mirror?"

The seeker hesitates. "Umm . . . no color?"

"That must be it, mustn't it? It reflects all colors, but it itself is colorless. In fact, its colorlessness is what allows it to reflect all colors. That's why it can even reflect black and red at the same time. Now, consider that your awareness is like the mirror—empty and open to reflect all colors. Unlike a physical mirror, it also reflects sounds, tastes, smells, textures, feelings, and thoughts, yet, just like the mirror, it remains empty, free of all that it reflects. Is that consistent with what you experience? Please look. See if your awareness has a color. Is it yellow? Purple?"

"No, it's colorless."

"Is it sour or sweet?"

"No, it's tasteless."

"Walking through the valley to get here this morning, you saw rocks and wildflowers, and the vultures circling overhead. You felt the heat of the sun and heard the sound of the streams, and perhaps you thought of your family back at home. All those came and went within your awareness—arising, changing, vanishing—but awareness remained, ever the same, ever untouched, just as it remains now. Is that your experience?"

"Yes."

"All right. What about this?" The sage holds the apple in front of the mirror again. "What if I keep holding it here—for a day, a week? Will the red color stick to it?"

"No. Nothing sticks."

"If *you* look at the apple for a day or a week, will the red color stick to your awareness?"

"No."

"And the same will be true for the other experiences reflected in your awareness. Sound, touch, taste, smell, thought, feeling. Nothing sticks to the mirror of awareness. In fact, do we have to wait for the objects to be removed for the mirror to be free of their qualities? Please take your time. Consider carefully. *Look* carefully."

"Hmmmmm . . . No. My awareness remains colorless even while reflecting colors. If I taste honey I'll be aware of sweetness, but my awareness itself still has no flavor. Clarity, emptiness is its quality. Freedom from all reflected qualities is the quality that allows it to reflect them."

"Very good. And that must include the thoughts and feelings that awareness reflects, whether the feelings are happy or sad, mild or intense. Awareness is always free of them, even while they're present, and even if they're present for many years. As you say, nothing sticks."

The seeker looks uncertain. "But wait. There's a widow in my village whose husband died seven years ago. She's been sad ever since. It would seem that the sad feeling has stuck to her awareness."

"Yes, it would *seem* that way. That's a common sight, isn't it? But is it so? The sadness has been present, reflected in her awareness, for seven years, just as the red of the apple could continue reflected in the mirror for a long time. But only if we keep holding the apple in front of it. The widow keeps holding on to her sadness. Her awareness remains free, but she doesn't know it yet."

"How can she know it?"

"Let's return to that question in a moment. First, let me ask you this: Where is the body in this scheme of things? Is your body the mirror of awareness, or is it, like the thoughts and feelings, something reflected *in* the mirror? . . . You look confused. Let's put that another way: Do you experience your body?"

"Yes."

"Yes. It's something you experience. When you were a little boy, you experienced a different body. When you're an old man like me, you'll experience yet another body. Actually, there have been many bodies, and there will be many more, as it changes incessantly. Who or what experiences all those bodies?"

"Well . . . *I* do."

"Indeed. You are not the body. You are the experiencer, the unchanging awareness that's aware of the always-changing body. You are the mirror, and by nature you're free of body, thoughts, feelings, suffering, sadness, fear, and anything else you may ever reflect, even when they're present. Nothing sticks to the mirror."

"Yes, but . . . it doesn't *feel* that way. When bad things happen, I feel pain. If there's a fire in my village and people lose their homes, telling them that they're free and their grief is merely a reflected sensation won't ease their suffering. Telling suffering beings that they're free doesn't seem compassionate. Compassion requires me to house them, clothe them, feed them."

"It absolutely does. We always attend to the practical first. You and I are able to enjoy this conversation because we've had breakfast and aren't distracted by our rumbling bellies. But why is it that people don't feel free of their suffering, when in truth they are pure, untainted awareness that *is* free? Whether it's your widow or your fire victims, why does the mirror seem lost in the reflection and stained with its colors? Because the reflection is what we're in the habit of paying attention to. When you look in the mirror to check if your hat is on straight, you see the hat, not the mirror. Precisely because awareness is such a *good* mirror, with no cracks or discolorations, without even shape or edges, we see everything else and forget the mirror. Because it's perfectly empty, open, and clear, we don't see it."

"Then what can we do?" asks the seeker.

"We have to take time to see the mirror—to become aware of

awareness. Then, when we're called by the business of the world, when our action is required to help alleviate suffering, we can act even while remaining aware of awareness. We can act from freedom."

"But *how* do we become aware of awareness? How do we see the mirror?"

"There are two ways. One way is practice—meditation, where we allow all the objects that are reflected in the awareness-mirror to fade temporarily into the background of our attention, so that awareness itself comes to the foreground. As for the other . . . well, have you found that this conversation has made you a bit more aware of awareness? We've been using words, but we've been using them to point to something beyond words: wordless, thingless, silent, clear like a crystal, always present, always free. Do you find that you have some sharpened sense of that right now?"

The seeker begins to answer, but then stops. For a long time he gazes down at his hands, then slowly looks around the hut, as if seeing it for the first time—as if waking from a dream. Then he looks back at the sage. The seeker's gaze, which till now has been lowered, deferential, is steady. His posture has straightened—he sits tall, and a smile spreads across his face. "Yes. I do have that sharpened sense. Right now."

"This is the second way: view."

The seeker places his palms together and bows toward the sage. "Thank you so much, Teacher."

The sage smiles and bows back. "Thank *you*."

CHAPTER 34

November 9, 2016

It's just past dusk and I'm walking north on Lincoln Boulevard, eating the exhaust and staring down the headlight glare of rush-hour traffic. Last night Yaffa and I stayed up late watching the election returns on my laptop. I was complacent at first, telling her, as I had for months, that there was nothing to worry about. Then the North Carolina vote came in, and as the night went on we were confused, then shocked, disbelieving, angry, and, finally, very scared. A crude, reckless, ignorant thug had taken over our country by stirring hate and selling empty promises to suckers. Eventually we got three or four hours of broken sleep, then awoke much as we did the morning after 9/11. Did that really happen? Jesus God, it really did.

Lincoln Boulevard is beautiful Santa Monica's least beautiful street. It's the unloved but necessary street that most cities of a certain size have: gas stations and tire shops, McDonald's and 7-Eleven, budget dental clinics and discount clothing stores, notary publics and sad-looking little legal offices. Stinkin' Lincoln, they call it. Poor, sainted, martyred Abe. The last time we were this divided, the blue against the gray, he gave his life to heal us, and we thought we were healed. But the gray has risen again, bathed in its old blood. Now it's the red against the blue, and Lincoln is just an ugly street.

Our car blew some kind of pump a couple of days ago, and now I'm walking to the mechanic's shop to pick it up—in shirtsleeves because it's eighty degrees on this November evening, but hey, global warming is a Chinese hoax, so not to worry. Cars have their windows rolled down, and as I walk past a clot of them backed up at a traffic light, I see a red Mustang, driven by a buff young Hispanic guy, in buzzed hair and white T-shirt, a rap tune pounding from his sound system:

> *Fuck Donald Trump*
> *Yeah, yeah, fuck Donald Trump . . .*

I give him the clenched-fist power salute and he salutes back.

In 1997, Ram Dass was working on a book about conscious aging. The first draft came back from his editor with a note saying it was too glib, too superficial. That night, as he lay in bed wondering how to connect more intimately with the anguish of aging, he had a debilitating stroke. Talk about on the nose.

This is my stroke.

This is my plunge into fear: fear that the good times are over, that chaos is unleashed, that my children and grandchildren will be denied the happy life that I've had and which suddenly looks like fragile, improbable luck—luck that may now have run out. I feel gut-punched, like I've had the wind knocked out of me and may never get it back. I feel dread. Hulking, lurking dread.

Miguel is the sweet, sincere Mexican man who comes to clean our house once every two weeks. He's like family to us: when his younger daughter turned fifteen we attended her *quinceañera*, an elaborate celebration in a hopeful little banquet hall in a shabby part of town. It probably cost him a few months' salary, and through the whole thing he ran around so nervously, trying to make sure everything went right and everyone had a good time, that he never sat down to relax and enjoy it himself. He's smart, hardworking, and selfless. If he'd been born into different circumstances he'd be some kind of branch supervisor or district manager, conscientious and caring about everyone on his team. As it is, he cleans houses to make a better life for his daughters. The older one is at UCLA Medical School, and when he talks about her future he says, "That's the dream." I've never asked about his immigration status, but once he said, "Well, I did what I had to do for my family."

Today, the morning after the election, when Miguel arrived at our door with his vacuum cleaner and his buckets, he looked like a ghost. I told him, "I'm so sorry," and he said, "We'll move to Canada." For me and my white friends, that's been the idle, joking threat, but for him it's no joke.

I walk past the Jack in the Box, the dry cleaner, the Walgreens that always has a couple of junkies and homeless guys in the parking lot. Miguel's kids, my kids. I think, How do we protect them? How did this happen? How could so many people make a choice that's so stupidly, unnecessarily, catastrophically wrong? How could they put the steering wheel of the world in the hands of this angry drunk driver, with all our kids in the backseat? Gullible, ignorant yahoos. How many years will it take before they slap their thick foreheads, do their remedial reading, and figure out that he's broken his ridiculous promises and broken our only world? Too late, too late.

And then comes another thought. These last several years, up till last night, I've been quietly celebrating humane, progressive change in our society, like almost everyone I know here in the blue bubble of Santa Monica. But all this time, out in the red states, those same changes have made people fear for the future of *their* children, *their* grandchildren. I think they're wrong—in fact, I think they're backward and infuriatingly dim. I'll probably go on thinking it for the rest of this life, and they'll go on thinking I'm wrong. In our opinions we'll remain irreconcilably divided, red and blue.

But in our fear we're one. Some newscaster last night cited a survey saying that half of Republicans are afraid of Democrats and half of Democrats are afraid of Republicans. Gandhi said, "The enemy is fear. We think it is hate, but it is fear." Our fear divides us, but at the same time it strangely unites us. Their fear feels to them just like mine does to me. Once again: different people, different circumstances, same feeling. Could there be some dark Law of Conservation of Fear, which dictates that there must be a constant amount of it at all times, that it's never destroyed but just batted like a tennis ball, back and forth over the net of world affairs? Must we keep taking turns forever being resentful and scared? Does this never end? Are we chronically, terminally screwed?

I look to my left. In the western sky, shining above the ocean that I know is just a few blocks behind the car wash, I see the evening star: beautiful, brilliant Venus, named for the goddess of love. And as I do whenever I see her, I think of the Buddha and the story of his awakening—how, stricken by the universality of suffering, the chronic screwedness of human life, he left his father's palace, sought teachers, meditated, practiced austerities in the jungle, grew more frustrated, till finally he sat beneath a huge tree and vowed not to leave the spot till he found a solution, even if he had to sit till his blood and bones and flesh turned dry. After forty-nine days of struggle, after exhausting all his other moves, he finally stopped struggling. He let go and went into free fall, into what he had been all along—clear, simple, sublime, and, till that moment, somehow overlooked. Simple beingness itself, resting blissfully in itself. He gazed upon the morning star, as we call brilliant Venus when she rises in the east ahead of the sun, and he saw her as radiant as his own being was radiant, as all beings are radiant, even those not yet awake to their radiance. And he said, "How wonderful, how wonderful! All beings are enlightened just as they are."

Thanks to what my teachers and my practice have shown me, I know that's true. I'm still in the process of awakening, not a full-grown

Buddha—yet—but I'm enough of a junior varsity Buddha to know I know this. Even if I don't see it clearly in every moment, steady and luminous as tonight's evening star, I've had enough glimpses to have faith in its presence all the time, even when it's clouded over by crappy events like a disastrous election or by my own cloudy vision. Not belief, but faith—confidence, the conviction that arises from experience and requires no belief. I'm like an infant that has finally attained object permanence, when it knows that the toy is still there even when Mommy holds it behind her back.

There's nothing to do but keep practicing. It's the same thing I said after 9/11 and the same thing I said when Maggy died: all our spiritual practice, all our meditative practice—these times, when these catastrophes happen, are the times we've been practicing for.

Of course, I also have to keep working on the earth plane, as effectively as I can see how, for the changes I think will make the best possible world for my grandchildren and all those red state grandchildren. But keep practicing, to keep sharpening the vision of that star. And do the work I've stumbled into, which, through some incredible grace, is to help others see it.

So I have to get the car and go home and pack. I'm flying to Omaha in the morning to lead three days of meditation workshops. Shine my little light. Deep in red country. Ommmm . . . aha!

November 10

Hotel room in Omaha.

TV news: the President-elect meets the President in the White House. He sits on the edge of his seat, leaning forward awkwardly, unsure what to do with his hands, his eyes like saucers—and I realize, *He's terrified*. Of course. He's in this boat of fear with the rest of us. Like us, he's a vulnerable sentient being that has come unmoored from its own nature, frightened as it tosses on the waves, looking to land on something solid and sure. Now he's landed on what he thought would be the highest, driest rock in the world. But it won't help. He speaks some polite platitudes for the reporters, but his eyes say, *Oh, shit—what do I do now?*

Divided in roles, united in fear. None of this changes what I need to do and say as a citizen. But as I take whatever action I take, I need to remember this, remember and extend the tendrils of my compassion to him and you and all others, to feel our commonality. Remember.

And then I remember one more thing: my long-ago conversation with my prison group about That Guy, as in, "Everything would be fine if it weren't for That Guy," and our conclusion that That Guy, whoever he is in any moment, always brings you exactly the teaching you need, the seemingly intolerable situation that you must learn to be OK in the face of. That Guy is always your guru. Even this guy on the TV.

When Ram Dass talks about his stroke, he says he was "stroked by God." OK, Boss—bring it on.

CHAPTER 35

The Magic Piano

Fun fact:

On most pianos, the soundboard—the curved plank under the strings that amplifies their faint vibrations—is too short to resonate with the bottom octave. It's physically incapable of sounding those low notes down at the left end of the keyboard. Yet we hear them. How?

Every note has overtones—a cloud of fainter, higher notes hovering above it and giving it "color." The soundboard does vibrate the overtones for each missing low note, and when we hear them our brain *infers* the note that should underlie them; our neurons fire at the right frequency to produce the experience of the bass note that the piano doesn't make. No tree falls in the forest but we're there to hear it, so it makes a sound.

If the mind can make piano notes, what else might it be making? How much of the world we think we live in is just the world we think? It's as if we see concentric ripples spreading outward from a point on the surface of a pond, and we mentally create the pebble that should have been, must have been, wasn't tossed there.

This is certainly true of many of our fear scenarios. One June, back in my high school teaching days, a just-graduated senior came to visit me at home. As I poured tea, he struggled for a good hour or more to come out to me. This was clearly as hard for him as walking through a wall, and I felt honored to be the one he felt safe with. But for years, the whole school had tacitly assumed he was gay. Everyone knew, and everyone knew that everyone knew, except him. At last he wrenched out his tearful confession. Then, as we talked about his years of sneaking and faking, it gradually sank in that he had spent his whole high school career worrying about revealing a dark secret that was a secret to no one. He'd been dancing his dance of dread to the overtones of a nonexistent note. As he stood at the door to leave, he laughed and said, "Gee—now I'll have to find something else to be neurotic about."

As in this case, the more emotion we attach to the thing we imagine, the more real it seems. The energy of intense feeling fuels the brain's powers of magic conjuring, as successful salespeople and politicians know. Perhaps you've dreamed that you were in a heated argument with a friend, and when you woke up it took a minute to sort things out and convince yourself not to pick up the phone and yell at him.

Or perhaps you've been convinced that your partner has thoughtlessly slighted you, and as you brooded on it you got more and more steamed, till you finally spoke up . . . and found out it was all a misunderstanding. Oddly, if that anger is strong enough, when the truth comes out you may feel a little deflated. You've invested so much emotional energy in writing that scene, casting yourself as the noble injured party and your partner as the callous tormentor, that it's a letdown when the show is suddenly canceled. This is one reason that marriage is such a fine laboratory for awakening—you get so many opportunities to believe something passionately, only to have it flame out before your eyes, and then see what's left when the smoke clears. Fooled me again! Hopefully, you and your partner have a good laugh and remember some of this for next time, when the roles are reversed.

The Deepest Note

After we've had enough such experiences, we may find ourselves led to a question:

Could there be some *fundamental* false inference at the root of *all* our self-inflicted drama; some deepest silent piano note, way down at the very end of the keyboard, underlying all our crazy overtones; something that seems really, really real, as real as it gets, deserving of all the emotional investment we can possibly give it, but which is ultimately as insubstantial as a dream? You already know the answer. If what we most deeply are is empty, open, mirrorlike awareness, boundless like the sky, then we're not the separate, isolated self that we take ourselves to be. The separate self is the deepest false note, and it's where all the trouble starts.

We've heard the sages' reports that the separate self, a.k.a. the person, has no substantial existence. It's not a thing, not a hunk of stuff. *Person* comes from the Greek *persona*, "mask," implying that it's not what we are but something we look out through. Behind the mask, peeking out through the eyeholes, what are we? If it's yet another person, another thing, then we'll have to ask what looks through *its* eyeholes, and so forth, in an infinite regress of Russian dolls within dolls—an absurdity. That leaves the possibility that we're not a person or thing at all, not a hunk of stuff that *has* awareness, but awareness itself—open, formless, free. If that turns out to be true, confirmed by our own experience, then it changes everything.

Then all the roles we've imagined for this person are just roles—roles to play while wearing our mask, overtones that imply the absent fundamental tone. They're things that we do, feel, think, but not what we are. So . . .

You're not your name.

You're not your family, your nationality, your culture, your religion.

You're not a husband, wife, mother, father, son, daughter, brother, sister.

You're not the team whose name is on your cap or T-shirt.

You're not your income.

You're not your place on the A, B, or Z list.

You're not your sex appeal.

You're not your career.

You're not your car.

You're not your résumé or your press release.

You're not your diploma, even if it's from Harvard.

You're not your neurosis.

You're not your diagnosis.

You're not your lifestyle.

You're not your addiction or your sobriety.

You're not a timeline.

You're not a long story wending its way toward a happy or tragic ending.

You're not your self-image or anybody else's image.

You're not a race, gender, or age.

You're not your personality.

You're not your attitude.

You're not your aesthetic gesture.

You're not your thoughts, your words, your deeds, or their impact.

You're not the summary bit of wisdom you imagine carved on your tombstone, or the first sentence you imagine in your Wikipedia article.

The list could go on. At one time or another you may have vaguely subscribed to most of these versions of what you might be: in the course of a day, you might rotate through several of them so seamlessly that you don't even realize you're rotating. Yet many of these definitions are mutually exclusive, so they can't all be true. Once we start imagining identities for ourselves, we can imagine anything.

So what? Why does this matter?

It matters because the separate self that you think you are is the one that suffers—the one to which fear, anger, anxiety, and craving stick. Because these roles are just big clusters of thoughts and feelings, it's easy for more feelings to stick to them. What you *are* is mirrorlike awareness, to which nothing sticks. When you say, *"I'm* afraid," you're talking about the personal self. If it's really just a false inference, a will-o'-the-wisp, then there's no one there to suffer. In one deft yank, we've pulled the rug out from under all your afflictions.

This doesn't mean we've gone all starry-eyed about life. There are still muggers and Mack trucks to dodge, flat tires on the freeway and hay fever in the spring, and there always will be. Shit happens. But the personal self is the one that shit happens *to*. If it's a construct, then we can deconstruct it and abide as pure, open, aware space, and the stuff all goes right through us. The old texts say that, for the unawakened being, the traumas of life are like lines carved in rock. For the one who has awakened, they're like lines carved in water.

And in fact this is exactly what you've been practicing every time you sit to meditate. Your fundamental instruction is, "Rest as awareness." Not just rest *in* awareness, not just be a person relaxing your grip and sinking gently into the silent ocean beneath the waves of thoughts, feelings, and sensations. But rest *as* awareness. Be, or, rather, notice that you are and always have been, the silent ocean—gracious host to the waves but never stirred by them. In time, that state of affairs spontaneously grows clear, both in and out of meditation.

The A/B Test

Here's one more way to play with this insight, to help awaken during our nonmeditating hours:

For just one day be on the alert, and note what versions of the separate self you trot out to invest your identity in: *Now I'm this role, I'm this body, I'm this hip attitude, I'm this sad or happy story*. We're like a coach putting players in the game: "Get in there, Romantic Melancholy, I know you can do it!" Don't try to stop this process of identification—just observe it as clearly as you can. Note every time you define your self, defend your self, prop up your self, inflate or deflate your self, justify your self. Note what all that *feels* like. Does it feel clear, mature, emotionally intelligent? Or petty, or grandiose, or both?

The next day, observe things in the same way, but don't be a self. Every time you observe yourself identifying with or propping up some version of personal selfhood, relax your grip on it. (Frankie says: Relax, don't do it.) Unclench your grip and relax back into simple, open awareness. Anytime a temptation to justify or glorify the little self comes up, throw it into the fire. And see what *that* feels like. Also, note how others respond when you come from this place of fresh openness.

If necessary, keep alternating days like this till you get the point and see how icky separate selfhood feels. You'll probably notice that it's like eating big quantities of blue cotton candy—you remember it having delighted you once upon a time in a state of lesser maturity, but now it gives you a stomachache.

Also notice which makes you busier: being a separate self or being free. At first the old way may seem easier because you've had so much practice. It takes some vigilance to notice it and drop it. But that's only because the old habit is ingrained. Free, open awareness, to spin one more simile, is like a vast, open plain, stretching on all sides to a clear horizon, under a cloudless, sparkling sky. The separate self, with all its busy stories and gestures, is like an amusement park built over the plain. It has plenty of entertaining features, but it's a lot of work keeping them all going: the Tilt-A-Whirl, the haunted house, the hot dog stands, the games of skill with their crappy prizes. Let's face it, it's pretty sleazy. *But I like the amusement park.* Sure you do. It's amusing. But not to worry. Nobody's going to take it away from you. All that changes is that you're no longer a prisoner of it, no longer invested in the belief that you *are* it, no longer stuck with its endless maintenance. Being a person is hard work. Being being is no work.

You relax as the open plain (rest as awareness), and it becomes clearer and clearer that the park runs itself. With greater maturity of consciousness, you may lose interest in a few of the rides: maybe you don't really need to go through the haunted house a ten thousandth time. Then they fade away like a dream, which is what they've been all along.

CHAPTER 36

Lord Shiva Kicks Ass

Let's talk about loss.

When you're hit by loss—you lose your job, you lose your spouse, you lose your health, you lose your cherished dream—it can be devastating. You can feel as if things have gone so utterly and hopelessly wrong that they'll never be right again. You can feel that the good times, the happy times, are now past, never to be revived, that joy has gone out of your life for good. If you're lucky, you have people around to encourage you, to reassure you that things will get better. It's all very sweet and sincere. You don't need me to be one more hopeful voice. Instead, let's pause for a moment and listen to the voice that we try to ignore . . . the one that says, *Hey—maybe things* won't *get better.*

And maybe they won't. Maybe you won't get a new job, recoup the value of your 401(k), or save your house from the repo man. Maybe your beloved country won't be rescued from the thugs who've seized power. Maybe you won't find a new partner who's sweet and understanding. Maybe you won't find a new partner at all. We don't know what you'll find. We do know what you'll lose: everything, sooner or later. On the day you die, if not before, you'll lose your partner, your job, your car, your house, your money, your country, your family, your body, and your mind.

It's always been this way and always will. Only rare, lovely little islands of relative comfort and tranquillity distract us from this fundamental human predicament. One such island was enjoyed for the last several decades by Americans with enough money and the right complexion, but every island eventually fades over the horizon, and then we're back in this same leaking boat, bailing water as fast as we can.

Yet a few people—Christ, Buddha, Al-Hallaj, Shankara, and assorted other sages—remain unperturbed. All along, they've told us not to invest our happiness in the impermanent. Just before his death, the Buddha said:

All constructed things must deconstruct.

He wasn't just warning us not to make some shaky start-up dreamer or Ponzi schemer the captain of our souls, or pointing out that every marriage ends in divorce or death. He was going more hard core than that, anticipating the Second Law of Thermodynamics, which describes how, over time, the neat arrangements of molecules that make up our universe must inevitably fly apart into messy chaos. Everything that's been put together—your house, your body, the Mona Lisa, your favorite shirt, your favorite planet—must eventually fall apart. Someday, as Charlton Heston discovers in *Planet of the Apes*, the Statue of Liberty will be just a bit of wreckage on the beach. It's pure, inescapable physics.

So why are the sages unperturbed? What can we learn from them? In the face of universal destruction, how can we fear less?

In 1688, the wealthy samurai poet Masahide lost all his possessions when his storage barn was destroyed in a fire. He responded by writing a haiku:

Barn's burnt down:
now I can see
the moon

We build up our career and our marriage, we store our treasures in our barn or in our stock portfolio or on our hard drive, and then they consume our attention. When they crash, it's a time of pain, but it can also be a time of vision. It's an opportunity to notice the underlying luminous nature of existence itself—Masahide's moon—which has been there all along. When everything that's material dematerializes, when everything perishable perishes, it's a chance to see what's immaterial and imperishable. Three hundred years after Masahide, a famous actor lost his Malibu house in a fire and commented, "It was so liberating." A dozen years after the Monica Lewinsky scandal, Bill Clinton told an interviewer, "Once you've been publicly humiliated like I was, it doesn't much matter what people ever say about you again for the rest of your life. And it's kind of liberating."

The Buddha spoke one more sentence before he died:

Through diligent seeing, be liberated.

Jesus said:

Lay not up for yourselves treasures upon earth, where moth and rust corrupt, and where thieves break through and steal. Lay up for yourselves treasures in heaven, where neither moth nor rust corrupt, and where thieves do not break through nor steal.

Clearly all our earthly treasures are doomed to slip through our fingers. But what are "treasures in heaven"? This heaven business can sound like some fairy-tale, Sunday school, Hollywood ending to our tragedy of loss, some opium-of-the-people pie in the sky when you die, until we remember that Jesus himself stated clearly that the kingdom of heaven is not on some postmortem cloud but within you.

He's even more to the point in the Gospel of Thomas, one of the Gospels that didn't make the cut—its teachings are so radical that it was buried in the sand and not recovered till 1945. There he says:

> The kingdom of the Father is spread out upon the earth, and people don't see it.

That kingdom, that luminous reality—the essential, liberative radiance of just being—is what we're walking around in right now. If we can relax and pay attention to it for even a moment, if we can just take a break from being hypnotized by our usual compulsive accumulation, that luminosity starts, even if only faintly, to come into focus. And if you make that attention a habit, the focus becomes clearer and clearer.

After Maggy and I finished raising our kids, we downsized and bought the charming little Tudor cottage of our dreams. She supervised some tasteful remodeling, I hauled in our books, we set up the grill on the patio and the cushions in the meditation room. The month we moved in, she was diagnosed with terminal cancer.

That night, I drove home from the hospital to the new house, which I could now barely stand to look at, sat on the front lawn, and howled and wept into the sky. She died six months later, and the life together that we had imagined was gone. The months after that were hard. The first time the reality of her gone-ness really hit me was at the A&P, when I found myself grocery shopping for one. I soon stopped going to that store—they always seemed to be piping in tragic love songs. I'd be picking out lettuce or bananas, and it would take all the willpower I could summon to make it out of the produce section without collapsing in tears.

But there was also something very precious about that time. The burning of that barn of imagination showed me the luminous moon of actuality. Where our marriage had been, there was now an empty space that I could have called loneliness or desolation. But I didn't call it anything, and by leaving it unlabeled I could experience it as just space, and in that there was great liberation. It helped that I had years of meditation under my belt. After she died, I wrote a haiku of my own:

> *My heart*
> *is broken*
> *open*

Maggy had years of practice and view under her belt as well. Once, she looked up from her hospital bed and asked me, "How do people who don't meditate deal with this?"

I shrugged: "I don't know." Her dying was her final exam, and she got an A. Two weeks or so before she passed, a friend called, excited, offering to bring some Tibetan monks to her room to do some special chanting for her. She said, "No, that wouldn't be authentic for me. That hasn't been my practice. My practice is just being without hope or fear."

That's a steep teaching. Everyone wants to get rid of fear and hold on to hope. "Keep hope alive," we tell each other and ourselves. We can make that work up to a point, but finally we have to recognize that fear is hope's flip side. They're both ways of betting our happiness on a particular outcome, of requiring that outcome for life to be OK. We can't invest our happiness in the hope of winning the game, the lottery, the election without buying the corresponding fear of losing. But what if we let go of both hope and fear? What would that be like? How would that freedom taste? And if that freedom sounds enticing, why wait till cancer or some other inescapable catastrophe pushes you to the wall before you open to it?

Consider the wind. The wind is nature's gardener, expertly pruning the trees. Every leaf falls exactly on time. Anything that *can* shake off *will* shake off, and, to the extent that there's such a thing as *should*, it should shake off. The tree also falls exactly on time. The only thing that makes any of this tragic is our concept of the tree as something with just those leaves in just those places, forever. That has never happened with anything, for anyone, anywhere. Persistence in the illusion of things or people or situations that will eternally conform to our preferences is a definition of immaturity and a recipe for anguish. When you choose maturity, you choose to spare yourself that agony.

In the Hindu trinity, Brahma is the creator, Vishnu the preserver, and Shiva the dissolver. Everything goes through the cycle of creation–preservation–dissolution: the budding, blossoming, and withering of a flower; the rise, peak, and fall of a civilization; the emergence, evolution, and destruction of a galaxy. The last phase is always just as necessary and right as the other two. Lord Shiva is the last one out of the building, the one who turns off the lights, who rings down the curtain and writes THE END. By embracing him, we undercut our own ability to cry, "Wait! No! This is a mistake!" In every cycle of existence, dissolution is the phase that's most conducive to awakening. In fact, Shiva is also the liberator. He turns off the lights, but he turns on the Light.

Dissolution sounds a lot like *disillusion*, and that, as the saying goes, is too much of a coincidence to be a coincidence. Usually we think of disillusionment as a bad thing, but why is being relieved of illusions bad? It's all Lord Shiva kicking our ass, kicking over our meticulously constructed castles of sand, mercifully kicking us awake from our dreams of endless empires and Ponzi economies and frozen effigies of our lovers, kicking us awake to the clear light of being, of awareness, now. Yes, it's true that the death of what we have known and loved best feels like the end of the world. But it's also true that the liberation that offers itself to us in that tender, vulnerable time of loss is proportional to our devastation.

At the end of the world, Lord Shiva dances. His kicking is part of his dance, and as he dances he holds up his right hand, palm forward, in the *abhaya mudra*, the universal gesture that means, "Be at peace. All is well. Fear not."

CHAPTER 37

Fear of the Lord

The comedian Adam Ferrara summarizes his Catholic upbringing in four words. Stretching out his arms like Jesus on the cross, his eyes glaring with reproach, he snaps, "I'm dead. Your fault."

But Catholics don't have a monopoly on spirituality served up with a couple of big scoops of guilt, shame, and/or fear. The school in New Jersey where I used to teach was founded in the nineteenth century by a Presbyterian minister, the Reverend Dr. John F. Pingry. Upstairs in the library, where generations of pubescent scholars have studied French, chemistry, and the cutie at the next table, hangs a large, heavily varnished oak plank, inscribed with Dr. Pingry's motto, from the Book of Psalms: THE FEAR OF THE LORD IS THE BEGINNING OF WISDOM. Cheers, everyone! I remember a skeptical science teacher once rolling his eyes at the plank and quietly sharing his own theory of religion: "The fear of wisdom is the beginning of the Lord." (Just for the record, there's also a block of granite behind the building, inscribed DR. PINGRY USED TO STAND ON THIS STONE TO MOUNT HIS HORSE.)

Westerners who turn to Eastern religions to escape fear-based spirituality are sometimes dismayed to discover that Hinduism and Buddhism, at least in their most old-school forms, have not just one but dozens of hell realms, as painstakingly customized as anything dreamed up by Dante. Commit certain sexual infractions and you can wind up dog-paddling in a river of semen, feces, and animal guts. Namaste! In some of the old pictures of these creative torture salons, the punishments are carried out by horned, bat-winged devils that look all too familiar to Westerners. At least these hells are not eternal; you spend a few eons there till you burn off your bad karma, then come back to the human realm to give it another try.

Judaism is probably the religion that has dodged these terrors most successfully, just by being vague. Ask the next five Jews you meet what their religion teaches about the afterlife and you'll probably get five shrugs. But even if you don't subscribe to any hellfire scenarios, you may still be affected by them in ways you don't realize. The Protestants who founded American society believed that worldly success was a sign that you were among God's elect. The poor, after a lifetime of deprivation, could look forward to an eternity in hell, and it was embarrassingly obvious to all the neighbors who the once-and-future losers were. This is the historical root of our famous Protestant work ethic; our compulsive busy-ness is driven by shame and fear.

Fear was injected even deeper into our legacy during the First Great Awakening, the revival movement that transformed Colonial-era church services from solemn, tedious rituals to get-down doomsday sermonizing. It was so effective at scaring the bejesus into people that congregants would weep, writhe, or faint, and in some cases commit suicide. One of the most prominent preachers of the era was Jonathan Edwards, known for such sermons as his 1741 greatest hit, "Sinners in the Hands of an Angry God":

> The God that holds you over the Pit of Hell, much as one holds
> a Spider or some loathsome Insect over the Fire, abhors you,
> and is dreadfully provoked; his Wrath towards you burns like
> Fire; he looks upon you as worthy of nothing else but to be

cast into the Fire . . . God will be so far from pitying you when
you cry to him that 'tis said he will only Laugh and Mock.

Certainly this kind of punitive God is useful for crowd control. When
you're trying to form a coherent society in a wilderness, whether it's
the deserts of the Sinai or the forests of the New World, a scary God
keeps us in line, so we can live side by side without killing anyone
(except witches and Indians). That kind of religion requires ritual as
well as hierarchy, so we can practice obedience: make your request in
the prescribed way, take two steps to the left, don't ask for bread, and
if you screw it up, God shouts, "No grace for you!"

These days, thankfully, the Soup Nazi God has yielded much of
the stage to a kinder, gentler God, with kinder, gentler devotees. We
have contemporary religious commentators like Kimberly Winston,
who has written:

If the concept of God has any use, it is to make us larger, freer,
and more loving. If God can't do that, it's time we got rid
of him.

There's plenty of material to support both views. Some revisionist
interpreters nowadays even spin the words "fear of the Lord" as "awe
of the Lord" or "reverence for the Lord." That goes down a lot easier,
but unfortunately the original Hebrew word *yirat* clearly means "fear."
And right or wrong, the hellfire guys were the fathers of our country.
They're in our national DNA—Jonathan Edwards had eleven children,
and his descendants included thirteen college presidents, each in a
position to influence the thinking of thousands. Even if you feel personally immune to this stuff, it echoes in our cultural memory. It's
worth trying to sort it out.

So . . . is God a mean guy, justifying your worst fears? Or a nice guy, another good reason to relax? Is God a stern parent ("When your father gets home, you're in big trouble") or a soft, pliable parent ("Time for cookies and milk")? Most religions offer, in some form, both of those answers, because both modes of being are so basic to human life. Some offer way more than two. The answers in Hinduism, like everything in Hinduism, are especially rich and varied. There are dozens of mother goddesses alone, from gentle, nurturing Lakshmi, who stands on a lotus, floating on a tranquil lake, with gold coins pouring out of her hand, to fierce Kali Ma, with wild hair, ferocious eyes, and protruding tongue, wielding fearsome weapons, clothed in severed arms and heads. Sometimes we need a fierce mom to protect us.

But wait. There's something wrong with this whole line of questioning. We've already discovered that when we look for the person that *we* allegedly are—the daughter, the salesman, the jokester, the seeker—it deconstructs before our eyes. What's left in its place is awareness, beingness, conscious open space, without boundaries. So, is God a cuddly person or a prickly person? None of the above. If little old me is nonpersonal boundlessness, certainly great big God must be nonpersonal boundlessness as well.

The personal God is the projection of the personal, separate self. It's what infinity looks like when you look as a person. When we look up at God (or look up *for* God), as long as we're looking through the distorting lens of the person we think we are, we'll see a person. Once we remove that lens, the sky above us is clear. There's no one up there to fear and no one down here to fear him.

Thus our pictures of God (who warns us in the Commandments not to picture him) may really be selfies—images of the self we think we are, with all its charming and alarming traits, projected onto a giant screen in the sky, where we can view them more clearly, watch them collectively, and see how they play out. In that sense, religions are like epic superhero movies. If the film is going to sell tickets, the protagonist must be both Man—ordinary, moody, Clark Kent-ish, so we can identify with him—and Super, so he can take us to infinity and beyond.

These movies can be inspiring, terrifying, or baffling, to express the full spectrum of human life in all its most inspiring, terrifying, and baffling aspects. But it may be time to cull our playlist. Once upon a time, the horror movie God—the Freddy Krueger God—could do only limited damage. But now that we have drones, computers, and WMDs to carry out his will, he threatens our survival. Again, here's Adam Ferrara, ranting in a sarcastic snarl that sounds somewhere between Jackie Gleason and Bugs Bunny:

> God's gonna get us all killed. Terrorists convince thousands of people to kill themselves in the name of God. I can't convince two of my friends to help me move. And I think human arrogance will be the demise of civilization. Look, if you think God is talking to you, and you understand God, and God needs you to kill somebody else for him—if that's what you truly feel—just sit down till that feeling goes away. 'Cause I'm fairly certain if God wants somebody dead, that guy is dead, OK? He don't need you—he's got the key to the lightning cabinet. So just settle down, you arrogant, finite, carbon-based life form.

No one can tell you what to think or feel or do about God, but I think most of us can agree it's time to kiss the old Divine Boogeyman goodbye and good riddance. No eternal tormentor to inspire our fear, no righteous warrior to justify our anger, no masturbation monitor to ensure our anxiety. But where do we go from there? Some people will go with no God—"above us only sky," as John Lennon sang in "Imagine." Some will go with a loving God, perhaps with wonderful results. (I have evangelical Christian friends whose good works in saving African children from starvation put my laziness to shame.) But there's another possibility. You've heard it, but you may not have *heard* it:

God is love.

Not lov*ing*. This is not just the angry old man in the sky upgraded to a mellow old man in the sky. God is *love*, not someone or something that loves. But how can God be a human emotion, a feeling? It can't. We cited earlier these words from Rupert Spira:

Love is not a feeling; it's lack of an other, of otherness.

We'll be exploring this notion further. But for now, if there's something that speaks to you in these two assertions—that God is love and love is non-otherness—perhaps just let them float gently somewhere inside you. Don't necessarily even think about them. Just let them mix in the test tube of your heart and see what chemical reaction takes place.

It might turn out that the fear of the Lord *is* the beginning of wisdom, but only the beginning. The end of wisdom—the goal, the culmination, the end point, the end of the story—might be love.

CHAPTER 38

Valley of the Shadow

I was scared to death of death.

I was seven years old when I realized I was going to die. *I was going to die.* This was not an encyclopedia topic, this was not a school report, this was not those hungry children in Africa guilting me into cleaning my plate, this was not cowboys on *Gunsmoke* or pioneers on *Wagon Train* clutching their strangely bloodless gunshot wounds, going limp, and now a word from our sponsor. This was Dean, me, this kid right here, sweating in my bed, imagining a forgotten grave under a lonely tree, with oblivious strangers strolling six feet above my head, as if I had never existed, forever.

My parents were more or less atheists, with no spiritual reassurance to offer. Eventually I saw that as a blessing, as it spurred my search and left me free to embark on it without a lot of baggage. But that was later. And a religious rationale might not have helped anyway. I also learned later that even the people who believe that they believe in some kind of heaven in the sky will often force-march their poor, spent bodies through every last-ditch medical intervention. I think most people, regardless of their alleged creed, are haunted by the same fear that gripped me at seven. To get through the day not paralyzed by that fear, we've perfected the art of looking away from it, just as we look away from the glare of the sun, so habitually that we forget we're doing it.

That's a glaring omission. If we're going to deal with this thing, we at least have to acknowledge it. Once, in Rehoboth Beach, Delaware, I saw a seagull swoop overhead, on its way from the ocean to a nearby grove, with a big fish wriggling desperately in its beak. I wondered if—and hoped that—for at least one moment, as the fish soared through that incomprehensibly wide-open dimension of sky, it looked around and thought, *Wow—I'm flying! Far out!*

When our culture does consider death, it often gets things wrong, sometimes spectacularly wrong, as in Dylan Thomas's "Do Not Go Gentle Into That Good Night," in which he urges his dying father to furiously resist what he calls "the dying of the light." This is good, rousing poetry, but it's very bad advice. This is calling for courage, rather than serenity, to address the one thing we definitely can't change. Talk about using the wrong tool for the job—talk about flunking the final exam! We can file this poem under SWAGGERING OBSTINACY, along with that damned "Invictus":

> *My head is bloody. but unbowed.*

Yeah, that's what happens when you keep slamming your head into things.

Slamming your head into things also keeps you from seeing clearly. When we finally relax out of those doomed heroics and pay attention, we have a chance to see what the sages saw, the reality that let them face death without fear, rage, evasion, or macho posturing: The light does not die. Whatever dies is not the light. You are not what dies. *You are the light of the world*—the light of awareness, which shines for a time through this form, this person, like light shining through a window, and does not cease shining when the window breaks.

Unlike our poets, you know this firsthand. You've experienced it many times. Every time you meditate, you're rehearsing for the time of dying. The world dissolves, the body dissolves, the senses and their objects dissolve, thinking and emoting and behaving dissolve, space and time dissolve. You relax your grip, everything dissolves, and you find out that when everything dissolves there's nothing to fear. Every *thing* dissolves—all the objects that have been dancing in the light, including the body—leaving only you, the awareness, the light.

Notice that I said *time of dying*, not *time of death*. There's no such thing as an experience of death—it's not an experienceable reality. *Death* is a concept that can only be conceived by the living. When they say, "Bob's been dead for six years," they're applying the concept of time to the absence of Bob's body from this world. That makes sense from their point of view. But from Bob's point of view, when he dies time dissolves, the world dissolves, the body dissolves, and "Bob," the person-concept he thought he was for a while, dissolves. All dissolve into timeless, worldless, bodiless, Bobless awareness.

This is the confusion I labored under as I tossed and turned at age seven. I was imagining Dean's "death" from the point of view of Dean living. The years and years (time) of lying six feet (space) under the earth (world) hold terrors only for the one thinking about it (mind). It has nothing to do with one who has dropped out of time, space, world, and mind. Thus the great fear, as expressed in Psalm 23, is not *the valley of death* but *the valley of the shadow of death*. The problem is not the actual, experienced reality but the shadow of fear it casts across the mind. And even shadows can be cast only because there is light.

The Lord is my shepherd, the psalm begins. We've already considered that the Lord is not a big angry guy or even a big nice guy, but that God is love—and love is not an emotion but non-otherness, non-separateness.

The Lord is beingness without boundary or limit. And *that* Lord safely leads the way, like a good shepherd, as long as I remain like a lamb: innocent, simple. That's a perfect description of natural meditation, where we abandon our efforts and strategies, stop pushing, and innocently allow ourselves to be pulled by the universal gravitation toward the delicious silence at the core of being, a.k.a. the Lord's mercy. Then the settling down of the turbulent mind happens all by itself: *He leadeth me beside the still waters.* And then we discover that we're not confined to the time-bound, space-bound, mind-and-body-bound separate self we thought we were. That vessel can't contain us: *My cup runneth over.*

The small self we think we are is like a whirlpool in a river. It never has a solid, separate existence. It's always nothing but river. One day the whirlpool dissolves, but nothing has gone anywhere, no water is lost. (No water was harmed in the making of this movie.) It has just runneth over into the river. The other little whirlpools say, "Hey, where's Bob? Gee, I'm gonna miss that guy." But Bob is not grieving. What *was* Bob is saying, if anything, "Wheeeeeee! I'm free-flowing water! Boy, it's great to be out of those tight clothes!" It's not that Bob's friends are wrong. Of course, from the point of view of the living—the world of forms—when a form that we love dissolves, we feel desolated.

But even in your desolation you may quietly notice that there's something precious and beautiful about the time of grieving. There's something about it that's a privilege. You get to grieve because you love, because you're a party to non-otherness. For you and the loved one, there's a sense of not-two, a sense of I-and-I, so it's natural to feel that something has been ripped away from you. But with a little quiet attention, it's also natural to notice that, because you're non-separate, nothing can be ripped from anything. Your love connection with the one who has dissolved beyond time and space allows you, on some level, to dissolve with them, to follow them into boundlessness. Every time you close your eyes and to some degree melt into simple beingness, you're melting into exactly where and exactly what your loved one is, which is exactly what *you* are—the one river. You may not even have to close your eyes. On the morning that Maggy died, the e-mail I sent out to our friends was headed NOW SHE IS EVERYWHERE.

In 1950, when Sri Ramana Maharshi was dying of cancer, his grieving disciples pleaded with him to heal himself. Calling him Bhagavan, "blessed one," they begged, "Please, Bhagavan, don't leave us! Don't go!" Ramana replied:

> They take this body for Bhagavan and attribute suffering to him. What a pity! They are despondent that Bhagavan is going to leave them and go away. Where can he go, and how?

Downriver

There's one more part of this picture to consider. After a whirlpool dissolves, what if its residual energy—its swirling momentum—persists for a while unseen, as an invisible, subsurface current? Then, somewhere farther downriver, that current takes form as a new whirlpool . . . or should we say it's the old whirlpool in a new form? This old-new whirlpool will keep popping up again and again in different forms, to continue its adventures and its evolution over a larger scale than a single lifetime allows.

As Ngak'chang Rinpoche, a lama I used to study with, once explained it, "If we're smart enough to recycle our cans and bottles, shouldn't the universe be smart enough to recycle us?" The engine that drives our every action is the desire for happiness. The whole universe of phenomena is engaged in the effort (actually *is* the effort) to perfectly realize its own essence, which is beingness, perfect happiness, *ahhhhhhh*. It can do that far more efficiently if it doesn't have to start from scratch with every being every time.

And so, it is said, the universe is like a school. You finish your freshman year in June, and then you're not seen on campus for a while. When you come back in September for your sophomore year, are you the same person who left in June? Kind of yes, kind of no. If you have an especially bad year you can be held back, and if you have an especially good year you might skip a grade. When finally you learn what the whole thing was about—when you wake up to the infinite OK-ness that's the essence of the universe in which you've been studying—you're done, you graduate, and you don't have to keep coming back. The Buddha, as he sat meditating through the night in the hours before his final liberation, is supposed to have clearly seen all his previous births, seen how they all led perfectly and inevitably to that moment. Many people have more fragmentary memories of previous go-rounds; you may have had some yourself and not recognized them as such.

If this sounds like Fantasyland to you, that's fine. If it works that way, it works that way, and if it doesn't, it doesn't. But for some people, especially those who've had a lot of confusion or frustration in this life, it can be helpful to know that it may all be part of a bigger picture. It's like having a bad hair day: tomorrow will be better. Those who have found themselves completely overwhelmed or baffled by human society may just be relatively new to being human. As they approach the end of this life, rather than think they blew their only chance and feel bitter about what they didn't accomplish, they can just know that they're the new kid in school: they'll be more comfortable next term. We're all on a long, unwinding road. When it runs into a big rock, it may dead-end for a while or even go backward, but only far enough to get around the rock.

Each rebirth, we could say, is like a chapter in a long novel, with lots of characters and complex, interwoven plotlines. A character who is your enemy in one chapter might disappear for a while, then come back as, say, your best friend or your spouse—whatever it takes to advance the project of unfolding your heart, your recognition of the non-otherness of others. One chapter might be set in the countryside, one in a prison. Some chapters might be filled with ease and romance, some with misery. But when we get to the end of the book, we realize (as the Buddha did that night) that everything was part of the story, and happened exactly as it had to happen. Nothing was a mistake. It was a great read.

And the moral of the story is to keep opening. The simplest, most direct way to do that is to always be kinder than necessary. And keep meditating, relaxing out of the rigid borders of small selfhood—the body, the thoughts, the emotions, all the life-circumstances—and into the big freedom of what you are, the big river of what we all are together. It becomes more and more obviously the open space in which you live every moment, which you *are* every moment. Then you live in joy, and when it's time for this body to drop away, it's obvious that there's nothing to fear. In a universe of non-otherness, the plunge into the Great Unknown turns out to be a reunion with yourself.

This Way Out

No matter how this lifetime/chapter of the adventure has gone for you, and no matter whether you suspect there's a next one or not, the traditions generally agree that the end of a chapter, far from being a calamity, is an especially opportune time to open into joy and freedom. In case we haven't already found the space of perfect OK-ness by the end of life, that blank bit at the bottom of the last page of each chapter gives us a peek at the perfectly pure, white, unspoiled paper that has underlain the whole story all along.

As we've seen, our core practice of resting as awareness is a perfect way to just be while dying happens. But for those who feel drawn to them and ready for them, there are also powerful meditative breathing techniques that can help ensure a clean, blissful, expansive exit. You'll most definitely want to practice the drill before the fire, which can come anytime but is guaranteed to come sometime. You do have to find out where the fire escape is, and for that you have to go up to the roof.

Imagine-feel your in-breath to begin at the bottom of your feet and travel all the way up your legs and spine to the inside of the top of your skull. (Or, instead of the feet, you can start at the base of the spine, especially if you're sitting cross-legged.) Use the ujjayi constriction at the back of the throat, and breathe slowly and fully. At the end of the in-breath, remain for a little while, feeling the breath-energy still at the inside of the top of the skull, pressing against it. Then, as you breathe out, feel the breath-energy bursting through the top of your skull and shooting out like a fountain, going out and out in all directions into endless space. Then start the next in-breath.

At first you may feel more or less identified with the body, and the breath-energy may feel like something moving through you and bursting out of you. But after a while you're more identified with the breath-energy moving through the body and through space. Finally you're just space. The body is something you've left far behind you. You've gone over the rainbow, high above the spinal chimney top, where the troubles of the body and world melt like lemon drops.

Actually, you can do this with any breath, anytime. You can do it as you're falling asleep, which, as the waking world fades from view, is a lot like dying. But in every moment you're dying out of the old, being reborn into the new. Just get with it . . . breathe with it . . . it's all good. The Cat in the Hat says, "It is fun to have fun but you have to know how." My wife, speaking from over the rainbow, way up high, says, "It's all fun as far as I can tell."

By the Book

Traditional societies have often had some form of how-to manual that is narrated or sung to the dying person. That is, the *acutely* dying person. Ngak'chang Rinpoche was once invited to come to a hospital and give a talk to the staff who worked with dying people. He replied, "And who are these non-dying people I'll be talking to?" Step One is to realize that we're all in this soup together. Step Two is to know there are more skillful ways to handle the situation than to rage, rage against the alleged dying of the light, and Step Three is to know it's a deep privilege to be present at the time of someone's exit and, if appropriate, to help that exit to be graceful.

The how-to manuals may be simple or elaborate and may or may not include techniques like our breathing method, but they share the same basic message: *Everything's fine. Let go.* For people with a strong connection to a particular form of the formless infinite, it may be enough to say something like, "Just melt into the embrace of Jesus." But in case it's useful, here's one short, secular, culture-neutral version of the manual. If (and only if) you find yourself in a situation where it's medically clear that a loved one is on the way out and they're receptive to this sort of approach, you can use these words or something like them. And you can ask your loved ones to use it with you when your time comes.

Hey! Hi, [insert Name here]! Please pay attention now.

(We start with an exclamation and address the person by their first name to catch their attention, which may be preoccupied with assorted bodily earthquakes and psychic fireworks.)

Now your body is dying.

(Bang. No fooling around, no euphemisms or evasions, no pleas to "keep fighting," no smiley-faced assurances that they'll be out of bed in no time, playing tennis or celebrating on their favorite barstool. Does that sound brutal? It's not. It's real and it's compassionate. *Com-passion* means "feeling together," and it can only arise when, together, we recognize truth and feel its impact.)

Don't panic. This is normal. This is not a mistake. It happens to everyone. Don't take it personally. Every single being has gone through this door before you or will go through it after you. You're in the right place, and this is the right time.

You're perfectly safe.

You're done with this lifetime now. Don't worry about unfinished business. You're leaving right on time. When you came into this life, you took on a sense of being a person called [Name]. That person had a series of adventures—some scary, some wonderful. Sometimes [Name] felt happy, sometimes sad, but that's all done now and you can let it go.

You've done as much as you could do and learned as much as you could learn. You did a good job. Sometimes you may have doubted that, but you played the role exactly as you could play it. Now you're done with that role, and it's time to let it go, to take off that costume, which was always tight in places. What a relief!

You're not the role. You're not the body. You're not the name. You're not the memories or thoughts. Those things will be going away now, and that's fine. Let them go. They've served their purpose. As you release them you feel lighter and freer. What a relief!

As the body gets closer to finishing its work, it may have moments of discomfort or pain. Don't panic. Don't be caught up in it. It's happening to the body, not to you. Pain is your cue to release the body, let it go, and come out into the free, open space beyond the body. There's nothing to be afraid of. It's like breaking out of a shell. It's perfectly safe. Everyone does it.

You're not the body or the senses. You're the free, open awareness that experienced through them for a while. Now they'll be fading away, and that's fine. You don't need them. Awareness remains. Awareness remains. You remain. You are free, open awareness, boundless like the sky, like open space.

This is a beautiful and precious time, a time of truth. This is a time of opportunity, when you can melt back into what you've been all along—free, open awareness, like open space.

This world will be fading away now, right on time, fading like a dream. It just evaporates. You can let it go. Let go of the person you were in the dream. It's easy. As you let that go, you'll wake up into a bigger, freer, more wide-open reality. Don't hold on to any dream. Let it evaporate. What remains is you: free, open, joyous awareness. There's nothing to fear. It's perfectly safe. It's perfect. Let go and just be. Let go and just be.

CHAPTER 39

Love Is All Around

The Vietnam War was heating up . . . civil rights marchers faced tear-gas and police dogs . . . Watts was in flames . . . and Jackie DeShannon was on the radio, singing "What the World Needs Now Is Love."

It was a wistful pop waltz with a big string section and a euphonium solo, and in the era of the Stones and the Kinks it sounded pretty fluffy. But it was hard to argue with the message in 1965, and it's hard today.

Imagine that, through some miracle, this song's plea was answered—that, even for five minutes, everyone dropped their thoughts about the other guy or group, saw each other through the eyes of love, and wished each other happiness and peace. Imagine that everyone relaxed into timelessness, released their litanies of past injuries and future fears, and, with a cry of relief, flung their old habits of judgment and blame into some festive bonfire. Imagine that they smiled, danced, and took the pain of others to joyously crack open their hearts. Yes, of course, the idea that everyone would do such things is a crazy dream, but I've been doing them and you've been doing them, and that's two. Just seven billion to go.

We've been calling those practices meditation. Fine. But the more you do them, the more you experience how they soften and melt the edges that make us feel separate. That's called love. And in that crazy dream where everyone joins us, hasn't this love cast out fear—as promised—and cast out rage and worry and craving along with it?

In *this* world, outside the dream, so many people seem desolate, bereft. Perhaps once upon a time they gave and received love in a clear, exhilarating stream—with their beaming parents, with their magic lover, with their beautiful child. But in time things got complicated. The stream's flow dwindled, or was diverted, or was polluted, or stopped, and now they fear it's gone for good. Some never had it to begin with, and no matter what pleasure or success they attain, they feel shut down or hollowed out or bitter. There's been much public psychoanalysis of our seriously broken leader, and the evidence points to a loveless childhood. He could wind up being history's clearest case of personal damage metastasizing into global damage—a big baby crying for attention, crying for love, breaking his toys, breaking the world.

But all this sense of loss is based on a definition of love as something that can be lost—a *feeling*, which runs in a stream between two points, two persons, its flow constrained by the rocky banks of circumstances, always in danger of being blocked or drying up. Now, as our view grows clearer, we can see that the stream is in fact a current, running through the ocean—water flowing in water. It connected two waves, called self and other, I and you, setting them free from their old isolation and limitation. But the current itself is not love. Love is the ocean. Through the current, we found our connection to the ocean and its vast expanse. But the ocean is always there, and we've never been apart from it. We can never be deprived.

Yes, of course, when you finally find the lover you were born for, and then in time your lover disappoints you or leaves you or dies, it's devastating. I know, I've been through it. But it's not the end of love.

We say, "My heart is broken," and there's certainly emotional bro-kenness, but the *heart*—what you are at the core and what life is at the core—cannot be broken. That current of personal emotion was always a clue to the love that's wider than any emotion, bigger than any person, the love we melt into when our edges melt—everywhere, oceanic, needing only for us to open ourselves to it. It's the love that is, as Jackie DeShannon sang, "No, not just for some but for everyone"—the kind that could make our crazy dream come true.

But our experience is our experience. How can it be that people feel fragmented, incomplete, as if torn from something bigger, longing to be whole again, when the sages swear there's nothing but wholeness? Whoever or whatever it is that will supposedly restore our wholeness seems to have stood us up. We're standing on the corner, looking at our watch, tapping our foot, saying, "When is The One, (or) The Next One, (or) the Messiah, (or) the good dope, (or) the orgasm to end all orgasms, the revelation that will make my head explode, nirvana with extra cheese—when's that gonna show up?" And all this time, say the sages, he-she-it has been waiting for *us*, right in front of our eyes and right behind our eyes, waving, whistling, trying to catch our attention. "Hey, over here! In here!"

When's your date gonna show up? *This* is the date, this is the moment, wherever you are, whatever's going on, right now. We just have to relax, be open, pay a little attention.

The door is everywhere. We can use anything.

Feel It in Your Fingers

For example, right now, please lay your hand on some surface, palm down: a book, a desktop, a sofa cushion, whatever's available. Let's say it's a tabletop. Look away from it or close your eyes. Notice the sen-sation, the *actual experience* of this contact between your hand and the tabletop. Experience it pure, as would a newborn infant, who has no associated concepts or memories.

Do you experience two things, the hand and the tabletop, or one thing, the contact?

Go slow—take your time with these observations.

Notice clearly that only contact is experienced. To have any notion of a hand or a tabletop, we would have to rely on concepts and visual memory to interpret the sensation and fill in the picture.

Does this sensation of contact have a location? Don't think— experience.

No. Location can exist only relative to other experiences, which right now, from our newborn point of view, are absent. Any notion of location will just be a concept superimposed on the actual experience.

Does this sensation have a size? Does it have a time, other than now? Does it have a definite boundary? Notice. If you were to make a visual representation of the sensation on a sheet of paper, would you use a fine-tipped pen to draw a clear, crisp outline? Or would you need something like watercolor, to make it more nebulous, more like a smooshy, soft-edged mist? Pay attention, notice.

Now, what is this smooshy sensation made of? When we ask that question, concepts or images of nerve endings or tables may arise, but those are just thoughts, not the experience. The sensation itself, the actual experience, consists of nothing but awareness, arising in the form of the sensation. Be sure. See if there's anything else present in the experience besides awareness.

Now notice the one that has been experiencing all this. That's simple. It's called *I*, and by now it's very familiar. It, like the sensation, is nothing but awareness, and its quality is open and empty like a mirror, boundless and edgeless like space.

And now notice whether there's any distance, any separation, be-tween this I-awareness and the sensation-awareness.

(Go slow.)

There's no separation, is there?

So . . . where before we seemed to have several things in our experience, interacting with one another but separate—tabletop, hand, contact, I—now we have only one thing: awareness.

Are our other experiences like this? Please notice whatever sound is present. Notice whether hearing consists of anything other than awareness, and if there's any separation between the hearing-awareness and the I-awareness.

(Take your time.)

Now notice the passing thoughts. Can you find a clear division between one thought and the next, or is it all a smoosh? Is there any ingredient in this smoosh of thinking other than awareness? And is there a clear division between that thought-awareness and this awareness, I, the experiencer of the thoughts?

. . .

What have we learned?

There is no separation, no fragmentation, no alienation.

There is only wholeness, continuity, intimacy.

Our old picture of life—in which I'm a little puff of consciousness locked inside a body, forever separate from an outside world of objects and people, struggling through sporadic connections and fragile feelings to bridge an unbridgeable gap—that picture is purely a product of thought. Our actual experience is that there's only awareness aware of awareness—spacious awareness aware of itself. There's no gap to bridge, no separation possible. It's one smoosh, and that smoosh is love. Again, in the words of Rupert Spira (who taught me to explore in this way), "Love is not a feeling; it's lack of an other, of otherness."

If you didn't "get" this exploration, please come back to it soon and repeat it till you do. This is too important to miss.

In fact, this stupid-simple experiment of our hand on the tabletop opens up the possibility that our crazy dream could come true. It shows us that Jackie DeShannon was half wrong: Love is *not* a thing that there's just too little of. It's the only thing there is. God, for lack of a better word—that which is everywhere, everything, the infinite arising as every bit of the finite, the ocean arising as every wave and current—is love.

Consider the wisdom of "Love Is All Around" by the Troggs, another fluffy, beautiful pop song of the sixties (later featured in virtually every romantic comedy starring Hugh Grant). The song speaks of feeling love in your fingers and in your toes, feeling it in the wind, feeling it grow, till ultimately you feel it in everything, all around you, all the time. In the light of our exploration, this silly lyric turns out to be literal, profound, life-revolutionizing truth. Every single contact you make with the world through your fingers or your toes, or your ears or your nose or anything else, is love, actually. In every moment of clear, simple experience, unmediated by thought, the dualistic concepts of *you* and *world* melt into the nondual smoosh. And so the feeling grows—more precisely, our *recognition* of this wholeness, this love, grows. Every "thing," every "person" we experience is non-separate from "us," the experiencing awareness. There's never two of us here. What remains is spacious, edgeless, undivided.

Take this exploration into your daily life and keep corroborating it. Love is all around. The contact of your bottom with the airplane seat, of your hearing with the engine roar, of your skin with the too hot or too cold or just right temperature of the cabin air—improbably enough, crazily enough, it's all love, all God kissing God. It has only taken us a few minutes to arrive at this insight, but now we have a lifetime to confirm it at every step, to take it wider and get it clearer. It's everywhere you go.

God to Earth

Of course, even as we say this, our lifelong, ingrained habit of equating love with a fragile emotion between individuals rears its head, raising objections. "But I *like* personal love! I *love* personal love!" Well, yeah, me too. But no problem. Oceanic God-love doesn't negate anything. It affirms everything, and it certainly affirms every kind of love-current. Love for your partner, your children, your family, your friends, your teachers, your planet, with all its human and nonhuman beings. This is how we bring God-love to the earth plane: Thy will be done on earth as it is in heaven. The nice thing about boundlessness is that there's always plenty of it to go around. It pervades everything and elevates everything. You open to oceanic love, and then, more and more, marriage, friendship, signaling your turns, ordering your breakfast, and everything else becomes great big, loving, oceanic fun. Taking out the garbage? Wheeeeeee!!!

And more love means less fear. People sometimes imagine that moving through this world with an open heart will make them delicate, weak, vulnerable to being hurt. But in fact this love makes you strong beyond strong. Look at the Dalai Lama, look at Gandhi and Dr. King and Nelson Mandela. Do you think Jesus and the Buddha were dainty snowflakes?

This love has been trying to come through you all along—just stop holding it back. How do you grow your hair out? Just stop cutting it. You start to get a knack, a subtle feel for how to let this love wash through all your actions in the world, as you complain to or thank the customer service rep; as you ride home from the airport, chatting or silent, with the cabbie; as you hug your parent or child for the thousandth first time; as you mingle bodies with your partner for the thousandth first time. (In the timeless freshness of the exploded moment, every time is the first time.)

In the tarot deck, this process of channeling higher love through earthly life is depicted in the card of the Lovers. The Adam and Eve figures represent every couple, but also every I and you, every self and other, in every interaction, including passing each other anonymously on a crowded city sidewalk. They stand upon the horizontal plane of

the earth—the finite, relational plane—but their connection is through a third point, the apex of a triangle. This is the infinite, represented by the Angel of the Lord and a solar disc. The Angel embodies non-otherness: it's androgynous, incorporating both male and female, lover and beloved, I and you. The solar disc is empty, with light beams radiating from it—the spacelike, formless emptiness of the infinite from which all our forms radiate, and to which, following the beams back upward, we return every time we melt out of separateness.

It's when we're exiled from the Garden, removed from the Angel's presence, that our fear and our sorrow begin. Fortunately, no one has exiled us but us. We've got to get ourselves back to the Garden, and now we know how. Just reach out, touch anything or anyone, and let yourself melt.

As you begin to consciously cooperate with this process, you'll probably notice sticking points, places of resistance, which are places of opportunity for opening. The most dramatic of these are often in marriage. "You always hurt the one you love," says another pop classic (reaching back to the forties now). That's because the one you love threatens the separateness of the little self that you thought you were. You and the other are always on the brink of melting into the not-two, the I-and-I. This, I think, is the deep reason why husbands abuse wives. This is the reason for cruel sarcasm, and for the proverbial postcoital cigarette. After the intense melting of sex, we feel we need some way to retreat to the private, separate realm, to rematerialize ourselves. *If I can feel this smoke in my lungs or this sarcastic edge in my voice, I must be a separate person. Whew! Saved again!* (I'm speaking more to men now. Women are generally more clued in. Note that in the picture, the man looks straight across to the woman and she looks up to the Angel. This is a wiring diagram of marriage as a spiritual path. Woman intuitively knows to surrender to the Big It. Man, if he's smart, surrenders to woman, and through her to It.)

If you let yourself fully love her, you *fall* in love. Whoopsy-daisy! You tumble out of your phallic tower of ego and go plunging into the Sea of Love, where "every atom belonging to me as good belongs to you," says Walt Whitman. Then you're really in the soup. So (fear tells you) you need a way to stay separate, tucked neatly into your outer form and your well-practiced roles. Whether you make her an object of abuse or an object of worship, you've made her an object, so you're off the hook. But if you drop both concepts, drop the fear that feeds them, follow her lead, look up to the Angel, and dissolve together, that's much less work and much more fun.

If we dare to use it this way, our love is a power tool for setting us free from the limiting, small self—the persona—behind which we've been hiding. "Love," says James Baldwin, "takes off masks that we fear we cannot live without and know we cannot live within."

The depths of philosophy, the heights of religion
The so-called mysteries of the East . . .
This is what it comes down to:
Your hand on the table
Your foot on the earth
One big smoooooooooosh.
Every contact is a kiss
You (awareness) kissing the earth (awareness) with
*   each step (awareness)*
You kissing the sky with each thought
God kissing world
Love loving love
Written on wind, everywhere you go.

In this, what is there to fear?
Where is room for worry or craving or rage?
And when their traces arise
See that that also is a kiss.
Don't be afraid of fear

Don't be enraged at rage
Don't worry about worry
All is well.

Do what you need to do:
Feed the cat
Teach the child
Put out the fire
Do the job
Pay the rent—
But in all this
Find the kiss
And then with each look
Each listen, each touch, each thought
You kiss what's there
And it kisses back—
At last you'll see that
That's all it's ever done.

Sometimes this will all be clear
Obvious, simple, delighting.
Sometimes (maybe now)
It will sound foolish, obscure, impossible.
But the glimpses were not wrong.
Stay encouraged
Stay in courage
Stay for the encore
Stay in your core
Where the kiss always is
And dare to bring it to the waiting world.

Every moment kisses you
Everything kisses everything
All is well—
Fear not.
In all this
Find the kiss.
In all this
Find the kiss.

And So . . .

Together we've explored many practices and insights. I've made many outrageous claims. (The best way you can improve your life is to sit down and do nothing. Right.) We're ending with the most outrageous claim of all: that the God (for lack of a better word) that you sought in your pain, the love that will cast out your fear and all the distortions of life arising from it, is right here, at your fingertips, needing only a little attention to begin its healing work.

Fortunately, I'm not the first one to tell these cockeyed tales. The sages have told them forever, and sometimes people have listened. If you've tried even a fraction of the practices I've suggested, if you've seen even the dim outlines of the view I've tried to convey, then you've had glimpses of the great clearing that awaits you. Whatever else happens after you close this book, please don't forget those glimpses. Then, sooner or later, you'll follow this short path to its end. Out of habit and inertia you may go back to pain, but you can't unsee those glimpses, and you won't go back for long.

You can drop your fear and your sorrow anytime. It's easy, I swear.

ACKNOWLEDGMENTS

Thank you to all those who have shown up to awaken together and allowed me to play some role in the process.

. . . to those who have hosted my sessions.

. . . to those who have contributed their generous suggestions, assistance, and encouragement, including Michael Ames, Katherine Bailey, Marilee Burton, Fu-Ding Cheng, Fu-Tung Cheng, Buzzy Cohen, Albert Cortes, Matt Emenheiser, Sam Epstein, Adam Ferrara, Lyn Genelli, Richard Gilbert, Phil Goldberg, Zahava Griss, Jason Litak, Jodi Manning, Sean McAnally, Renée Missel, Day Rosenberg, Gina Salá, Ted Schultz, Sara Sgarlat, Dave Stanton, and Jim Vincent.

. . . to Brittny McCarthy for graciously and gracefully posing for the photos.

. . . to Amanda Shih, the Wonder Woman of TarcherPerigee.

. . . to my publisher, Joel Fotinos, who has guided me wisely since a previous millennium, and who continues to see before I do, shimmering somewhere in the ether, the book I need to write next.

. . . to my mentor Jeremy Tarcher (1932–2015), dearly missed but living on in the books—and the books to come—of the writers he grew in his garden.

. . . to Yaffa Lerea, love friend and infinity buddy, heart wrangler, the brains of the outfit, ambassador to the earthlings, and, in an astonishing stroke of luck, my brilliant de facto editor of first resort.

. . . to my teachers.

Photo by Andrew Turman

DEAN SLUYTER (pronounced *slighter*) has taught meditation and led workshops and retreats since 1970, from Ivy League colleges to maximum security prisons. A grateful student of sages in several traditions, he has completed numerous retreats and pilgrimages in India, Tibet, Nepal, and the West. Dean's books include *Natural Meditation*, winner of the Nautilus Award for best book on body, mind, and spirit practices. He has appeared frequently in national media, including *The New York Times*, National Public Radio, Coast to Coast AM, and *O, The Oprah Magazine*. When not writing or teaching, Dean makes music and happily rides his Vespa through the streets of Santa Monica. His website is **DeanWords.com**.

Deepen your experience and insight with
Natural Meditation

"If you thought you didn't have the time, focus, or discipline to meditate, this book is for you. The approach is both simple and fun, but don't be fooled. It's powerful because it's doable—and truly transformative."
—LISA OZ, host of *The Lisa Oz Show*

NATURAL
MEDITATION

A Guide to Effortless
Meditative Practice

Dean Sluyter
author of *The Zen Commandments*

A NAUTILUS BOOK AWARDS
GOLD MEDAL WINNER

"A rare combination of insight, clarity, wit, and pragmatic common sense."
—Philip Goldberg, author, *American Veda: From Emerson & the Beatles to Yoga & Meditation*

"If you were going to read one book on meditation, this would be the one."
—Shiva Rea